Heart of Darfur

Heart of Darfur
Lisa French Blaker

HODDER &
STOUGHTON

First published in Great Britain in 2007 by Hodder & Stoughton
An Hachette Livre UK company

Copyright © Lisa French Blaker 2007

A CIP catalogue record for this title is available from the British Library

ISBN 978-0-340-95230-6

Typeset in Minion Pro and Helvetica

Author photograph (cover) by Fiona Tomlinson
Photographs by Esther Prinsen

Printed and bound by Griffin Press, Australia

Hodder & Stoughton policy is to use papers that are natural, renewable and recyclable products and made from wood grown in sustainable forests. The logging and manufacturing processes are expected to conform to the environmental regulations of the country of origin.

Hodder & Stoughton Ltd
338 Euston Road
London NW1 3BH
www.hodder.co.uk

INTRODUCTION

What is it like in Darfur? people ask. Is it as bad as they say? And they lean forward, wanting to know the worst, drawn to the questions the way a child is drawn to a story of a wolf in the forest.

Darfur is the best and the worst I have ever seen. I lived and breathed them both through 2005 and 2006. On a good day the sun shines, the grasses dance in the breeze and children laugh. On a bad day the heat strips the skin from your body, the smell of burning hangs in the air and everything feels hopeless.

To many in the West the conflict in Darfur appears complicated and overwhelming, even unsolvable. So they walk away, unable to face the reality. But if you pause for a moment and look a little closer you will find that behind the horror and the conflict there are people not so different to you and me. Their story, like ours, is closely entwined with their past. Each day they put one foot in front of another as they try to survive in Darfur.

Learning a little about Darfur opens your eyes to the lives of those who live and love and die there. Perhaps you will find it is not as complicated or unsolvable as you first thought, though it is far from easy. You may be surprised by Darfur. Through the overwhelming sorrow and heartache you may even see hope and beauty. And perhaps then the story of Darfur will touch your heart.

****

Sudan is the largest country in Africa. It is a land of mountains, marshland, desert and coastline with extraordinary beauty and endless space. It is also a land of conflict. Conquerors, slavery, domination and tribal warfare weave their way through the history of Sudan, impacting upon lives and communities in every corner of the country since time immemorial.

In recent history war exploded in 1983 when the military regime in Khartoum, the capital, pushed south to expand its Islamist agenda among the African Christian and pagan communities. The tribes in the south united under the Sudanese People's Liberation Army (SPLA) to fight the government. The following twenty-one years were awash with murder, atrocities and loss. In 2004 an agreement was reached between the government in the north and the SPLA in the south; peace, a share in the south's substantial oil wealth and the possibility to secede in the future. That conflict has faded from everyday news, but tensions remain high.

Darfur also has its history of conquerors, domination and slavery. For the people of the land, the Fur, Birgit and Zaghawa tribes among them, it has been a history of change at the hands of others. With hundreds of tribes, most with their own dialects and even distinct languages, uniting Darfur under one ruler was always going to be difficult.

The semi-arid province in the far west of Sudan covers an area of 300,000 square kilometres. It is the size of France and equal to one-quarter of the size of the United States. The Sultans, Egyptians and the British all failed to govern it well. Tribal conflict, neglect and poverty left Darfur a fractured state. But the people continued with their nomadic and pastoral way of life, most practising Muslims and living in relative peace with periodic fierce tribal skirmishes.

Government representation, roads, hospitals, jobs and development passed them by.

As the people in the south drew breath in 2004, safe at last from the war, the people of Darfur were stumbling into another conflict as brutal and as vicious as any in the south. In 2003 many of the tribes of Darfur drew together under the Sudanese Liberation Army (SLA). The SLA claimed to be standing up for the people of Darfur, believing that the government was neglecting the province and favouring ethnically Arab people in government and jobs. More recently, rebels have described themselves as Africans fighting an Arab government. But the lines are never so clear in Sudan; there are Arabs and Africans on both sides of the conflict and all are Muslim. All are hurting, some more than others, as this conflict enters its fifth year in 2007. And it shows no sign of losing momentum. It only worsens as the days pass.

****

But what does this all mean and what is it actually like in Darfur? people still ask. Life in Darfur is coloured by the conflict. Whichever side they live on, in government or rebel areas, people see and feel the effects of war every day; the sound of Antonov planes and helicopters, vehicles with tinted windows roaring through town, soldiers walking with weapons through the marketplace and long queues of people, broken and damaged by the war, sitting outside clinics and hospitals waiting for help.

When you talk to someone who was born and raised in Darfur you look into a weary face. But it is a face that smiles and loves as well. When they laugh it is a laugh of joy and gratitude for the simple pleasures in life: family, friendship and safety. When they talk they often tell a tale of tradition, loss and pride in their tribe. Through the conflict they try to hold their families together, clinging to the hope that one day life will be better. And when they cry the tears exhaust and consume them, tearing at their soul and bringing them to their knees. There are a lot of tears in Darfur.

Into this conflict many international humanitarian organisations have come to bring relief; Médecins Sans Frontières, the International Committee of the Red Cross, Oxfam and the UN's World Food Programme to name a few. They bring humanitarian aid to the estimated six million people living in Darfur. Most are entirely dependent on humanitarian aid to survive. Médecins Sans Frontières (MSF) has been present in Darfur since 2003. The organisation was founded in 1971 to contribute to the protection of life and the alleviation of suffering out of respect for human dignity. This is done primarily through medical action, but also includes work on water, sanitation and food programmes. It is an organisation of volunteers, both medical and non-medical; people who are committed to help others in precarious situations. In Darfur they provide humanitarian assistance to all sides of the conflict. It is an uphill battle in a land where fighting persists, wave after wave, and the civilian population continues to suffer while the key players refuse to talk or listen to each other.

If you follow me now, I will take you on a journey to Darfur — to share with you the reality of my work in a land of conflict and loss, beauty and hope. I will introduce you to some of the people of the land, their children and their dreams. So that in the end, when you sit back in your chair at home, you will know what it is really like in Darfur — the worst *and* the best. Your heart may ache and despair, and your tears may sting for a moment. But through it all you will have touched another world, seen the reality of life there. Perhaps your heart will have been touched by the extraordinary people of Darfur.

CHAPTER ONE

I arrived in Khartoum in the oppressive heat of a September night. Exhausted and dishevelled, I stood in the doorway, bags at my feet, and looked around the living room of the 'expat house'. Fans whirred noisily high on the ceiling, sending eddies of hot air across the room.

The mats on the polished wooden floor lay crooked and upturned where they had been shoved aside to make way for shoes, empty bottles and discarded bags. Small groups of expats sat or sprawled on sofas, listening to music or watching television in the dim light. Arnold Schwarzenegger cut swathes through enemy lines in one corner while Moby crooned softly in the other.

I paused there, trying to find a friendly face, a helping hand to my room. But everybody just slumped in exhaustion, closed to new arrivals and lost in their own private thoughts. No one stepped forward. The loneliness and exhaustion of the last five days roared around me. I wanted to drop to the floor and cry. Tears came too often those days. The clinic nurse in Amsterdam the day before had been the last straw. Because of a mix-up with the MSF Sydney office I had arrived in Amsterdam without having had the full array of vaccinations and medications required. A grave offence, I gathered.

****

Time was short and my evening flight from Amsterdam to Khartoum was confirmed, so the only solution was a mad dash across town to a clinic to get the necessary vaccinations. I was given a hand-drawn map of the back streets of Amsterdam and shown to a rickety black bike in the courtyard of Médecins Sans Frontières, on Plantage Middenlaan.

'If you ride quickly you will be back in time for your taxi,' said Eva, the MSF human resources officer. 'If you miss the taxi then I don't know what you will do. You will let a lot of people down.'

After two days with no sleep en route from New Zealand, my body was not entirely ready for the challenge. But what else could I do? I slipped the instructions into my pocket, unlocked the bike and hurled myself into peak-hour Amsterdam traffic.

'Out of my way!' I bellowed as I pedalled furiously. 'Girl in a rush!'

Twenty minutes later I sat in front of the disgruntled clinic nurse, my vaccination book on the table beside her, watching as she tapped my details into the computer. The name on her silver badge read 'Elena'. She hadn't greeted me as I walked into her office and I felt uncomfortable and unsure of myself. The rest of the clinic was quiet, doors closed and corridors empty.

'Why didn't you come here earlier?' she demanded, eyes on the screen. 'Why has this vaccination schedule been so disorganised? I'm very tired, you know. It's been a long day and I was ready to leave before MSF phoned about you. You are unprepared for your mission.'

I stuttered my apologies and tried to make myself as small as possible, apologetic for the intrusion and extra work I was so obviously causing. On and on she went, her long nails clacking across the keyboard as she kept firing unanswerable questions in my direction.

I looked up at the clock on the wall as I listened to her. I was going to be late. There was nothing more I could think of to say to her and apparently I was just about to let many people down. Despite my apologies and my pride I didn't have the strength to stop the tears that welled up in my eyes from falling.

'Oh,' she said, glancing up when she had finished. 'You're crying.'

I nodded.

'Well, I suppose it's not all your fault. Come with me and let's get this over with.'

I followed her out of the room.

Vaccinations dispensed with, I made it back to the office in record time. I don't remember the roads — I just pedalled as fast as I could, repeating the mantra 'I'm not going to let anyone down!' over and over in my mind.

This was not the first time I had negotiated these back roads and alleyways. My first two missions with MSF had also been fraught with late preparations. Last-minute appointments, late buses and a lost alarm clock had left my nerves jangling and my heart pounding. Surely this time I would get it right, I thought to myself when I arrived in Amsterdam. Third time lucky, wasn't it? But despite my careful packing, the concentrated hours of organising my belongings and making sure all my paperwork lay in neat piles by the front door, I still got it wrong. So much for being an expert at international travel! East Africa, Sri Lanka and South Sudan had obviously not sharpened me enough.

By the time I made it to Schipol airport that night my shirt was wet with sweat, my shoulders aching from the weight of my rucksack and the added kilos of extra post I had been asked to carry to the projects in Darfur. I slid my passport across the counter and dropped my luggage onto the weighing scale with a heavy thud. I had made it! My knees were shaking and my headache begged me to rest.

'Here are your boarding passes,' said the woman behind the counter, pushing the paperwork towards me. They would be my stepping stones from Amsterdam to Cairo to Khartoum. 'Have a nice holiday.' She smiled a polite, elegantly dressed smile and turned to the next customer. What a start to my third mission — my holiday of a lifetime.

****

After five days of travelling through seven countries with little sleep, my body swimming with a cocktail of vaccinations and anxious not to let anyone down, I finally caved in. Why am I doing this to myself? I thought as I lay on my bags, out of sight on the living-room floor of the expat house in Khartoum. This is pointless. Eventually I managed to rouse myself enough to get up again — the mosquitoes were getting the better of me. A young woman walked over from one of the sofas.

'Hi. My name is Alice. You must be new here,' she said as she put out her hand to take my bag. 'Let me show you to your room.' And the tears started to fall all over again.

Over the following months I saw many expats come and go from that front room. Late-night arrivals, bright excited expressions, and weary tear-streaked faces. Some carried rucksacks crammed with chocolate and cheese, others carried small worn-looking packs with only the essentials. And sometimes mine was the closed face looking out blankly from the sofa, trying to avoid eye contact with the fresh open faces of the new arrivals and ignoring their endless chatter.

'It's so good to be here,' they'd burble. 'I'm looking forward to this so much. I really want to make a difference here. This is an amazing opportunity.'

And I would lie there, bruised and despondent after another six weeks in the field, and close my eyes and ears to their enthusiasm. Just wait till you've been there a while, I'd think. Wait until you've been kicked in the teeth a few times and seen all your work lost or dismantled. Then come and tell me what an amazing opportunity this is.

But all of that lay months in the future. As Alice led me to my new room I remember talking excitedly, while I wiped away the tears.

'It's so good to be here. This is an amazing opportunity!'

She didn't respond.

When my bags were unpacked I climbed onto my bed and listened to the whistling hum of the air-conditioning unit in the corner. I remembered Amy, the Belgian nurse I met on the way to Zanzibar all those years ago, and sighed. Her enthusiasm and passion for her humanitarian work was what had inspired me to work for MSF. I pictured her bright eyes and the salty sea air and I had wanted to be like her — to share in her adventure and her commitment to making a difference. I had given up my home, job and car in New Zealand and come halfway around the world just to be in Khartoum to try to find a life that made more sense than the aching emptiness of my work at home in New Zealand. I had to make it work in Darfur — I didn't have anything else.

****

Two days later, on September the 29th, I was back at the airport, all packed and ready for my next step closer to Darfur. Some people underestimate the size of Darfur. It takes over two hours to fly in a straight line from Khartoum to the capital of South Darfur, Nyala. Hours of hot, flat, barren landscape, stretching out thousands of kilometres below. The occasional road, long and straight, leading to a village would catch my eye, leaving me wondering how on earth people survived down there. With scarcely a tree or shrub in sight it seemed like a vision of hell.

Sarah, Matthew and I departed the house together just before 5 a.m. that Thursday morning. They were an English couple; both working as part of the management team in Nyala. Two very experienced MSFers, they had worked in countless countries around the world over the last decade: Colombia, Somalia and Uganda, to name a few.

In my comfortable Auckland apartment only months before I had felt numb and restless. I tried to readjust to city life after my last mission — to return to work, visit friends, realign my dreams and plans to fit in with the people around me. There was no one else with my discontented restlessness. I was the odd one out. At night I sat in the dark and looked out over the lights of the city. A distant, aching need dragged at my heart, whispering of the world that waited for me. A world of heat, frustration and vast African night skies. After months of tears and aching I knew what I had to do — I had to go back to Africa. Then the phone rang one night and I heard Sarah's voice inviting me to Darfur.

'What's that noise in the background?' I asked, struggling to hear her voice over a rumbling din.

'I'm standing in Kalma Camp,' she replied, raising her voice. 'You can hear a few thousand people standing around me wondering what I'm doing talking to myself, standing in the sun in 35-degree heat. Why don't you come and join us?'

I said yes in a breath. Four weeks later I sat next to Sarah in the taxi and listened as she talked of her dreams and adventures.

She described a life that I had barely touched during my last two missions. I want your life, I thought. I want to travel and explore and to help others, to be part of something real.

The sky was still dark as we drove to the airport, and night sounds filled the air — crickets, bats and mosquitoes. Those who have travelled in Africa will know the warm, noise-filled excitement of an African night. It never sleeps. Even before dawn the streets were busy. Minibuses plied the main roads, attracting more and more passengers until the doors wouldn't close and the exhaust pipes dragged on the ground. Along the dusty unpaved footpaths women were setting up little stalls, their wares slowly unpacked from plastic bags and cardboard boxes and assembled with care. There were tea ladies and women selling peanuts, cigarettes, oranges and more. The men arrived later, their smarter stalls built with plywood or corrugated iron, locked overnight on the footpath. They offered everything from phone cards to shoe polish.

Our driver sped along the city's dilapidated back roads, emerging onto the main highway from a long potholed track that zigzagged through dark suburban neighbourhoods. He pulled out onto the tar-sealed road and quickly pushed his way through the traffic to the inside lane. A curious feature of Khartoum highways is the single lane in the centre. In order to travel on this lane our driver negotiated concrete barriers and other hooting, speeding drivers also shunting their way in. Once there, motorists raced madly in either direction, using it as both a high-speed lane as well as a place to turn. In theory it sped up the flow of traffic. In practice it was a motor strip of Russian roulette — anyone could take their chance on it and everyone was at equal risk. As we hurtled towards the oncoming traffic I closed my eyes and breathed in the hot, humid air. Surely my work in Sudan wouldn't end in carnage in Khartoum, I thought.

Having survived the journey to the airport, we stepped out of the car to gather our luggage. Our brief was simple — the three of us were to check in our bags at the main counter and wait in the departure lounge for the first World Food Programme flight of the day to Nyala. But what's simple in Africa?

Walking towards the main entrance I heard shouting and yelling coming from inside. Between us and the X-ray machine in the far corner surged a hot, anxious crowd of people, all pushing and heaving bags and boxes as they inched towards the machine under the bright lights. Every passenger had to put their bags on the short conveyer belt to have it X-rayed before proceeding to the other side of the room to enter the departure hall. There was only one door.

Five flights were departing at the same time as ours. About 400 people jostled in front of us, ready to shove and crush their way through that doorway to freedom; holidaymakers, politicians, refugees, each with their own reasons for wanting to leave. Sarah, Matthew and I looked at each other, eyes wide, and shrugged.

'Here we go! Follow me,' said Matthew as he launched himself into the mêlée.

Western etiquette has its place in queues and offices. A door opens here, an elderly lady is let through there. In the pre-dawn light of a crowded Khartoum airport there is no etiquette. So we pushed and heaved and shoved and shouted with the rest of them. When a gap appeared, Sarah, who was the shortest of us, would force her way in, shouting, 'I'm in, follow me!' Follow her? To where?

With each push I found myself packed ever more tightly in the anxious crush of humanity. What amazed me was that some even seemed to be enjoying themselves. They were smiling! I kept pushing with all my might, the rucksack on my back battering people as I moved. With a twist of my shoulders I knocked someone to the right, then to the left. As my frustration levels rose and the sweat started to pour, I became more confident and I gave in to the crowd mentality. I was starting to enjoy myself too! I wanted to get to that X-ray machine as much as anyone else in the room, not caring what I had to do to get there. That was how the game was played.

For a moment I lost sight of Sarah and Matthew. I swivelled my head, searching for Sarah's red scarf. Ahead of me an overweight Sudanese businessman in a suit lifted his knee to crack the back of the knees of a man in front of him, squeezing into the space left by the fallen man. Beside me an English expat stood cursing, his round pink face glistening with perspiration, patches of wetness spreading below each arm and across his chest. Soon his neatly ironed blue-and-white checked shirt was limp, the carefully rolled sleeves sodden.

'You people are mad!' he shouted over the din. 'Let me through. I work in Darfur. I'm trying to help you people!'

Nobody was paying any attention.

Finally he let his bags fall and bellowed, 'I don't have to put up with this, you know. I'm British!' That was a bad mistake, dropping his bags. Even I realised that. Four men threw themselves towards the space he'd left as his bags fell and trampled over them, one of them knocking the Englishman backwards, a briefcase catching his shoulder as he staggered. I turned away as he started to shout again, muttering under my breath, 'Talking gets you nowhere, buddy . . .'

After ten minutes of struggling I was beginning to tire. The weight of my rucksack was starting to pull me down and the strength to hold on to my daypack and the laptop computer was dwindling. The stress and heat were really starting to take their toll. Two nights' sleep in Khartoum had done little to ease my tiredness after a week's travel. The sights, sounds and smells of the city had both excited and assaulted my senses, leaving me tense and jumpy. By sunrise, enveloped in the madness and crush, exhaustion set in.

Directly in front of me an enormous box — perhaps a parcel abandoned by someone who had given up the struggle — blocked my path. A man to my left suddenly lurched towards me, driving his elbow into my shoulder as he launched himself up on to the box and into the crowd beyond. He had obviously done this sort of thing before. I felt myself falling forwards, my feet trapped behind the heavy box. Sensing my weakness, the crowd pushed even harder against me. The feeling of powerlessness and suffocation was terrifying. There was nothing I could do and no one who would care what happened to me.

As if from nowhere I heard Matthew's voice.

'Give me your rucksack,' he shouted. 'We're getting out of here!'

I felt the straps loosen as he lifted the pack from my shoulders and threw it headlong onto the X-ray machine. I hadn't realised I was so close.

'This is bloody ridiculous,' he gasped, his long curly hair dripping with perspiration. 'Even by African standards this is madness.'

With my rucksack gone and Sarah relieving me of the laptop and daypack I had clenched in my numb hands, I lifted my feet over the box on the floor and followed them along the wall to the entrance. The crush continued unabated as we drove ourselves against the flow to retrieve our bags on the other side.

A security guard stopped us as we stepped through, his hand on Matthew's shoulder.

'Where's your ticket?' he shouted. 'No ticket, no coming in.'

Matthew knocked the guard's hand away and roared, 'You want to see my ticket, then you sort out that bloody mess,' gesturing over his shoulder at the crowd. 'Forget it. We're going in!'

With that, he marched forward, Sarah and I trailing limply behind, our clothes drenched with sweat and shoulders hunched. Welcome to Sudan, where only the strongest survive.

****

Various agencies and reports estimate the number of people killed in Darfur's war at 200,000–400,000 since 2003. They speak of the displaced in millions — two or three or four million. The true scale of the conflict is unknown to any of us. Families living on the run for months slowly bury their children, one by one, as they succumb to malnutrition and disease. Newborn babies lie buried in shallow graves, their fathers missing or dead while the family flees the fighting. Thirst, hunger and malaria are the killers. The number of dead exceeds our worst estimates. Often it is only the strongest and the luckiest who survive. Our Khartoum airport experience was nothing compared with the strength we needed in the months to come.

****

We arrived in Nyala after lunch. We waited until the other passengers had exited the plane before rising from our seats, still not fully recovered from the stressful morning. Walking across the deserted tarmac I breathed in the cool air, and closed my eyes to the sun concealed behind clouds. The light gave those first few moments on the ground a feeling of calm and respite after the chaos of Khartoum.

In spite of all the stress it felt good to be back in Africa. I was born in Africa, in a small, elegant town in apartheid-weary South Africa. After emigrating to New Zealand as a child, life changed forever. Perhaps it was for the better, but still my heart longed to be back in Africa. Any excuse took me back — to climb Mt Kilimanjaro, to work in Johannesburg, to travel for months through East Africa on the tail wind of a glorious three-month working holiday in Tanzania.

My second mission with MSF took me to the Nuba Mountains in Sudan, to a place of lush, tree-covered peaks and valleys filled with rivers and ponds. I woke every morning there with a smile on my face. I loved being in Africa.

****

I looked around as we emerged from the terminal. The airport was tidy — bougainvillea bushes splashed colour across the walls, white, pink and red, and the white-painted stones along the verge were neat and orderly against the newly cut grass. As a government-held town in Darfur, the military presence was strong. White government helicopters sat in ranks at the end of the runway. Soldiers at a military checkpoint at the gateway to the airport watched visitors down the barrels of their guns, their heads just visible above the brown sandbag walls. Land cruisers with open backs and dark-tinted windows sped through the town every day. On the back of each vehicle, four or five policemen clutched the rear of the cab, scrutinising the people around them through dark glasses. Curfews were common. Orders to stay indoors after dark would be issued by government officials after a skirmish in town or reports of unrest in the camp on its outskirts.

Nyala is a big town, serving as the capital of South Darfur. It is like many towns in Africa, with one tarred road leading from the airport to the marketplace, the others gravelly and sandy. The roads are well planned, lying perpendicular to each other — straight lines of order in an otherwise chaotic place. Pedestrians, donkeys, horses, three-wheeled tuk-tuk taxis and cars all vie for space on the narrow, bustling streets. The sand and baked-mud alleyways give way here and there, deteriorating into gullies and trenches strewn with plastic bags, broken shoes and empty soda bottles.

When the wind blows, eddies of sand rise and hide passers-by in a hazy cloak. Every week convoys of huge trucks enter Nyala, dusty and overloaded, transporting goods from Khartoum to supply the thriving markets. Displaced people and a burgeoning community of aid workers living in and around the town ensure a constant demand for goods.

Kalma Camp sat on the edge of Nyala. In an area only 1 km wide and 6 km long over 80,000 people lived and struggled to survive every day. All were drawn to Nyala and its relative safety as the fighting around their villages intensified. Government troops fought with the Sudanese Liberation Army (SLA) in vicious battles, while Janjaweed militia moved through the state attacking villages and stealing cattle. Villagers were slowly being cleared from their lands. The town was unable to accommodate such an influx so humanitarian agencies set up the camp to provide the essentials of life — food, water, shelter and healthcare. In the barren wasteland of Kalma the displaced people wait. They wait for the Janjaweed militia to go away, to stop stalking women as they leave the camp in search of firewood. They wait for food and supplies from aid agencies. And they wait for the fighting to stop so they can go home. Some have been waiting for over three years. Living under sheets of plastic, their homes a tiny scrap of earth, they sit and wait and pray. Sometimes they get angry and fights break out. When that happens, the aid agencies pull out quickly and local police stand at the gates and watch. For a time, Kalma becomes a lawless territory, a bedraggled, miserable state of exhausted souls. Soon enough, though, conflicts defuse, arguments resolve, and life returns to 'normal' for a while.

In the early days following my arrival I often walked the streets, catching a glimpse of everyday life in the homes behind the high brick walls with their ornate iron gates. Women hanging washing on long ropes that criss-crossed the courtyard, children running and playing around the flapping sheets. On the streets I saw donkeys, their front legs tied together to stop them running away. They wandered and hobbled through the heat of the day as they snuffled and searched for food in the sweepings and gullies. Children played with balls on the side roads, jumping and shouting each time the ball disappeared from sight, then racing each other to retrieve it. Cars, vans and tuk-tuks slowly picked their way amongst the potholes and trenches. I felt at ease, enjoying the smiling faces and colours of another African town. I soon learned to look further and realised that all was not as enchanting as it first seemed; hungry faces, thin children, big guns and night-time curfews were part of the undercurrent of daily life.

The week I arrived, the MSF team I was to join had been evacuated from their project in the government-held village of Saleem. Everyone was tense, fearing more fighting. An attack on Saleem on September 19th had resulted in a total withdrawal of MSF from the area. SLA fighters had launched the assault from their stronghold in the hills to the east and south, these grassy heights offering them some protection in the days and weeks preceding the attack.

The SLA managed to take control of Saleem for several hours before being pushed back into the hills again by the government forces. The sound of heavy fighting was heard for hours before the evacuation, with helicopters and Antonov planes supporting the government troops from the air. Small arms, AK-47s and rocket-propelled grenades were used by the combatants on both sides.

While the attack unfolded, the MSF team crouched in their bomb shelter. Their compound sat directly in front of a government building, an obvious target during the battle. All the local staff had fled. Many of the residents of the town were on the move, trying to find shelter from the danger in a place with few solid buildings and only one bomb shelter.

As the day wore on, the SLA troops were forced out of the town by heavy fighting and a window of opportunity presented itself for evacuation. A helicopter was scrambled from Nyala and made its way to Saleem, flying low and slowly. A white helicopter flying to the scene of an attack would surely be an obvious target to the SLA fighters below. It could belong to the government. But even in a bush war the commanders on both sides carry satellite phones. MSF constantly builds on its good relations with both sides of any conflict so that when the time comes to evacuate, help is only a phone call away. The team of expats and some local staff were evacuated safely and brought back to Nyala to recuperate.

Where other agencies pull out in times of danger, MSF can be reluctant to evacuate a project too hastily. When the local population are under fire MSF tries to maintain its presence, standing as a witness to events and ready to treat the wounded as they arrive. The first principle of MSF's charter is 'to provide assistance to populations in distress'. Bullies are less likely to do harm if they know someone is watching. It's a simple theory which can bring about powerful results. MSF was awarded the Nobel Peace Prize in 1999 in recognition of their humanitarian work. But sometimes it is too dangerous to remain. Such was the case in Saleem on the 19th of September.

****

And so started my first week in Darfur. The hours stretched into days as I waited for my call to join the team going back to Saleem. Each morning I walked to the MSF office, seeking out anyone who would talk to me or brief me on the situation. I stood at each doorway, a hesitant smile on my face, not wanting to intrude and painfully aware that I was just another new girl making demands on their precious time. The answers were always the same: 'Come back later. No. Too busy. Can't stop.'

I would call in at the dining shelter before heading back to the expat house after each fruitless attempt. The shelter was spacious, with a long wooden table stretching across the room. Twenty or so expats gathered around it each day, talking, complaining and laughing as they took a lunch break in the middle of the day. Its walls were layers of soft mosquito netting put up in an effort to keep the flies and mosquitoes away during meal times. In the 35°C heat the sweat ran freely, my shirt clung to my back and my eyes ached. But there in the shade of the dining room I found a brief respite from the heat of the day. I sat and watched the netting as it billowed in the light breeze, hot wind blowing gently through the soft walls. My eyes would often focus on the flies trying in vain to find a way in, to get closer to the food. Without radio or television to distract me, I had to find another pastime. It soon became fly spotting.

Most flies were fooled by the netting, buzzing against it in frustration. Occasionally one did make it through a gap in the nets, not knowing that the food it sought sat covered on the table — their reward was always one step out of reach. But in the heat and confusion of the billowing nets the triumphant fly would invariably get tangled again, its body trapped between white layers, not knowing whether to move forwards or backwards. Some days, transfixed by the flies, I was even moved to help the trapped adventurers, whispering encouragement as I lifted open the net, showing them the way through. What else was there to do? By day's end I would count the number of dead flies tangled in the mosquito nets, their legs trapped in the holes, their wings spent. And I would tally the number of successes — those I'd helped get through and those which had made it on their own. That was my day's achievement and, in a small way, it brought me satisfaction.

After four days of waiting for news of Saleem the stupor set in. I woke early each morning, the heat of the day creeping into my room as the sun rose. The whitewashed walls were blinding in the full sunlight, so I soon learned to rise at dawn to enjoy the calm, cool air and gentle light while I listened to the birds and savoured my breakfast. Cornflakes with caramel-coloured sugar grains, milk made from a tin of milk powder I found sitting on a windowsill, and a bowl of fresh fruit — mangoes, bananas and oranges. It was a feast for a king. Sitting alone in the cool air, I revelled in the quiet luxury, happy to be there during those early morning hours. Cradling my cup of Earl Grey tea and watching the morning star fade, I was at peace.

But by mid-morning each day I felt lethargic and empty. With no work for me to do — the evacuated team huddled together talking and planning, their backs turned outwards — I felt excluded. They were planning their return to Saleem and it didn't seem to include me. My daily trips to the office produced nothing, so each time I returned along the dusty side streets to the expat house where I lay on my bed and watched the ceiling fan turn.

When the team returned to Saleem it would be without me. There was clearly no place for me there, the new girl with no experience in war. My previous missions evaporated and my experience meant nothing. Perhaps they saw me as a burden, more work in an already unbearable situation. Their project had been evacuated, their patients scattered and who knew what damage had been done. My enthusiasm meant little to them and my heart felt heavy.

I had forgotten that in Africa nothing happens quickly. You wait endless hours and weeks and months and hope that your turn will come; your work, your visas and permits or your money. When it eventually does you embrace the reward and life seems easier for a while. For the rest of the time, though, you wait. Patiently and endlessly. And I am not a patient person.

The days fell into a predictable routine as I shuffled between the office and the expat house. Hours stretched into each other, shapeless and tiring at times, lightened by the laughter and friendly faces of other expats at others. Craig, Liz and I often met in the late afternoons to pass the time. Craig was waiting for his place in a team in West Darfur. After nearly three weeks of waiting for travel permits and favourable weather to drive, he was no nearer to leaving. His hair grew longer and his new beard proved to be his new hobby as he inspected it each day, combing and trimming it carefully. Liz worked in Kalma Camp as a logistician, her energy boundless and enthusiasm still fresh since her arrival a week before mine. We had worked together on my last mission, so I knew her laugh and sharp wit well.

We lay on narrow rope beds in the shade and talked about anything and everything — our reasons for being there, our passions, disappointments, dreams and frustrations. Many people ask me why I keep travelling to faraway places like Darfur to work. I have many reasons, but one is surely for afternoons such as these. All too often at home we rush and work and stumble through the day, with no time to really relax and talk and listen to each other. In the hustle and bustle of Western life we lose touch with ourselves and our friends. I love the honesty of those lazy times in the shade, the quiet simplicity where we can talk and be heard.

And then there are the parties! Humanitarian workers know how to enjoy life, throwing themselves into parties and gatherings with a frenetic enthusiasm. The escapism of laughter and music, men, women and food, lift them for the moment from the hardship and suffering that fills their working days. Thoughts of rape, malnutrition and injustice temporarily fade in the hours after dark when the parties begin.

****

On Wednesday night I stood in the kitchen, filling my water bottle at the filter for the fifth time that day. Through the wire netting on the windows I heard someone calling my name.

'Lisa — there's a party at the Spanish Red Cross tonight. You want to come?'

'I'll meet you in ten minutes,' I called back. 'I'll have a shower and meet you outside.'

What I wasn't prepared for was just how many glamorous and beautiful clothes the others had brought with them to Darfur. Standing in my clean trousers and neatly ironed T-shirt I felt decidedly underdressed beside the other women in their shimmering silk blouses, fitted skirts and designer jeans. Bracelets, necklaces and earrings shone in the kerosene lamplight as we stood waiting for the tuk-tuks. I had brought nothing like that with me!

Six of us squeezed into two tuk-tuks and headed off into the dark to find the party. We meandered along bumpy lanes and crossed the single tarred road in town several times before it occurred to me that we were lost. But sitting there on the front seat, my arms wrapped around the open frame to keep me from falling out, laughing and chattering with the others, I didn't care. We arrived at the Spanish Red Cross expat house late. The guard let us in through the arched gateway, nodding and whispering as he led us to the front door. Dozens of candles lit the entrance and hallways, soft cushions lay scattered on the floor, and from upstairs came the sound of music, laughter and shouting. Peter, who had been in Nyala longer than any of us, led the way up towards the party.

It's true that the Spanish know how to have a good time. On their rooftop palace they had laid out mattresses and cushions, trays of food and glasses of soda. The mattresses were covered with expats, reclining and laughing in the candle light. In a state where alcohol was banned we drank only water and soda, fruit juice and lime. But they had made an alcohol-free cocktail, fresh fruit juice filled with pieces of watermelon and pineapple. The huge glass bowl on the floor gave the illusion of something more exotic as I dipped my glass in, fishing for fruit. Liz and I stood together and looked out over the darkness of Nyala. The intermittent electricity supply meant that no one could count on night lights, but that evening many houses were lit, their windows glowing yellow in the warm night air.

'Welcome to Nyala,' said Liz, holding up her cocktail. 'May the party never end!' We made a toast and turned to join in the dancing.

****

Five days after my arrival I woke to good news — I could accompany the first convoy back into the field to assess the security situation. I barely had time for my morning ritual of tea and star gazing as I rushed to get ready. This was what I wanted — to be out there, helping people, being part of the team. I look back on my idealism now and smile. I thought that through my presence things would somehow change, that I would make a difference there. How naïve I was. But on that Monday morning as I hurried out the front gate to the MSF office everything seemed possible.

Standing in the quiet of the morning waiting for the other expats to arrive, I felt shy around the confident local staff and their war-weary faces. They knew each other well and shouted greetings as more of their number arrived. They shook hands and rested their right hand on each other's chests in the greeting of brothers. Cigarettes were passed around and identity cards checked before

Dave called everyone to attention. We all stood in silence while he addressed us.

Dave was a veteran of many missions. His army stories were long and slightly repetitive, always beginning with 'When I was in Afghanistan ... or Bosnia ... or Pakistan ...' as he closed his eyes and dragged on his cigarette. As the project coordinator for the team he was the most senior person there, so I listened to the stories every time, trying to learn from them as we drove.

Dave asked to see everyone's ID cards and work permits before we left. Any worker, expat or local, who was apprehended at government checkpoints without a valid card or permit would jeopardise the entire trip. Permission to travel would be withdrawn and we would be sent back to the office to wait days or weeks until the new paperwork was completed. The morning check was mandatory. So we queued up to hand him our cards. My shiny new plastic sleeve stood out against the others, theirs worn, peeling and smudged.

We headed out of town in a small convoy, two land cruisers packed and ready for work. Dave and I sat in the front vehicle with the driver, Musa, and our translator, Adam Ali. I had barely made eye contact with the pair at the office, but now I sneaked glances at them as we drove. Musa sat behind the wheel, the only driver of Mobile 32, the land cruiser he drove every day. He didn't know his age exactly, but guessed he was twenty-nine or thirty years old. He sat on a thick, colourful cushion. It was his trademark companion on every journey, he told me. Standing only 160 cm tall, he needed the boost of the cushion to see clearly over the hulking bonnet of the vehicle. When he shook my hand it was warm and gentle.

Adam Ali, our translator, looked like a dignified man, his polished shoes and neatly ironed trousers contrasting with the rattling, untidy boxes and barrels around us. His MSF waistcoat hung loosely on his slim frame. Below it his blue business shirt was freshly laundered, the singe marks of last night's ironing showing on the collar. In his top pocket he carried two pens, a heavily embossed fountain pen and a black biro. His handshake was strong and his gaze direct. He looked to be in his early 30s, his face smooth, laughter lines around his eyes.

Toby drove behind us with the rest of the day's team and the equipment for the clinic. One expat nurse, two local nurses and one translator sat in the back. They would run the clinic while I watched. Toby was Canadian, short and taciturn. I could tell he enjoyed the chaos, scrutinising boxes in the pharmacy in Nyala and sitting on them while he made notes in a tattered exercise book and hummed. He thrived on the endless meetings. As the logistician in Saleem he was responsible for managing stock and coordinating administration. More often than not, though, he stood in the sun and smoked, staring thoughtfully into the distance. His portly stomach strained against his belt, his MSF T-shirt tucked tightly into his trousers. 'Can't talk now,' he'd say. 'We've evacuated.' I turned to look at Toby's vehicle as we drove out of Nyala, just behind the plume of dust and sand that boiled up as we sped along in front. His arm hung out the window, clutching the handle above the door as he bounced on his seat.

We approached the first military checkpoint after just a few minutes. Musa pulled the vehicle off the road, down a short slope and glided to a stop in front of a thatched shelter as two uniformed men emerged. Across the road ahead of us a string of old car tyres blocked the way. The message was clear; the road ahead was not open to just anyone. I took off my sunglasses and scrabbled in my daypack for my ID card and work permit. Climbing out of their vehicles, Dave and Toby walked over to the soldiers waiting in the shade.

'Salaam aleikum,' Dave greeted them. 'Kula kwess?' he asked in his pidgin Arabic. Over the coming months I was to discover that those two phrases, 'Hello' and 'How are you', were the sum total of his Arabic vocabulary. Delivered with a smile, though, they passed for a salutation in a land where introductions and greetings can go on for ten minutes or more as acquaintances enquire after everything from one's wife and children to the health of one's cattle.

The soldiers remained unsmiling, their faces tight. We were the first humanitarian agency to leave the government-held area since September 19th. Where were we going and what did we think we would see? they asked, walking over to our vehicles and peering in each window, looking carefully at the staff and frowning. Even with permits in order and local commanders informed of our movements, permission to travel could be withdrawn at any time. My heart was in my throat as I waited and watched in the back seat. Then with a curt nod they gestured for us to drive on.

Dave climbed back into our vehicle and Musa slowly drove forward, across the open sandy ground beside the checkpoint, until we had passed the blockade. Then, with the engines roaring, we pulled back up the slope and onto the tarmac road. I sighed with relief and put my sunglasses back on as we resumed our journey.

We turned off at a bend in the main road, a spot without signposts or markings, but known to all who worked in the area. We drove into the bush, following dusty tracks that only Musa could see. Under trees, down river banks and across sandy river beds. The flat savannah-like landscape was dotted with thorn trees and scrub. In the distance were low hills, long and flat, their rocky faces shaded in the early morning light. The MSF flag pulled and tugged in the breeze, showing the world who we were. In a land where the rules of war apply, every party is known by the colour and shape of their standard. Ours flew brightly every day and it was respected.

The two vehicles, roofs laden with boxes and barrels, slowly made their way further from Nyala, deeper into the 'other' side

— SLA and Janjaweed militia territory. The dust rose, a warm wind blew and the early-morning sunrise cast hazy light through the clouds of sand. I caught sight of myself in the side mirror, a smile on my face. It was finally happening — the chance to be part of life, of an extraordinary reality and to try to make a difference.

We stopped after an hour to have tea and meet local leaders. Without telephones, handsets or the Internet, villagers all over Darfur nevertheless find out what has happened after a raid or attack, who did it and where. The information spreads like wildfire, the news arriving long before the return of the dead. In a place where attacks occur without warning and lives are stolen without permission, people learn to rely on themselves.

While Dave talked with a local leader, the sheik, the rest of us crossed the sand track and ducked into a small coffee shop. The low thatched roof covered a deceptively big area, with a beaten earth floor and loosely thatched walls. Here and there chickens sat in the cool shade, their mouths open, panting in the heat. By 8 a.m. the temperature was already over 30°C, the air thick and dusty. My skin was covered in a fine gauze of sand. I wiped my eyes as I stood in the shadows.

Musa led us over to a corner and pulled two woven beds close together so we could sit. In every tea and coffee shop in Sudan the beds are the same. Four customers can sit together, the frame creaking and settling into the sand as they relax. Some have ramshackle weaving around a strong wooden framework. On others great gaps and tears in the woven ropes leave brittle holes that defy the weight of even one customer. But they are still used. Nothing is ever wasted. On that day, however, four of us sat comfortably, leaning together as we waited for our drinks.

The woman who ran the coffee shop sat in the centre of the room, carefully preparing food for the evening meal. I watched as she finished making a pile of kisira, bitter-tasting crepes the Sudanese use to dip into sauces and stews. Perched on a little four-legged stool, her knees drawn up to her chest, she ladled the batter onto the hot, flat pan over the fire. It bubbled and steamed for an instant and was cooked in seconds. Turning, she dropped the finished kisira onto a pile beside her, each paper thin and perfectly round. The whole routine looked effortless, pouring and cooking, lifting and turning. A routine born of a lifetime of experience.

As she worked, I examined the woman's face in the dim light. It looked lined and tired, her skin dry. A blue scarf covered her head, hiding her hair and ears. She narrowed her eyes each time she poured the liquid onto the pan, the only sign of her concentration. When she had finished she called for some milk. A little girl, perhaps eight or nine years old, came running in carrying a bucket in her hands, half filled with frothy white milk. She stood and watched her mother, one hand resting on the tired shoulder beside her. Her arms and legs were long and thin below her faded green dress. Malnutrition affects more than just the weight of the children; their height and mental growth suffer as well.

Heating the milk in a pot, the woman waited for the first bubbles to appear on the surface while she stirred the embers and added charcoal below. On a side table sat six glasses, small thick-sided cups for serving hot sweet tea, coffee and milk. She lifted each glass and dipped it into a pottery urn beside her, rinsing each one in the murky brown water and holding it up to the light to check its cleanness. When they had all been washed she reached under her stool for a metal drum full of sugar. 'USAID oil' read the battered silver-and-blue label, a relic from the past that had found new purpose for a resourceful housewife. She carefully measured four round spoons of sugar into each glass, filling them halfway with the golden crystals. Then she lifted the pot from the fire and poured milk into each one, leaving a foaming lip around the top. When the milk was ready the little girl carefully lifted each glass onto a silver-coloured tray and carried them over to us. She nodded as she held out the tray, indicating that we could each take one.

If I don't get bilharzia from this it will be brucellosis, I thought. Parasites in the water or bacteria in the milk — what a choice. But how could I refuse such a conscientiously made gift? So I nodded my thanks and reached for my glass.

We spent an hour sitting in the cool, quiet coffee shop while Dave talked and asked questions about the safety of the area. Yes, he was assured, all was safe up ahead. There had been no disturbances since the attack. We could continue on our journey.

When my hot milk was finished I pushed the empty glass into the sand the way I had seen others do. Thanking the woman in my halting Arabic, I made my way back outside. On either side of the road there was little activity — it was a small dusty village, poor, with neglected lean-tos and crumbling market stalls. The prosperity of Nyala obviously didn't reach this far. Even the children appeared small and dusty, sitting in the shade or crouching behind thatched walls as they observed us and our extravagant circus of vehicles and equipment. The rest of the team emerged from the coffee shop and we clambered back into the land cruisers and drove on to Tala, our destination for the day's clinic.

We arrived in Tala at 11 a.m. The local community was not expecting us — it wasn't the usual MSF clinic day and the previous clinic had been cancelled because of the attack on Saleem. We stood around in the sun and waited while the guard opened the cavernous white MSF tent that served as the clinic, standing on tiptoes as he reached up to undo the clips holding the tent closed. I moved into the shade of a thorn tree while the others pulled the boxes and tables from the vehicles, setting up the clinic quickly and efficiently.

'Is there anything I can do to help?' I asked Sam, the expat nurse.

'No, just watch what we do,' he replied. 'In a few weeks you'll be running this clinic, so I hope you're a fast learner.'

I smiled, but inside my heart sank. Great, I thought. Another MSF project where I'm thrown in without any instructions. In Sri Lanka my desk was neatly polished and my chair dusted, but the instructions from my long-departed predecessor were nowhere to be found. In the Nuba Mountains my colleague left after three months, leaving me to make sense of a tangle of paperwork and order forms, reports unwritten and tally sheets missing. The painstaking untangling had taken months and I swore I wouldn't do it again. But here I was in wartime facing another hot, busy mission without instructions. I rubbed my eyes and took a deep breath. I can do this, I said to myself.

Outside the tent, Adam Ali and Musa were sweeping the waiting area. Six logs dug into the sand served as the frame for the rakuba, or shelter. The thatched roof had long since fallen into disrepair and we had neglected to bring a tarpaulin to provide shade from the midday sun. Musa shook the mats as he unrolled them, a shower of sand raining down as he worked. They were laid down for patients to sit on, the men on one side, women and children on the other.

The patients started to gather under the shade of the thorn trees, not interested in the hot, shade-less waiting area. Most were just curious passers-by, on their way to the market or coming to have a look at the morning's activity. I sat on a chair next to Sam and watched while he examined and treated patients. He was born and raised in Sierra Leone, a survivor of war himself. He was a veteran of many missions. With his dark skin and smiling face I mistook him for a local staff member when we first met. But his confidence and authority in the team quickly revealed he was in fact the chief organiser of the clinic.

With no curtained room or privacy in the giant open tent it seemed temporary and makeshift.

'How long have you been running a clinic here?' I asked Sam.

'A year,' he replied. 'They don't really need a clinic, but by giving something to the community we can ensure safe access along this road. The theory is that if we treat their wives and children they won't attack us.' He smiled. 'It's worked so far.'

I watched as Sam and his translator examined and talked to patients, laughing and writing as he worked. I wondered if I would ever be as confident and at ease as he appeared to be. After a while, however, I became tired of hearing the same old complaints from different patients. General body pain, burning feet, and the infamous 'gas in abdomen' were brought to the clinic for healing and treating. After a lifetime of work, dehydration, malnutrition and the stress of living in a war zone, all the adults suffered the same complaints. None were life threatening, they were the result of a desperate life of subsistence and war. What they didn't seem to understand was that MSF couldn't take away their chronic ailments. Twelve paracetamol tablets would not cure all their ills. But still they tried. Perhaps I would have done the same in their place.

Excusing myself, I stood outside the back entrance of the tent and looked around. The landscape was barren — kilometre after kilometre of flat land, long grass and the occasional tree. Established family compounds lined the main road and spread out along sandy tracks. Here and there the long, plastic-covered roofs of temporary shelters belonging to displaced people shone in the sunlight. After previous attacks some families had moved closer to this town and had received goods from one of the aid agencies that enabled them to build waterproof shelters.

Beside the tent, in the shade of a tree, sat a young mother holding a little baby on her lap. A patient card lay on the sand beside her, small stones weighing it down in the light breeze. The baby hung limply in her arms, its head lolling back and eyes closed. The mother was just sitting, watching the activity in the waiting area, her attention not on the baby. I walked over to have a closer look.

'Salaam aleik,' I said. 'Can I have a look at your card?'

She stared at me blankly but smiled when I reached for her patient card. In most clinics a card was a sign of importance, no matter how old it was or what the complaint had been. It was a sign that you were important, that you had been seen and had received treatment. Even while their homes burned people would go back to collect their patient cards to keep for the future.

The card showed that the baby had just been seen by Sam. Diarrhoea, severe dehydration and malnutrition were diagnosed because the baby was being fed exclusively on goat's milk. When Sudanese mothers ran out of breast milk they often fed their babies with water and goat's milk. The milk was too rich; full of fat but deficient in so many nutrients it was not meant for humans. Contaminated water and rich milk often led to diarrhoea, dehydration and death in babies under one year. Beside the young mother stood a soda bottle filled with rehydration solution. On the patient card was a carefully written schedule for her to follow. It was written in English.

'Water? Baby?' I asked, pointing to the bottle and the baby.

She smiled and shook her head. No, she was saying, not for the baby.

'Wait here,' I gestured. 'I'll come back.'

I ducked back into the tent and looked for someone who could translate for me. Musa sat at the dressing table, cleaning his scissors. Our versatile driver also dabbled in minor surgical procedures and could do a number of tidy dressings with ease.

'Musa, would you come and translate for me?' I asked. 'I've got a lady outside and I don't think she is giving the treatment to her baby.'

We walked back to the tree and crouched down beside her.

'She says the doctor gave her medication because of the goat's milk but she will wait until she gets home before starting it,' he translated. 'She has another sick child at home so she will share the treatment.'

'Please tell her to start the rehydration treatment now and tell her I will go and get enough for her other child,' I said, reaching for the bottle.

Musa translated my words, explaining that if the baby did not get the treatment now it would probably die. He measured the solution into the lid of the soda bottle and gently tipped the water into the baby's mouth. The water spilled from its lips. A voice from inside the tent called Musa's name. He stood, passing me the lid.

'I have to go now. But she knows what to do,' he said.

I sat with her a while, slowly coaxing the baby to drink. Little by little he started to move as the life-sustaining rehydration solution trickled in. If there is one treatment above all others that gives me satisfaction to administer it is oral rehydration solution. Before your eyes children and babies stir and waken, the simple solution replacing valuable lost sugars, salts and water. Hold a baby on your lap as you feed it water and you will never forget the life-giving satisfaction as it starts to work.

By 2 p.m. the number of patients had dwindled, leaving a queue of men sitting in the sun, all complaining of the perennial general body pain and burning feet. Dave had completed his security talks with local leaders and the men were given their weekly dose of paracetamol. The day's work was done so we dismantled the tables and helped the guard carry them all to his 'garage', a small thatched rakuba beside his house nearby. On a piece of wood outside he had drawn the MSF symbol with charcoal.

'MSF,' he said in English, smiling and pointing to the sign. 'MSF good.'

I smiled and nodded.

We drove back to Nyala slowly, everyone tired in the heat and the local staff thirsty on their Ramadan day of fasting. My stomach growled with hunger. I wasn't fasting but it had seemed unfair to sit and eat while the others worked. So my cheese sandwiches stayed wrapped in their tinfoil at the bottom of my bag. I sat on the back seat, grinning to myself, satisfied with my one contribution to the day. The baby had been drinking when we left and it looked awake and alert.

'Musa, do you think that baby will be okay?' I asked, leaning forward and speaking to him as he drove. 'Now that it's drinking rehydration solution it looked better, don't you think?'

'It did look better and it will be okay,' he replied. 'For today,' he qualified. 'But tonight it will be fed goat's milk and dirty water again and it will die. Tomorrow or next week. What else does the mother have if she has no other milk and no clean water?'

I sat back. The young mother had smiled and nodded as Musa and I talked to her before she left the clinic. Yes, she understood, she said, thank you. I told her she should not give her baby goat's milk and that she should find clean water. The solutions were obvious. But I hadn't thought about what was practical for her, what she could actually do. In the months that followed I learned a simple recipe for diluting goat's milk to make a palatable, nourishing drink for babies. If mothers had access to water from a borehole they had clean water in abundance. But clean water remained elusive — there weren't enough boreholes and local leaders ensured that every jerry can filled with water had to be paid for. Some families could not afford to buy enough water. Even in war man seeks to profit at every level.

My first attempt to help and to be useful had been useless. And that baby would die because of it. I sat quietly for the next two hours, lost in my thoughts. If I was going to make a difference I would have to learn how to do things better, and fast.

CHAPTER TWO

A volley of gunshots and a head-on collision welcomed me to Saleem. By the time I stepped from the vehicle my nerves were taut and my head throbbed with an ache that pleaded for calm.

We left Nyala just after dawn, driving along dusty tracks and through deserted villages. Government and SLA skirmishes and increasing tribal friction in Saleem had left the situation tense. But after ten days of lethargy and distraction in the expat compound in Nyala at last it was time to do some work. The rest of the team had left for Saleem early one morning five days before, not saying goodbye or including me in their plans. My seat on the helicopter was taken by someone else, someone more useful than I. With all my nursing experience and a folder full of certificates and diplomas I was an outsider and I knew it.

But finally my turn had come. Approaching Saleem my eyes were alert, looking for signs of the trouble I had been told lay waiting. Reports of troop movement and intimidation in the town continued every day. None of this seemed real to me. I had no experience of active conflict, having sailed in on the wake of war in Sri Lanka and the Nuba Mountains. With peace in the air in both missions life had been sweeter, if not easier. I only knew that I wanted to join the team now and end my weeks of waiting.

Crack!

Crack!

A series of shots flew at our vehicles from the trees to our left. I looked around wildly, trying to see who was firing at us, looking for a place to hide. All around us were fallen trees and thorny scrub; there was nowhere to hide. Musa stopped the car suddenly and we were all thrown forward. Through the rear-view mirror I saw Steve fling open his door and stride out into the field, swearing.

'What the fuck is going on?' he shouted.

The last thing I would have done was to shout at a concealed gunman. I sat in the car, wide-eyed, clutching my seatbelt. Musa leaned forward and switched off the engine.

'It's okay, Lisa. This is no problem,' he told me quietly. 'This happens many times.'

Musa and I sat in silence, my heart racing and shoulder aching where the seatbelt had tightened as we braked. The sound of a gunshot — my first sign of real war — was frightening. It had a sharp, high-pitched sound, not the slow, fat noise I'd heard on TV. These were bullets, real and present, and they were meant for us. Or so it seemed.

A soldier appeared out of the trees, a gun held in both hands, his face unsmiling. I heard talking. Steve stood, his palms held upwards in the open and non-threatening stance I became so familiar with over the following months of fighting and negotiation. After several minutes they shook hands and Steve turned and walked back towards us.

'Arsehole,' he muttered as he passed. 'And he's probably only 15 years old!'

I nodded and raised my eyebrows. I looked round at the others. Musa smiled his slow, soft smile.

'Don't worry. This is how the life goes,' he said, reaching forward again and restarting the engine.

Steve's voice crackled over the radio. 'Let's move forward. *Slowly*, Musa.' And we pulled away, leaving the soldier behind us, standing alone in the field.

Sitting in the back of our land cruiser was a barrel of chlorine powder. It was for cleaning and sterilising in the clinic. After the sudden braking the lid had become dislodged and soon the air was filled with the sharp, stinging smell of chlorine. I wound down the window and leaned out, breathing in great gulps of warm air to drive the chlorine taste from my mouth. My head started to hurt. When I could bear the fumes no longer I turned to Musa.

'Doesn't that smell bother you?' I asked.

He smiled and shrugged. The local staff in so many places were accommodating, unwilling to speak out or make problems unless a situation was serious. They were careful and undemanding for much of the time. Sometimes I appreciated it and at others their apparent passiveness drove me crazy. I suspected Musa and Adam Ali would have put up with the acrid stench for hours.

'Can we stop for a moment?' I begged. 'I have to do something about that smell!'

'Call Steve on the radio and ask him first,' advised Musa. 'He doesn't like surprises.'

I reached for the radio, unfamiliar with the codes and radio etiquette of Darfur.

'Um. Mobile 32, this is Lisa. Can we stop for a moment? There's a bad smell in here.'

'You've got one minute,' came the curt reply. 'And remind me to teach you how to use the radio properly when we get to Saleem.'

I winced at his tone.

Musa stopped the car and I asked him if it was safe to get out, hesitant after my fright with the gunman only minutes earlier. He nodded. I stepped out onto the sandy track. My back ached from the long journey and I stretched in the sun, my shirt wet from the drive.

I walked round to the back of the vehicle and reached in to look for the container, hidden far behind Adam Ali. I avoided turning to see Steve's exasperated expression and concentrated instead on tightening the loose black lid. It took my mind off the fact that I was the only one standing outside the vehicle in what felt like the most dangerous place on earth. All around me was silence — even the birds were in hiding. When the lid was secure I ran back to the passenger door and quickly hopped in. Two minutes later the nauseating smell started to fade as the wind blew through the open windows. I leaned back against the headrest, eyes closed.

****

We entered the town through two military checkpoints. I stayed seated while soldiers gathered around Steve's vehicle. I watched them talking in the rear-vision mirror. Take off your sunglasses and smile — those were the rules I'd been taught about checkpoints. I held my sunglasses on my lap, but the smile just wouldn't come. I still felt shaky after the shooting, and the soldiers' unsmiling faces were intimidating. My skin felt cold in the morning heat. They all held guns. In the shade beside each checkpoint sat a machine gun, propped up on a metal tripod, a soldier lying on the sand behind it. A long brown belt of bullets was strung through each, ready to fire.

They waved us through at last and soon we were in Saleem. Its wide sandy streets were a smaller, tidier version of Nyala. High thatched walls hid small compounds, round pointed roofs peeked above the fence line. Donkeys stood in the shade of great, sprawling trees, their front legs hobbled together.

Steve's car drew ahead and we followed him towards the

new MSF compound. When the team returned a week ago their priority had been to build a new compound. Their proximity to a government building had proved dangerous during the recent attack. So they moved to a new part of town and built a new base for the compound. The trouble was that none of us was sure where it was. At an intersection Steve's car stopped, its brake lights dim in the morning sunlight. Musa kept on driving, nearer and nearer, not registering the stationary vehicle ahead.

'Wait, stop, careful!' I said, putting my hands out.

BANG!

We crashed into the car in front, our bull bars tearing its rear bumper and crushing the back door. We were all thrown forward as we slammed to a halt. My head smacked forward then back, bouncing off the headrest. The engine cut out with the sudden halt. We sat in silence, metal clicking quietly in the heat.

'Oh no,' groaned Musa. 'Oh no.'

Steve's door flew open and he stormed over to my window.

'What the hell do you think you're doing? I can't believe you fucking did that! Can't you fucking drive? Get out of that car and look at what you've done!' he bellowed.

We all shrank in the face of his fury. Musa climbed out and they surveyed the damage. Steve stood shouting, his face rigid with anger. My neck ached and my head was starting to throb. I don't think I want to do this any more, I thought. After two impatient weeks of waiting I wanted to give up at the start.

****

I was shown to my little round tuckul, or hut, on that first day and I sat down on my new bed and took a deep breath. It was my space, my retreat and my escape from the noise and fury outside. I loved it from the start. Home. I spent the rest of the afternoon unpacking and slowly putting my signature on my new home. By tea time my toiletries and photos filled the single shelf, a sheet of poetry hanging from the sorghum thatched roof. That night I crept into bed early. My body still ached from the loud, hot, jarring day and my head pounded. I lay there and blinked in the darkness. The oppressive, chaotic heat of Khartoum was gone; the horn-honking, crowded streets of Nyala were far distant. Instead I was surrounded by the cool night air of the village, crickets and frogs filling the dark with their calls. At the front gate two guards sat talking quietly, pausing now and then as they drank their hot, sweet tea. Above me in the thatched roof birds rustled and whispered as they settled for the night. Hearing them made me smile. In spite of all the frights and stresses of the day, I was happy. For as long as I could remember I had wanted to be here, far from anywhere, working to make a difference in a place where I was needed. I pictured myself sitting in the dark in my inner-city apartment only a few months before. So many nights I sat, waiting, wishing, aching for some unknown change. I tried to fit into life in Auckland, to laugh and play and work like the others. And through no fault of my friends and family my restlessness remained, a constant reminder that I didn't belong. But on that first night, with the murmuring birds in my roof above, I was at peace. I pulled up the covers, a smile on my face and fell asleep.

****

Within days the aches had faded and it became obvious that there was so much work to do. My two predecessors had left without even leaving a note. Since the attack on September 19th the whole project had been in a state of upheaval, the expat compound and the clinic in disarray. Working for MSF you learn to think on your feet, looking for opportunities every day and using common sense to piece together a plan to make things work. If you can't do that then you won't survive. As I started to realise the extent of the upheaval my mind was spinning, looking for solutions and a way to bring order.

As the only female in the team my role lay with the women and children. Paperwork, building and staffing issues were for the logisticians. After any attack the priority is to talk and listen to people and treat their wounds. That much I knew. And there was no shortage of wounds.

There were four of us working together — Steve, Toby, Sam and me. There was no time for formal introductions. But I kept my eyes open as I watched the others and tried to learn something about them. Steve was the toughest nut to crack. His background in the British military gave him the experience and the cynicism to deal with the authorities and to understand the subtle intricacies of diplomacy. Moments where I would have given up in exasperation I watched as he played the game with various officials, talking, listening and discussing his way to his chosen outcome. The local staff obviously respected him immensely but I still felt shaken by his eviscerating temper. There was little time to get to know him anyway, as he powered through his days with a smouldering cigarette in his hand, his head hidden in a cloud of smoke while he sat hunched in front of his computer.

Sam was already my favourite, after our clinic in Tala. He was from West Africa, his voice a gentle lilting relief from Steve's rapid-fire orders. Sam worked as a nurse, the most experienced medic in our team. Under his guidance I learned how to work under stress, watching while he smiled, encouraged and slowly nodded through the most difficult situations. Nothing seemed to shake him. At the end of the day he sat quietly in the shade, refreshed by his evening shower, and he would sigh deeply.

'How was your day, Lisa?' he asked each evening. 'Are you happy?' He was my rock, my guiding companion in the overwhelming exhaustion that quickly became the pattern of my work.

And then there was Toby. As our logistician he was the one who kept our warehouses well stocked, the staff salaries paid and made our work possible. His slow Canadian accent made him sound easy-going, a voice never raised in anger or agitated with the daily frustrations. With his broad shoulders and equally broad belly, he moved ponderously through each day, often talking to himself as he worked.

Each of us had a specific role, with tasks that required us to work at full throttle to complete them each day. There was no time for slowing down and no one to pass any unfinished work to when the load became too heavy to bear. But all those insights and thoughts lay weeks in the future as I settled into my new life in Saleem.

****

I stood under the kitchen shelter helping Selwa and Halima, our compound ladies, prepare dinner several days later when the guard called my name.

'Lisa, there's a woman for you.'

Peeling potatoes and eggplant was not a priority but it gave me a much-needed opportunity to get to know the ladies, the only other women in our compound. Their giggling and chatter was soothing. Putting down my knife, I told them I would be back soon. The Arabic I had learned in the Nuba Mountains seemed a source of hilarity to the ladies. It was far from classical Arabic, more of a pidgin version that the remote tribes had used to communicate with their far-off neighbours. Selwa laughed at my Arabic and nodded. She mimicked my voice and I heard them laughing as I left.

I followed the guard to our after-hours consultation room, a small mud brick hut in the middle of the living compound. It had been built by the team the week before, discreetly off a lane behind our compound. Anyone entering the lane could be visiting family, or searching for a lost goat. Only a few people knew of our entrance, those who needed our help after our clinic had closed for the day. Government officials insisted that there were no problems in the town and that life had returned to normal. But intimidation and threats by government soldiers towards people suspected of supporting the SLA were increasing. It was worrying that the number of visitors to our compound was increasing, and several times that day I was called to our consultation room to treat another victim of senseless violence.

Ducking in through the doorway, I greeted the two women waiting for me with a smile and a handshake and sat down on the narrow rope bed beside my translator, Adam Ali. His neatly ironed trousers and business shirt were still clean and unwrinkled despite the day's work and heat.

'This is a hard one, Lisa,' he said. He had heard many accounts of intimidation, torture and worse in the past. If *he* judged this one as hard then I knew it would be bad for me.

Miriam was forty-five years old. Her eldest daughter was thirty, her youngest child was seventeen months. Her children were her life. She sat on the edge of the bed, hands twisting the fabric of her dress into ever-tighter balls, and told me her story softly, her eyes on the floor.

The men had entered her family compound around 3 p.m. four days before. She knew them from the town — passing them each Wednesday on market day — they owned stalls selling meat and vegetables. They claimed to be searching for her husband. She was from the Zaghawa tribe, a group repeatedly attacked since the September 19th attack because both the government and

Janjaweed militia suspected all Zaghawa of supporting the SLA. It was true there were many Zaghawa leaders in the SLA, but the rebel movement also drew support from other tribes, calling itself the army of the people of Darfur. This meant little to the authorities in Saleem.

The Zaghawa are a semi-nomadic tribe from the north which originally settled on the land to farm. They moved with the seasons, cultivating and building temporary communities where they could. When the war intensified many found themselves on the wrong side of the ever-changing battle lines. Those living in Saleem had been there for twelve or fifteen years, but they were always referred to as guests, not residents. Their years in the community meant nothing in the face of growing tribal tensions.

'Your husband stole our cattle and now he must pay!' the men's leader shouted at her. 'You people are all the same — Zaghawa thieves, taking what isn't yours!' They entered all the shelters in the compound, kicking over chairs and buckets, yelling at the children inside.

Miriam knew it was a lie. Her husband had been killed in a raid two years ago. There were no men in her compound. But she kept quiet. On her back she carried her baby daughter. On her hip she held her grandson. Both were seventeen months old. As the men shouted, the babies started to cry.

The leader walked up to Miriam and shoved her backwards with a blow to her chest. 'Give me your baby,' he demanded, pulling at her grandson's arm.

'No!' she cried as she stumbled backwards trying to protect both infants.

'Boil some water!' he ordered. 'A big pot on a hot fire.' He grabbed again at the baby and wrestled him from her. 'We are going to cook your baby and then you will eat it!'

Miriam fell to the ground, screaming 'No, no, no!'

Carrying the baby to the warm embers, he dropped him on the sand. 'Now!' he shouted.

'Who are you?' she cried. 'How can you do this? Our God cannot allow this.'

'*We* are your gods,' he said as he stood over her. 'We do what we want.'

Miriam didn't remember the exact sequence of events that followed. The men carried her and the babies out of the compound, stumbling and crying. Nobody helped her; no one was brave enough. At a time when everybody was afraid and tribal loyalty meant more than friendship, no one was prepared to stand up to help a Zaghawa woman.

Miriam remembered standing on the edge of the dry river bank just outside the town, her hands bound in front of her. Her daughter was still strapped to her back, her grandson lay on the ground beside them.

'Kneel down there,' the leader pointed to the sand. 'When you fall, the dogs will find you first.'

They started to beat her on her head, shoulders and back, the blows raining hardest on her baby daughter. She let herself fall forwards down into the sandy river bed. They followed her down and continued to beat her. Then her grandson was thrown down on top of her.

After some time she regained consciousness, her face covered in sand, flies buzzing across her skin. She didn't know how long she had lain there. The men had returned and they lifted her up. They carried her out of the river bed, put her on a donkey and took her to the local jail. There they laid a charge of theft and the police put her into a dark cell with her baby daughter. For two days and two nights she lay there waiting.

'The police gave me one cup of water and one piece of bread

every day. I wasn't hungry. I was just crying for my baby. I didn't know where my grandson was,' she told us.

On the afternoon of the second day her Oomda, a senior community leader, came to see her. He knew she was missing and rumours about her disappearance had led him to the local jail.

'If he had not come for me, I would have died there,' she said.

She sat in front of me, still wringing the cloth of her dress. Her bruises showed up as dark swellings around her neck and forehead. The burn marks left by the ropes on her wrists were raw and painful. Beside her, her sister held the baby girl, her little head swollen and her lips dry. Her grandson, it transpired, had been found alive in the river bed and was now in the care of relatives.

I sat in the darkening hut and my tears fell. She told her tale without emotion in her voice, not looking at me once as she spoke. But I could picture her story in my mind, see the events unfolding. Several times I wanted to shout 'Stop!' — but it was her story, not mine. *My* emotions were not going to help her. I felt a lightness in my head, my fingers tingled. This was not just a story in the newspaper or an appeal on television. I couldn't turn the page or change the channel. She sat in front of me; I could hear her breathing, smell her perfume. And my hands shook with anger and fear.

Are experiences like Miriam's too hard to hear about and merely an 'unfortunate' result of tribal conflict? I felt the bile rise in my throat. I didn't have the answers and surrounded by the brutality of her story I felt hollow. I know that my belief in intrinsic goodness, my trust in others, was changed forever with her story. Snapped with a single tale.

When she had finished talking I thanked her quietly for talking to us. My voice shook and I didn't trust my legs to stand. She had taken an enormous risk by talking to us. The unrest was not to be discussed publicly. The officials in town seemed to want all Zaghawa to leave, quietly and without complaint. Those who stayed faced serious trouble every day.

I reached over to the toddler and examined her wounds. She was breastfeeding again, Miriam told me. But she needed a proper examination and undoubtedly medical treatment. It was nearly sunset, though, so I gave Miriam some paracetamol for the baby and asked them to return to the clinic in the morning. It would be unsafe for her to be out on the streets after nightfall and she had suffered enough already. Adam Ali and I watched in silence as the two women rose and ducked through the low doorway as they left. They walked slowly across the compound, pulling their wraps over their heads. They let themselves out quietly into the alleyway.

'Inshallah,' Adam Ali sighed, shaking his head as he wiped his eyes. God willing.

****

On Tuesday morning the whole team sat around the breakfast table and made plans for the day. The local staff had heard talk of a large group of people camping in a river bed 35 km away. They were from the Zaghawa tribe and were too afraid to return to town.

'Should we go and look for them?' Steve asked. 'We should really be in town to talk to the security people and keep an eye on things here. What do you all think?'

He looked round at us. Steve included everyone in his discussions: drivers, nurses, translators, local staff and expats. Each voice was heard and counted. I was still cautious about putting my thoughts forward. Steve's sudden outbursts unsettled me. His temper singed all those around him with its ferocity. But it is wise to listen and talk to everyone in a place like Saleem, when your security and your life depend on the people around you. You never know which rumour or piece of information may be the one to save yourself or others.

Ahmed had heard in the market that the displaced group was running out of water. Their nearest water source was four hours away by foot. Adam Ali had met a woman who had just returned from the group with her two children. Both had fallen ill with no shelter and contaminated water. One had died on the way back to town and the other was seriously dehydrated in our clinic.

The decision was made — we were going to find them. The group in the river bed were clearly in a desperate state. Their needs were urgent. Discussions with the security officers in town could wait until tomorrow.

Nevertheless, every journey outside Saleem required the permission of the local authorities, government security officers, intelligence officers and the military. We drove across town and parked the vehicles under the tree outside the security office.

'What do I do?' I asked Steve as I climbed out of the front seat.

'Come with me and I'll introduce you,' he said. We crossed over to the two men sitting against the white wall. 'But don't say anything.'

The men stood up as we approached, resting their AK-47s carefully against the wall.

'Salaam aleikum,' they both said, shaking hands with each of us in turn — Steve, me, the two drivers Musa and Ahmed, and Adam Ali our impeccably dressed translator.

'How's the day, gentlemen?' enquired Steve. 'I hope we're not interrupting anything.'

Around them lay various pieces of disassembled AK-47. Springs, bolts and levers sat in piles on a sheet of dirty grey cloth. Spent bullets lay scattered about on the sand. Each time we visited the security office over the following months we found them cleaning and refitting their weapons with endless patience.

'No problem,' they assured us. 'We have the whole day.'

Steve introduced me as a new team member and explained that we were just going for a drive to show me the area. 'Maybe we will go south,' he said casually. 'Take a look at the old river beds and hand pumps. But not for long.'

The more senior of the two looked at Steve carefully.

'Why do you want to go to the river beds?' he asked. 'What will you find there?'

'Nothing, my friend,' Steve answered easily. 'I just want to give Lisa a guided tour. She will be here a long time, helping your people.'

They both regarded me, unsmiling. I looked back, trying to appear as though it made no difference whether we went or not, and I smiled. Men are the same the world over — so predictable when a woman smiles! Both men smiled back at me, and the younger one winked.

'Okay,' they agreed. 'You can go. But be back here by 4 p.m. We will wait for you.'

With that we all shook hands once more and turned back to the vehicles. My knees felt weak.

'What if they find out you lied to them?' I asked Steve as we walked away.

'Do you think they'd let us go to the river bed if they knew it was full of Zaghawa?' he said. 'They'd rather see them die out there than receive any help. We told them what they were capable of hearing. Besides, there's no one in the riverbed who will tell them where we went. They will never find out.'

Climbing back into our respective vehicles, we slowly retraced our way through town. The reality of the attack started to take shape in my mind as we passed burnt walls and deserted streets. A heavy feeling settled in my chest.

****

The landscape around Saleem was beautiful. Wide open stretches of savannah, long grasses and gently rolling hills in the distance. With access to water and undisturbed by fighting, the farmers had been able to cultivate their fields. Here and there stood neat rows of crops, branches and trunks of thorn trees fencing them off from wandering goats and cows. Little rakubas stood in the middle of each field, small lean-tos with thatched roofs where the children would shelter while parents worked in the fields during the heat of the day. They all stood empty now.

The area between Saleem and the hills was no-man's-land, an area that was held by both sides at different times but by neither side permanently. The sandy track led us closer to the hills and further from the government-held town. Rumour had it that many of the townspeople had fled into the hills where a small lake and proximity to the SLA gave them some measure of security.

Driving up the first steep track I heard Steve calling on the radio. The sound of his voice always made me jump, waiting for either the shouting or a rebuke to come.

'Stop the car but stay inside,' he instructed. 'I want to talk to Ahmed.'

We halted for a few minutes while the drivers and Steve talked through the open windows. Which direction should we go in, what landmarks would guide us? he asked them. In Darfur our daily work was full of such uncertainties; routine and planning altered with the hours. I kept quiet, still unsure of my own opinions and hesitant to speak up.

After an hour or so we veered off the track and started crossing grassy fields as we searched for the river bed. We had rough directions, but in this landscape rivers and villages changed with the seasons and place names varied according to the names of transient village leaders. Al Wadi and Sheik Hassan one month became Al Wahid and Sheik Musa Ibrahim the next. It was all very confusing.

We drove on for another twenty minutes when Ahmed slowed down and looked to the west.

'Look. There they are,' he pointed.

In the distance I could see spots of colour, scraps of fabric tied to the trees, but my eyes blurred in the heat. I blinked to clear my vision. As we drew closer the river bed became clearer. It was filled with people, hundreds of them. They huddled together under trees in groups, some lying beneath pieces of plastic. Children crouched together under shrubs, stealing what shade they could in the fierce midday heat.

There were no aid agencies here, no colourful UN tarpaulins to protect them from the sun. There were no queues for food or lines at the hand pumps — the usual sights that we see on our TVs. Instead there were hundreds of families, most with children, crowded together in the barren, sunbaked river bed, trying to escape the heat, the fighting and their fear. Most had fled in the night, carrying their children and a few possessions as they walked through the no-man's-land and over the hills to escape. Without water or food they sat in the river bed and they waited. Waited for what, I didn't know. There was nobody coming to rescue them, no aid agencies queuing to relieve their suffering, no one with spades to bury the dead. They were alone. And they waited.

Steve's vehicle pulled ahead and stopped beside one of the shelters. We followed as he got out and stood there, hands on his hips.

'Jesus Christ,' he sighed. 'Not again.'

I watched as he and Musa walked forward, shaking hands with a group of men who had risen to greet them. I stood looking around, taking in the bleak surroundings and listening to the sound of plastic in the trees, pulling and snapping in the wind. It was one of the saddest scenes I have ever encountered. Utterly desperate and totally forsaken.

Steve turned to me after a while and called out, 'They say there are some very sick children here. You go and see what you can do and I'll go and talk to the sheiks. See what they need.'

I nodded, glad to be able to do something useful. Ahmed and I pulled the silver box of drugs and equipment from the vehicle and set off with two men.

'The children have been sick for days,' one of them said as we walked. 'We think they have malaria. But we have no treatment for them and we can't go back to the clinic in Saleem — it's not safe. We are just watching them die.'

We followed them to a small grove of trees beside the river bed. A girl, perhaps five years old, lay in the shade. Her mother sat beside her, legs outstretched as she stroked the child's head and arms with long, slow strokes. She was singing softly. I knelt down beside them and put out my hand.

'Salaam aleikum,' I said as we kneeled. 'My name is Lisa.' Ahmed opened the silver box and we set to work.

The little girl's temperature was 41°C, her body burning in the shade. She lay on a piece of red cloth, her eyes closed as she panted for breath. I balanced the little malaria test on two sticks I found in the sand, pricked her finger with a small needle and waited for enough blood to start the test. I watched as Ahmed counted the six drops of buffer solution onto the tray. Within minutes the result was clear — she had cerebral malaria, a killer in any country. Taking off my backpack I emptied my water bottle into two cups that sat on the sand beside her. The family had no water containers and the ten-year-old child sent to collect water for the day had not yet returned.

Without prompting, Ahmed started to explain to the family what the test showed and how the girl needed to take the treatment. As a driver for MSF, Ahmed had experience with every side of the project: performing malaria tests, administering drug treatment, doing mechanical repairs and negotiating with the military. Before the war he had worked as a laboratory assistant in Nyala's general hospital. He had mapped out his future and chosen a wife. Once he qualified he was going to save for a house in one of the smarter areas of Nyala. Then he would marry and settle down to enjoy his life. But it wasn't to be. The war had stolen his dreams. Family members were killed, others came to live in his small house as they ran from their villages in the east. He had more than twenty people to feed and look after in his home, so he had to look for a job that paid more money. He found work with MSF.

He told me all this as we drove that morning, his face sad. But when he finished talking he turned to me and smiled.

'But that is how the life goes, Lisa,' he said. 'Maybe next year the war will be finished and I can find a safe job.'

As I knelt in the sand I smiled at him, grateful for his help and relieved by his skill.

Within minutes a crowd had gathered around us, some holding out sick babies and others asking us to come to their shelters to see the sick. We agreed that what they needed was a more organised clinic, so Ahmed quickly explained to them why we were there and told them to bring only the sickest to see us beside our vehicles. That said, we half ran and half walked back to the vehicles, Ahmed dragging the heavy silver box through the sand.

Adam Ali had already pulled the metal trunks from the back of the land cruiser and set up tables and chairs in the shade when we arrived.

'I knew you were busy so I have prepared everything,' he said, smiling.

I sighed with relief. Where would I be without these two men with their smiling faces and willing hearts?

Over the following ninety minutes we saw an avalanche of patients. Babies with diarrhoea, children with malaria and adults suffering from dehydration. Forgetting my stethoscope and thermometer, I worked at a frantic pace, touching, feeling, listening and palpating as I examined each one. Antibiotics, paracetamol, malaria treatment and rehydration salts flowed from the drug box as we worked. Ahmed switched roles again and now worked as the pharmacist, giving instructions as he dispensed plastic bags of tablets and watched while children swallowed their first dose of malaria treatment. Names and ages became irrelevant, histories were brief. What was important was what we could see and feel in front of us.

Behind the vehicles Steve crouched in the sun and talked into his satellite phone, relaying his findings to Nyala: numbers of people, their immediate needs and security concerns. He turned now and then to look at the crush of people around us and counted them quickly with a practised eye. All of this was noted and the logistical wheels were set in motion back in Nyala. Plastic sheeting, jerry cans and medications were ordered and would await the next vehicles to Saleem for distribution to this frightened and exhausted group.

Miles from anywhere we worked as a team, doing something to meet the needs of these people and helping where nobody else was. Our little medical group laboured without pause, diagnosing illness, treating wounds and organising patients. Through the frenetic activity I felt calm. I was part of something that mattered and for the first time in so long I fitted into my life.

But all too soon it was over.

'You guys have to pack up now if we're going to make it back to Saleem by four o'clock,' Steve called out to us just before 2 p.m.

But still the crowd queued and pushed, asking, pleading and begging for more time. 'My son, my baby, my father . . . please . . .' I looked around at them all and felt my heart sink.

'We can't leave them, Steve,' I said, feeling overwhelmed by the need. 'There are people here who will die without treatment.'

'We have to go or we'll not be any use to them in the future,' he replied. 'Pack up now! With luck, we can return in a few days.'

Closing the lid on that blue metal trunk was one of the hardest things I had ever had to do. Saying no to those men and women, telling them that we were out of time and had to leave them. You can divorce yourself from that reality when it is presented to you on television or in the newspaper. But when it's you standing in the blistering heat, a crush of pleading bodies surrounding you, your boots burning on the hot sand and you must look those people in the eyes and say no, then it hurts. With sadness and a throbbing head, I closed my eyes and turned away.

I knew we had to go, to check in with the security officers in Saleem after our 'scenic drive' in the bush. Back to shake hands with and smile at the very people who had driven these poor people into the bush, to struggle and die alone. We drove back to town in silence, Ahmed, Adam Ali and I in the second vehicle. We all felt exhausted by the day's events, drained by the scale of the need that we had left behind.

As I stood beside Steve outside the security office in Saleem shaking hands, I felt sick.

'Welcome again in Saleem,' said the younger officer. 'I hope you had a good time.'

I smiled as I'd been taught and looked at my boots, saying nothing. I just wanted to go home.

We didn't make it back to the river bed for months after that day. War has a way of upsetting plans and throwing priorities into disarray. Other needs surfaced in Saleem, we found more groups of displaced people, and security limited our movements to the south. The little girl with malaria whom we treated in the shade died — her father returned to town weeks later and gave us the news. I have never forgotten those people, waiting for us to return. I think of the hot, stinging wind, the sound of the plastic being whipped by the wind through the thorn trees and I see them watching me. Who knows where they are now, where they moved to when they realised that no one was coming back to help them. That is the reality of war; the waiting and the despair. And it keeps me awake at night.

****

As the days passed we stood witness to more and more injustices, still more wicked acts committed by the people we shared the town with as they intimidated, raped and murdered others in and around Saleem. Some days there was occasional gunfire, a plume of smoke or we noticed that the clinic seemed quieter than usual. Other days the shooting and screaming lasted long into the night.

My mind simply couldn't comprehend the reality around me, the horror of the lives of the villagers who were targeted in the smaller attacks. Instead I concentrated on my work, treating patients and trying to create some routine in my days. If I could control the small space around me then perhaps the rest would become less chaotic and out of control. The other three in the team, Steve, Sam and Toby, were focused and stressed and they moved about in a haze of cigarette smoke from dawn to dusk. There was no time to chat, to reveal tiredness or to cry. It was enough to simply make it through each day.

The days and nights crowded and tumbled into one another in those first months. I tried to hold the outreach programme together, to supervise the local staff in the clinic, write reports, reorganise the chaotic, mouse-infested pharmacy, to order drugs and do assessments of displaced people living out in the bush. When a critically ill patient was brought to the clinic, Sam and I were called to treat them. We'd spend hours in the small, hot treatment room trying to rehydrate, suture and heal our patients. We saved some patients, but we lost too many.

At night my mind raced as I tried to think of ways to work more efficiently. Perhaps if I got up earlier or delegated more? But I already started work at 5.30 a.m., and with a skeleton team of four people there was no one to delegate to. Each person carried more than their share of the load through each day. It never occurred to me that perhaps the load was actually impossible.

Even so, there were windows of time where life felt good, when I rested and smiled with satisfaction. Brief moments of clarity and simplicity that came in gently and lit my day. They usually happened at sunset, when the light was softening and the burning heat had started to subside. I'd lie on my back, in the shade of the acacia tree, and watch the leaves move with the wind. The respite usually only lasted minutes, but in those days it was enough.

We all know that pleasure — the simple pleasure of a rest well earned. Perhaps on the first day of a long weekend after the madness of a busy week. When the hours of peace and relaxation stretch before you, work behind. That was how I felt and I loved it.

On Thursday afternoon of the second week in Saleem I sat with my back against the tree and drew circles in the sand. The promise of a whole day off on the Friday was intoxicating. Yes, I had only been in the project for two weeks, but the sixteen- and seventeen-hour days, with only one Friday off, had taken their toll and I was exhausted.

Steve, Toby, Sam and I ate dinner together, while the drivers and translators sat on mats in front of their tuckuls nearby. They were slowly working their way through the three-hour-long feast that is a Ramadan meal. After fasting all day they took great delight in drawing out their evening meal, talking, laughing and singing well into the night, stopping only to pray again before retiring to bed.

After our short meal I returned to my spot under the tree and waited for the coffee to brew. Tiny fire finches danced through the branches, flashes of turquoise and red as they flitted, calling to each other in short, rolling peeps. Perhaps they were also revelling in the evening bliss.

Toby found an old CD player in one of the tuckuls, a relic of somebody's hasty departure. Balancing on a little wooden table beside the tree, it played Toby's two CDs in ever-repeating loops: Van Morrison's mellow tones always followed by a mournful Portuguese singer, her voice deep and sorrowful. I lost track of how many times we listened to the music, over and over again. But that evening, with my stress and exhaustion fading, I loved every note.

When the coffee was ready Steve carried a mug over to me, pushing it down into the sand. Sweet, rich coffee, blended with a touch of spice and a hint of something I could never quite put my finger on. I didn't need to. It was perfect. I thought back to my early days in Nyala, the long hours of lethargy and fly watching. I had come here looking for an adventure, a way to stretch myself and grow while I worked to make a difference. My old fear resurfaced briefly, asking 'Who are *you* to make a difference — what have *you* got to offer?' And what if I couldn't cope with the horrors and stress of daily life, with the sound of gunfire and listening to more stories of terror? I didn't have an answer yet. I still wasn't sure what I could really do. But I had put my hands out, touched real problems and real people. And it was a start.

CHAPTER THREE

It is a curious fact of life, but the relationship between fear and passion is a close one. As I stood on the edge of the crowd, surrounded by armed soldiers and Janjaweed militia, I felt fear. Cold, heart-stopping fear. The commander stood watching us, his face stony, his authority absolute. And he said nothing. Through my fear and inertia I also felt more alive and alert than ever before. Colours and sounds seemed more brilliant and sharp. The sound of boots scuffing the sand around us was loud in my ears. And the clatter of the soldiers' grenade belts as they jumped down from their vehicles ripped through me. Fearful and alive in a single breath.

Steve and I arrived in El Wadi with Ahmed and Musa soon after breakfast. We made our way slowly along deserted streets in our rumbling vehicles. News of El Wadi's isolation after the attack of Saleem on September 19th had reached us in the weeks that followed. We heard stories of intimidation and violence, dwindling food supplies and medicines in the government-held town as villagers escaped. The SLA had launched an attack on El Wadi in the wake of September 19th, but had been pushed back into the surrounding hills by government forces. The Zaghawa tribe, among others, were being treated badly and threatened because of their presumed support of the SLA attack. But there were no outsiders to see what unfolded. We discussed the rumours amongst the team and decided we had to venture north to see the situation for ourselves. Four weeks after my arrival in Saleem I was about to have my first taste of fear.

The security officers in Saleem had been unhelpful as we left, closed and unfriendly as we explained our plans for the day's trip.

'Why are you going?' asked the tall one. 'What will you do there?'

We planned to visit El Wadi to see the situation for ourselves. If people were hungry, sick or afraid then there would be a reason for us to return later to run a clinic or talk to more people. And if all was well, as the local officials in Saleem told us, then we would return knowing that the people did not need us.

The official in Saleem wanted a report on our return; who we had found and what they said. I kept smiling.

'Inshallah,' Steve replied. God willing; the word with a thousand meanings. It could mean yes, no, perhaps, later, half truths or never. Inshallah to their demands. Inshallah to our obligations.

We drove into the village from the south, following the track used by commercial traffic in the past. Great chasms were gouged into the dry earth, signs of last year's rainy season. Streams and bogs covered much of the area from June to September, leaving the tracks almost impassable as mud sucked and oozed around unsuspecting wheels. But now it was dry. Our vehicles bounced and jarred along, veering suddenly to avoid the chasms and holes all around us. Clouds of dust surrounded us as Ahmed and I followed Steve and Musa. Our two land cruisers were the only vehicles in sight. Through the open window I saw Steve's arm resting in the sun, his cigarette ever present and hanging between his long fingers.

Standing in the market I looked around at the deserted town. Long roads, dusty and unswept, stretched ahead and down to the lake. Two donkeys stood in the shade of a tree, their front legs bound, heads hanging in the heat. In the distance I heard the rhythmic creaking of a hand pump as someone collected water out of sight.

Two men appeared from an alley, their white jelabyia gowns billowing in the hot wind. They walked towards us, smiling, arms outstretched to welcome us.

'Salaam aleikum,' they repeated, nodding and smiling as they shook hands with the four of us in turn.

'You must stay for some tea,' said the oldest, his grey whiskers and tired eyes hiding behind falling wrinkles. 'We have not many guests.'

Steve and I looked at each other. Not many guests in this strangled town of frightened villagers — it was no surprise.

He turned and shouted for a chair. In seconds a little boy emerged from the alley, struggling with a heavy metal chair. Its blue-and-white seat was torn and fading, its thin rusting legs dragging through the sand as he stumbled towards us. Being the only woman I was given the chair.

'Shukran,' I whispered to the boy. Thank you.

He looked at me with wide eyes and ran back to the alley.

And then the soldiers arrived. The heavy sound of a vehicle somewhere behind the low thatched buildings made everyone turn. A roar, the rough sound of gears changing and the vehicle lumbered out of the alley. Its camouflage green paintwork looked dull in the sunlight, the brown splashes ugly and crude. The driver slammed the vehicle to a halt in front of us making the engine stall. The dozen or so soldiers standing on the back fell and stumbled against each other, their guns clashing together. The scene would have been comical was it not for the enormous machine gun mounted on the back and the barrel of a rocket-propelled grenade launcher pointed at us.

Four soldiers jumped down, their boots landing heavily in the sand. They walked towards us, one stopping behind each of us. Their commander sat in the driver's seat, his hand on the wheel.

'One question,' he said in English. 'Why are you here?' He looked straight ahead, not at us, as he fingered the green lace around the steering wheel.

Steve walked towards him, always the negotiator, and smiled. But before he could speak, a second vehicle roared into the marketplace, with more soldiers surrounding another mounted machine gun. It drew to a halt behind us. We were surrounded.

I stood up, my mind empty and heart pounding. I walked over to Steve, looking for something familiar and safe in those minutes of fear. I reached out and touched his shirt, my hand shaking.

'Good morning, Commander,' he said, standing to attention in the hot sun. 'We have come to introduce ourselves and to offer our services to the people.' Respect means everything in this country. With weapons like theirs and absolute power this group commanded our utmost respect.

'I know who you are and we do not need your services,' replied the commander, his eyes still looking ahead.

Oh shit, oh shit, I said to myself. The barrel of an RPG sat inches from Steve's head. It looked lethal; huge and bulbous in the bright sunlight. What do we do now?

My hand dropped from Steve's shirt and I felt Musa take my other hand, giving it a gentle squeeze. He led me back to the shade and guided me to the creaking chair. In a moment of fear and my own helplessness, Musa rescued me with a smile. With his gentle touch he reminded me that he was there and that I was safe.

I sat on my torn throne and quietly worried my boots into the sand while Steve negotiated with the commander. I concentrated on the feel of my feet in my socks, not on the weapons that surrounded us. In moments like that there is no universal rule for action. I couldn't put up my hand and say, 'I am from New Zealand, you can't hurt me.' Or 'this is wrong; you have to let us go now.' The rules of war are flexible. The man holding the gun decides what he will and won't do. I kept my eyes on my feet.

****

Steve negotiated and the commander gave a little. Steve talked some more and after some time the unsmiling commander relented. We could have two hours to look at the sickest patients. Two hours in a village of 20,000 people, and again I was the only medical person. After all Steve's negotiations we had a window of opportunity to look, listen and learn about the problems in the town. My headache and pounding heart left me feeling unfriendly and withdrawn. I was in no frame of mind to take on a storm of patients all desperate to be seen; asking, tugging, relentless. But as the military vehicles reversed and disappeared back into the labyrinth of the market place, I knew we were lucky to be there. The guns were gone, the threat had lifted and we had two hours to help. There was no time to withdraw or hide from the need around us. I closed my eyes and sighed deeply, willing my spirit to carry me through the day.

****

After the soldiers had left, the marketplace was still. No birds, no voices, not even the sound of leaves rustling in the wind. Nothing.

I looked up as Steve walked past me, wiping the perspiration from his forehead. The day was already oppressively hot and it was only 10 a.m.

'Right, let's do some work,' he said. 'It's up to you now, Lisa.' And he climbed into his vehicle.

I sat a moment longer. Breathing in, breathing out. As I stood I knocked the sand from my buried boots. The elderly man who had first greeted us stood as I rose.

'No problem,' he said, smiling. 'We will help you.' He took my hands in his and gave them a warm squeeze. 'We will help.'

****

Half an hour later we were working frantically in our makeshift clinic, our vehicles parked under a tree on the edge of the market. Around us stood a crowd of villagers. About three hundred people had come running when they heard that MSF had arrived. A surging, crushing, impatient crowd, all talking, calling and shouting for attention. It was the peak of the malaria season and the general health of the community was poor. All around me their need pushed in. How do you prioritise when they all need help now? Children lay in the sand beside their mothers, women lay under sheets, carried to us on mats by worried relatives, babies with diarrhoea lay unmoving and dehydrated in their mothers arms.

Now. Now. Now.

My headache started to grip even tighter. Surrounded by the initial chaos and frantic need, I felt helpless and lost. Every face needed me. I felt paralysed. Musa rescued me again. He called to me, directed my attention, pulled my eyes towards the patients I had missed.

The rest of the team worked together; performing blood tests, taking temperatures, handing out medications and more while I examined and diagnosed patients as fast as I could. I scribbled prescriptions on pieces of paper and handed them to Ahmed.

Malaria, chest infections, abscesses and dehydration stood or lay in front of me, the patients exhausted by their wait, the stress of life under the military eye and the relentless advance of disease. Musa prioritised patients as he moved through the crowd, taking temperatures and lifting up blankets to look at those on the ground. His eyes were as sharp as any nurse's when he was doing triage. War is the ideal classroom for those without formal training. He had seen everything before.

'Over here, Lisa,' he called when he found someone seriously ill. And the family would carry them to me, lying them down on the sand between the two vehicles in our shady consultation area.

Steve's military background gave him the practical skills to deal with situations like this. Creating order from disorder, his methodical way of working soon had the clinic running more smoothly. Patients had numbered cards and a rope barrier stopped the curious onlookers from intruding on consultations. If only there weren't so many people.

At one point I stood up and screamed. I couldn't take the noise and crush any more.

'I cannot work if you all pull and push and shout at me!' I bellowed. My Arabic was poor but they understood. The crowd pulled back, their faces anxious and strained in the morning heat. I stopped working and climbed up the metal rungs to stand on the roof of the land cruiser to escape the heat and the crowd. Stretched out below me were hundreds of people, not the colourful, chattering faces of our routine clinics. These were frightened faces, tired and strained, wearing torn clothes and dirty jelabiya gowns. It was overwhelming.

I took a few deep breaths and closed my eyes. Then I scrambled back down to the ground. I moved through the children, checking Ahmed's malaria tests. The strips of white-plastic test kits were lined up on a piece of cardboard, revealing the horror of cerebral malaria. Eight out of the ten children and babies had malaria, and all needed treatment faster than we could work. The sickest of them lay in their mothers' arms, dehydrated and exhausted as the parasites stole their lives.

I stood unmoving beside Ahmed, giving in to the chaos and my helplessness again, when I saw Musa walking slowly towards me. His arms were around the shoulders of a young woman.

'Lisa, this woman needs your help,' he said softly. He sat her down on a wooden box and gently lifted the wet fabric from her chest. 'Her name is Hanan. She had a baby two weeks ago but now her breasts are very painful. She has fevers and cannot feed her baby.'

Beneath the fabric her young breasts lay in gaping, abscess-filled agony. Great wounds filled with pus covered every surface of each breast. Lifting each one in turn revealed cavities beneath, each the size of a tennis ball. Muslim etiquette and her modesty were gone as she sat swaying, her eyes closed as she tried to breathe through the pain. She was beyond caring who saw her wounds.

What do I do? Where do I start? I asked myself as her family watched me. Her mother held the newborn baby in a dirty green-coloured blanket. It looked so close to death and I didn't have time for the dying. The young mother needed wound swabs, a blood culture, intravenous fluids and antibiotics to start with. Her baby needed intensive nursing care, his tiny body dehydrated and exhausted with malnutrition. Instead I had five minutes to keep the flies from her wounds and to muddle together a plan to try to save her life.

I ran to the silver box that sat in the back of the vehicle, the box that saves lives. The silver box was our portable hospital, with a handful of everything you might need in an emergency. Needles, syringes, antibiotics in vials and packets of dressings. I pulled everything out of the box, leaving a confused mess on the floor as I searched for the treatment I needed.

'I need a carrier bag,' I called out to Ahmed. 'And a handful of paracetamol and antibiotics to treat an abscess.' Within seconds he raised his left arm, my orders filled and sitting in neatly labelled drug bags, all inside a brightly coloured carrier bag. He'd barely broken his rhythm as he dispensed drugs for the waiting children.

'Thank you, Ahmed,' I whispered as I grabbed the bag and ran over to the young woman.

I knelt beside her, my knees in the sand, as I started to treat her.

'What is your name?' I asked quietly. 'How old are you? You do have a beautiful baby. This might sting a little. Take a deep breath.' I kept talking to her, my Arabic imperfect, but the words trying to distract her from my work as I examined her carefully. I lifted the dress above her knee, injecting her with pain relief and antibiotics. Her thin leg shook, the muscle quivering with fever and hunger. I couldn't start cleaning and lifting her swollen, yellow-crusted breasts until her pain had subsided.

'Come with me, lie down here and I will come back in a few minutes,' I said, covering her breasts and leading her to the foot of a shady tree, away from the crowd. 'I won't forget you, just close your eyes.' She hadn't said a word, her eyes sunken and her body shaking as I talked. She lay down slowly, with a grunt of pain as she relaxed her muscles. I stroked her arm and hand, not knowing how else to show her that I cared. In her silence she grasped my hand and squeezed it gently. Then she started to cry.

'Lisa, another one for you,' Musa called out. 'There is a woman lying on a mat over there, bleeding down below.' He pointed to the outskirts of the crowd. Then he turned and walked back to look for more patients.

I walked over to Ahmed and Steve, both working at a frantic pace. They were diagnosing and treating malaria according to the protocol — textbook work that all non-medics could do safely and well. Steve was also responsible for making radio contact with our base in Saleem every fifteen minutes. He had arranged frequent radio checks because of the uncertain situation. This wasn't an ordinary day. Toby sat by the radio all day, ready to relay our situation to Nyala while we were out of Saleem. There was no sign of trouble but Steve had a feeling that things might change.

'Are you two okay?' I asked. Neither looked up.

'Yes,' said Steve. 'We're going as fast as we can, but they just keep coming.' I reached out and touched his shoulder.

'You are both doing a great job, guys.' They looked up briefly and smiled. We were in this together and all of a sudden I felt like I belonged, as though every vivid second was more precious than anything before. Maybe, just maybe, we could help these people. I turned away before they caught me looking sentimental.

I pulled some more drugs and equipment from the silver box, stuffed them into my pockets and ran over to the bleeding woman. She lay on a mat, groaning, her skin hot and fevered. I pulled the malaria test from my pocket and pricked her finger with a needle. I'd start with the obvious problem first.

****

Just at that moment, the soldiers arrived. Two vehicles roared up to the crowd carrying new soldiers and a new commander. The engines revved and the soldiers shouted as they jumped from the back of each camouflaged vehicle, their guns clattering and grenades swaying as they landed. Some were government troops and some were Janjaweed militia, Ahmed told me later. I couldn't tell the difference as we watched them walk closer. A group of soldiers started to walk towards the crowd, each carrying long camel whips. Women screamed, they started to run and the children began to cry.

Three of the soldiers started into the crowd, wheeling their whips in circles and making an almighty *crack* as they whipped the air. They laughed as they lurched at the crowd, taunting, intimidating and frightening.

Their commander stepped out of the first vehicle. His pale skin stood out amongst those around him.

'Your work is finished,' he said in Arabic. 'You will leave now.' Ahmed translated quietly, his eyes on the ground.

After the paralysis of my first moments of the clinic my body now felt alive and focused. I was *not* going to listen to a short, barrel-chested man telling me to stop treating patients. We were making a difference here and I was not negotiating.

Steve, Ahmed and Musa stood up and walked towards the commander. They stood in the hot sun and I could hear talking. I walked backwards slowly to Ahmed's table of paracetamol and malaria treatment and started to fill bags. The bleeding woman needed treatment and I was going to give it to her. Bugger the soldiers. One bag. Two bags. Three ...

'Stop now.'

I looked up and saw the commander pointing directly at me.

'Stop.'

His small eyes were dark, his face unsmiling. His camouflage uniform looked ill-fitting on his small frame.

'Fuck you,' I wanted to shout. The anger flared under my skin and I ground my teeth together. I looked at Steve, his back straight and unmoving in the sun. I put down the bags and walked over to stand with them.

'Give me your radios,' said the commander. 'And the keys to your vehicles. Remove the batteries from your satellite phone.' He stood with his hand outstretched. 'Now!'

I watched as Ahmed and Steve obeyed his orders. They handed

their batteries and keys to the commander. The two soldiers at his side took the goods and walked over to their vehicle, putting them on the front seat. Our safety and our lives were protected by that equipment. Without them we were alone. I looked at the others, then down at my feet. We really were alone.

For the first time in my life I felt truly afraid. A cold, shuddering fear like no other. This was no game where we waited for someone to call 'Okay, stop' from the sidelines. This was real, their guns were real and no one was coming for us. In Saleem Toby would have noticed our silence at the last fifteen-minute radio check, but that was not going to help us right now. We stood in silence, my skin burning in the sun. Behind us over one hundred patients shifted uncomfortably as they waited.

We stood like that for seconds, minutes or longer. I lost track of time. The commander watched us, looked at the crowd and kept silent.

'These people do not need you,' he said quietly. 'You will leave now.' His eyes rested on Steve. 'Now.'

Steve stepped forward, his hands palm upwards. I took a deep breath. Now we're in business, I thought. The consummate negotiator is about to begin. Ten minutes later Steve had found a way in, a point of negotiation. The commander had indigestion. For an extra five minutes of clinic time we would give him a month's supply of antacids. As I knelt at the drug box I wished for pellets of rat poison to give him instead. For a further five minutes his colleague wanted paracetamol for his toothache. I wanted to give him cyanide. And so it went. Steve negotiated thirty minutes of extra time in exchange for drugs. Everyone wants something in this world. In times of stress and danger you just have to find the key to their greed.

I left Ahmed dispensing the drugs-for-time to the military as

Steve, Musa and I went back to work. On Ahmed's wooden table sat a long row of malaria tests. Most of them were positive for cerebral malaria.

'Where are these patients?' I asked Steve, pointing at the tests.

'I think most of them ran away when the soldiers arrived,' he replied. 'They won't be back now, they're too frightened.'

'But they'll die without treatment. We have to find them.' I felt panic spread through me.

'They're gone, Lisa. We have to treat the ones that stayed. Look around — they need our help too.' He pointed to the waiting groups, still and silent in their fear.

I walked away from the table, my heart breaking. Those that stayed did need us, but what of the patients who sat hiding in their tuckuls and behind trees. They needed us too. I went back to the group under the second tree. The woman with vaginal bleeding was beyond my ability to treat. I knelt down and pulled a heavy, brown blanket over both of us as I started to examine her. Her dignity was somewhat preserved as I fumbled in the dark. I tried to find out where and why she was bleeding, but my Arabic failed me and my sight was poor in the dim light. Behind me stood a soldier, I could feel his boots on the mat against my own.

I stopped for a moment, my head hanging as I leant on my hands and knees. The heat under the blanket was unbearable, the smell of sweat and blood overwhelming. She could be miscarrying and things could get much worse.

'Oh God,' I thought, 'I don't know what I'm doing.' I couldn't just leave her. But without a speculum, good lights and some space I was achieving nothing.

'Please come to the hospital in Saleem,' I whispered to her, not wanting the soldier to hear. Taking patients away for treatment was not part of the commander's plan.

'Here is the treatment for malaria, but *please* come to the hospital.'

I pressed the bag of tablets into her hand. She wiped her eyes and looked at me.

'Mamumkin,' she whispered back. Not possible.

I drew the blanket back and looked around. The weapon in the soldier's hands knocked my back as I stood. He stepped backwards and adjusted his gun over his other shoulder. Around the mat stood her family, her husband clasped the blanket in his arms.

'Okay?' he asked, stepping towards me.

'The malaria is no problem,' I said quietly. 'Come to Saleem for the bleeding.'

He shook his head. 'Mamumkin,' he replied.

There was nothing more I could do. I turned away and walked to the vehicle without looking back.

'Lisa,' called Steve. 'We've just got another six or seven babies. We need help over here.'

I walked towards him, but stopped as I caught sight of a pair of thin legs resting behind the tree. The woman with the abscesses, Hanan — I had forgotten about her! She lay quietly, her eyes open as her mother gently poured water into her mouth.

'Pain?' I asked.

She shook her head and smiled. 'No pain,' she whispered.

Around us the soldiers stood in pairs, holding their weapons closely. By now I didn't care about them. I cared about my patients. I ran to the vehicle and collected more dressing equipment for Hanan's wounds. She deserved my patience and care as I cleaned away the pus, lifting each breast and wiping the cavities clean. But there was no time. Instead I worked quickly, packing the wounds with an antibacterial cream, usually kept for burn wounds. It would prevent the infection spreading and the flies from feeding from her wounds while the antibiotics started to work. It was all so undignified, so primitive. But she kept her eyes closed as the soldiers watched and I worked. It was the best we could do.

I handed her mother the bag of dressing material, giving her basic instructions on cleaning the wounds until I could see her again. Ahmed's carefully labelled antibiotics and paracetamol would bring her some relief in the meantime. But who knew when we would be back.

'Lisa!' shouted Steve. 'We need you *here*.'

Lying on the ground around Steve were six babies, quiet and panting for breath in the shade.

'We've got five minutes,' Steve said quietly. 'I'll start packing up now, so work fast.'

Ahmed and I worked in silence, malaria tests, injections, rehydration solution and wet cloths to cool their burning skin. He didn't need prompting. A mother stood by each baby, unwilling to be there, surrounded by soldiers but desperate for treatment.

'I need more time, there are more coming, please give me more time,' I whispered to Steve, nodding towards the new group of mothers who stood beside the vehicle. 'They ran away when the soldiers came, but their babies need treatment.'

'We don't have any more time,' he replied. 'Just keep working, keep your head down, and when he says "Stop", then you stop immediately.' He gestured towards the commander, who still stood in the sun watching us.

So we kept working. I held my breath, praying 'just one more, just one more, please.' Six, seven, eight babies. Then I heard a shout 'Stop! You must leave now!'

And so I stopped. The babies lying on the sand received their treatment and all were carefully lifted onto their mothers' backs, tied on with a soft sheet and they quickly disappeared from sight. The newcomers stood silently and watched while the drugs were packed into boxes and the vehicle doors shut. They held their babies tightly, surely knowing that their only chance for help was about to drive out of town.

The commander returned our keys, the radios and batteries. The two military vehicles reversed slowly, giving us room to leave. Their engines idled and the soldiers climbed onto the back, laughing and banging the butt of their guns on the metal floor. It was all a joke for them, a game of intimidation that they won every time.

I sat beside Ahmed in the vehicle while Steve talked with the commander. I couldn't raise my eyes to the waiting mothers, or look across to the woman who lay bleeding on the mat. What did the soldiers care? Inside my heart felt cold, my hands wouldn't stop shaking. Had we really made a difference? What would the soldiers do to the patients we were leaving behind? The commander had won, that much was clear. We drove slowly out of town, and no one said a word.

****

Over the following days the faces of the women we left behind in El Wadi haunted me. I went about my work, organising the pharmacy, meeting with the community outreach workers and dealing with staff issues, their complaints and demands. But their eyes followed me. Those women who stood quietly as we left El Wadi, their children sick or dying in their arms as we drove away. They were helpless and we left them.

In our compound in Saleem Toby had already established himself as a procrastinator, an inert body that achieved little, but still finding time to smoke an endless number of cigarettes while he thought about his tasks. He was our Canadian fossil.

'Toby, did you manage to find those staff lists I asked for yesterday?' I asked one morning.

'Ahhhh, no. I was looking for them but I remembered that the warehouse needed cleaning so I made a plan for the guys to reorganise it tomorrow. It's important stuff, Lisa.'

'Toby, did you get those staff lists from last week?' I asked again several days later.

'Ahhhh, no. You have to realise how busy I am. I had to make sure the guys cleaned the warehouse and it's taken all week. Maybe next week. Just relax.'

It was Toby's job to keep the project moving with logistical supplies. And with four expats, three staff from Nyala and over sixty local staff he did have his hands full. But his days were filled with tasks he never quite accomplished.

'Toby, Salah's salary is incorrect again this month. Can you fix it?'

'Ahhhh, I'll do my best, Lisa. It's all very complicated.'

Needless to say Salah's salary continued to be a surprise every time. He never quite knew what he would find when he opened his brown envelope at the end of each month. Oddly enough it seemed to be a surprise to Toby too.

By Tuesday night the frustrations of Toby's non-achievements and the haunting eyes from El Wadi became too much. I was tense and snapped at everyone, my body aching for solitude. I wanted to escape the frenetic activity and endless report writing. Our beautifully swept compound with its straight thatched walls and fresh washing on the line had become a prison. Every footstep outside the compound was watched by our guards, every journey was accompanied by a driver, Ahmed or Musa. The security situation could change in town in a flash; a Janjaweed raid, an SLA attack from the hills or nervous government troops firing into town. Each of us carried a radio, ready for trouble or to be called for another emergency. Every activity inside the compound was watched by

Selwa and Halima, the compound ladies. Simple curiosity and interest, I knew, but it became intrusive and tiring.

The sound of a gunshot somewhere in the village every day made me jump, my nerves stretched even tighter. Who had they shot? Why were they shooting? What would we do if the victim was brought to us — with no operating theatre or access to blood transfusions what more could we do but watch them die, slowly dripping on the clinic floor.

That night I walked slowly to the shower. The concrete slab of the shower stall was smooth, the heat of the day slowly escaping and warming my feet. The blue water barrel stood in the corner, filled carefully during the day by our local water supplier, Idriss. He led his donkey to the shade of the tree every morning and lifted the lid of the drum that rested on the cart. It took over an hour to fill the drum, one bucket at a time from the leaking rubber hose. There in the dark the water's surface reflected the stars, bright streaks of light in the rippled water.

I filled my little black bucket from the barrel and cup by cup I washed away the frustrations of the day. All around me the night sounds called; crickets, beetles, bats and faraway dogs. I heard women talking as they crossed a nearby path, laughing as they carried home their last buckets of water from the hand pump. The guards outside the gate were playing cards and every now and then one would shout triumphantly, the other grumbling and conceding before the next game began.

Toby's failings and my own frustration started to fade as I soaped and foamed, splashed and dripped in the dark. I sat on the concrete floor, my hair running cold rivers across my skin. Their eyes wouldn't leave me, though, even in the dark. The women with their dying babies always found me. With my eyes closed and my head hiding in my arms, I started to cry.

****

Later that evening I went to look for Steve.

'Steve, when are we going back to El Wadi? We can't leave those people. It's been five days and the children are dying with malaria.'

'We'll go when security permits, Lisa,' he replied, his eyes never leaving the computer screen. 'Militia movements, government permits, security concerns here in town — there are a lot of factors to take into consideration.' He reached for a cigarette, his head disappearing in a haze of blue smoke as he drew deeply, again and again.

'I'm doing my best,' he muttered.

I turned away. We were all doing our best but still women were being attacked, children and babies were dying from malaria unnecessarily and more areas of town were emptying as the unwanted tribes were pushed into the bush.

Suddenly the sound of gunfire ripped through the darkness. Heavy explosions, the blunt, high-pitched sound of rifles.

'Down, down, everybody down!' shouted Steve. 'Into the bomb shelter now. Heads down and run!'

We ran, crawled and fell down the sandbag stairs of the bomb shelter — Toby, Sam, the guards, drivers, Adam Ali and me. Steve crouched at the entrance and counted us as we went down, then he slipped down the stairs behind us. We fell and stumbled until we came to rest in the deep, dark tomb. The sandy floor was cold, my bare feet hurting from running and tripping over stones. Adam Ali held a kerosene lantern, its dim orange light giving us warmth as we drew together, shoulders resting against each other for comfort.

'Are you okay?' asked Adam Ali.

I nodded, my heart thundering in my chest.

Above and around us the fighting tore the night apart. Steve sat on the steps, his head to one side.

'There are more shots going out of town, not so many coming in. They've had a threat from the east,' he said quietly. 'Some are firing at a target at close range, you can hear the echo.'

I looked round at the others. Musa and Adam Ali looked straight ahead into the darkness, their hands clenched. The two guards sat together beside the steps, talking softly. Ahmed drew lines in the sand with his finger, counting the shots. Seven, eight, nine, ten. I turned away.

When the fighting stopped we sat in the cold silence of the bomb shelter.

'We will stay here for thirty minutes after the last shot is fired,' instructed Steve, looking at his watch. 'No one moves. I'm going to call Nyala and update them,' he said as he disappeared into the darkness above. We heard his voice, low and deep, as he spoke to someone on the phone.

I rested my head against the sandbag wall and felt the warmth of Adam Ali's arm against mine.

'Have you been down here many times?' I asked.

'Many times,' he sighed. 'Tonight was easy. Sometimes it comes much closer. Sometimes I think they want us.'

'Tell me about your family,' I said, wanting to change the subject. 'Pretend we're not down here. Pretend we're all sitting in your home.'

The others turned to listen. There in the dark we played make-believe. We were warm and we were safe, sitting around Adam Ali's table in the smart suburbs of Nyala, his wife and baby daughter with us as we talked and laughed quietly.

He spun tales of his family, painted us pictures of his dream home, its strong walls and new television set in the corner. Even in the depths of war we have our dreams. In Adam Ali's dream, life was good and we were happy.

****

The fighting in and around Saleem erupted more frequently in the days and weeks that followed. Threats and counter-threats, nervous soldiers shooting in the night. There were a dozen different reasons. In our area of South Eastern Darfur the SLA held huge tracts of land. Their area seemed to be expanding and strengthening with time. The tribes of Janjaweed militia held their traditional land, dotted around government-held towns. The Government of Sudan (GoS) forces held two towns in the heart of SLA land — Saleem and El Wadi. Surrounded on all sides by open savannah and rocky hills the GoS-held towns were always open to attack. A full-scale assault like the one on September 19th wasn't launched again during my three months in Saleem, but the threat was always there.

During daylight hours the soldiers demonstrated their strength — convoys of trucks sped through town along bumpy, sandy paths. Dozens of soldiers crowded on the back of each one, cheering or shouting as they drove. Uniforms, weapons and sheer numbers were always plain to see. I still met the outreach workers every day, but the track from the military camp to the town passed close to our meeting place. The roar of the engines and sound of the soldiers' shouts made us all freeze. I would watch them pass from behind our sorghum-thatched wall. My heart was still as I watched them, waiting for the day they would stop and come towards us. In the silence that followed each vehicle the outreach workers looked at their hands and rocked quietly as they sat. We moved our meetings to the clinic but we were never far from the sound of their voices.

At night, though, the soldiers kept to their barracks. The town became unpredictable and unsafe. An attack at night gave everyone a warning — the SLA are nearby and nothing is as it seems. SLA shots taunted the soldiers from the hills. I lay in bed and listened to the shots, telling myself to breathe deeply and not succumb to the breath-holding dizziness I'd felt in the early days. The Janjaweed presence increasingly frightened and intimidated villagers. Their horses were tied to trees in the marketplace, their sunglasses a sign of their anonymity and wealth. As the weeks passed the Janjaweed became more confident, sitting in the marketplace during daylight hours as we passed on our way to the pharmacy in town. They stole goods, attacked women and chased villagers on the outskirts of town. Moving at speed on their horses, with weapons across their backs, they were unchallenged and unafraid.

According to the government none of this was happening. There was no fighting, no attacks, the Janjaweed were an independent force out of control of government troops. The attacks on locals were exaggerated and the fighting simply tribal warfare. The reports of assault and intimidation that filtered through to us seemed endless. And our workload increased as the days went by. But none of it was really happening, they said. And life was going on as normal. But life was getting harder, that much I knew. I still had six months left in Darfur, but how would I ever get my work done with the sheer weight of patient numbers, after hours work and reports crushing me each day? In those days after our bomb-shelter experience the war started to become personal. They were my patients who were being terrorised, my colleagues being threatened in the marketplace and my sleepless nights that were suffering. And when it became personal, I started to share in their pain.

CHAPTER FOUR

I woke to the sound of gunfire. I lay in the dark, my heart pounding and I held my breath, waiting for the next burst. The thatched fence and my mud-brick walls were no protection from stray bullets. When the shooting starts you must stay still. And wait.

After an endless wait, I sat up and swung my legs to the floor. In the silence my ears were ringing. I felt for my torch on the floor but my fingers brushed the mat and felt only emptiness.

'Blast.'

My torch had rolled away in the dark again. As the bed moved with my tossing and turning the thin woven mat creased and bunched, sending cups, torches and pens rolling into the dim recesses under the bed. I scrabbled in the dark. After weeks of early-morning blindness I had organised my tuckul — my clothes and socks lay in a heap on an upturned cardboard box by the door. I pulled on my trousers and a woollen jersey and stood shivering in the darkness. During daylight hours the heat was suffocating, 40°C and relentless. Sweat dripped from my chin, my shirt clung to my wet back. But in the early-morning dawn the air felt bitterly cold. The warmth of the day fled through the desert sand each night, leaving us stamping to keep warm in the cold, dry air.

A soft light shone from the tuckuls across the compound. Musa,

Ahmed, Adam Ali and the guards were preparing their Ramadan breakfast. Celebrating the long Ramadan days they fasted from dawn until nightfall. As we worked — driving, talking, treating patients and negotiating — these men starved. In the searing heat of the day they hoicked and spat their saliva onto the sand. No liquid passes their throats during the daylight hours of Ramadan. But there in the dark they feasted. Plates of freshly made bread, sauce and sweet vegetable stews sat in colourful rows, brought by Halima and Selwa while I still slept. On the fire a kettle started to hiss and steam as they prepared their first and only cup of tea for the day.

I heard Adam Ali laugh and I envied them their dawn feast. They talked and they laughed, sharing their faith and their friendship in the close brotherhood of Ramadan. We had been waiting for two weeks and still our access to El Wadi was denied. There were many reasons for us to stay: insecurity, our small team size, the flood of stories the outreach workers were bringing from around the town. But it felt as though we were stuck in Saleem and there was nothing we could do about it. The frustration was driving me mad.

I walked over to the gas cooker and stood stamping my feet as the kettle started to heat. Above me the stars still shone and an owl called somewhere in the distance. If I could capture the essence of those first months in Darfur I'd fill it with those early-morning moments. The stillness, the icy breaths of dawn chill as I stood in the dark and the gentle sounds of the day as the village started to wake around us. The creak of the hand pump, the humming tunes as the ladies walked past the compound on their way to the open wells, and the desperate, mournful braying of donkeys that filled our waking hours. After the violence and fear of the gunshots, those moments of peace were soul food.

I poured my tea and walked over to the circle of plastic chairs.

'Sabal kerr, Lisa.' Good morning.

I turned. 'Sabal noor, Musa.' Good morning to you.

He stood on the edge of his prayer mat, his arms and feet glistening with water. Dawn prayers. His white jelabiya gown and prayer cap were immaculate in the half light — smooth and uncreased. He closed his eyes and started to pray, a quiet murmuring of blessings. Then he gently knelt and bowed his head to the ground, over and over. My morning ritual was watching him. With gentleness he gave thanks for every day. The pain, the hurt, the fear and the hunger of the day were still hidden. There in the darkness the day held opportunities untold and Musa was grateful.

In the days and months before coming to Darfur I dreamed of life far from home. In flashes and gasps I had touched the life I dreamed of. Standing on a hilltop watching the stars at night I felt a part of something bigger than myself. Sheltering from a storm and feeling the power of the wind and the thundering rain I felt it too. And sitting beside a patient's bed, talking and listening while their body suffered, I knew that there was more to my life. Somehow the inexorable drag of days in suburbia, trapped in an endless queue of traffic or drowning in the minutiae of life in the city dulled my dream and bent my intent. Simply surviving took all my energy, leaving me little time to dream.

Moving to Darfur was as much an escape for me as it was a step to help others. Perhaps we all dream of escaping. In the early-morning quiet of Musa's prayers I found my escape. Memories of social obligations and days of mindless frenetic activity at home faded with every breath. My days were now full of obligations and activity of another kind. The kind that matter. Purpose and clarity drew me out of bed each day. There was no time for self-doubt or reticence. If I didn't do the work, who would? And if I didn't try my best, who would pick up the pieces? No one. In the stillness of the dawn, Musa's peace was my peace.

****

I had inherited the outreach workers from the previous team. They were a group of women with big smiles and sheets of official looking paper. None of them spoke a word of English. Each morning we sat together on thin, sandy mats beside the clinic and they told Adam Ali and me their stories. Each pair of women was responsible for a particular section of town. They visited their sector daily, looking for sick children, giving health education and referring patients to the clinic. The outreach workers were our key to the community. They represented every tribe; their families and friends were our neighbours and patients. The government was telling us there was no problem in Saleem. Our outreach workers were telling us a different story.

Neema was twenty-seven years old. She was Zaghawa and she had lived in Saleem for fifteen years. The reports from her sector of town were the most disturbing.

'I would like you to meet my cousin,' she said that morning. 'She was hurt and I think she will leave town soon.' Neema fingered her skirt, pulling at a thread and avoiding everyone's gaze.

Adam Ali translated for me. He sat cross-legged beside me, his polished shoes sitting neatly behind him on the sand. He smelled of aftershave.

'We must be careful, Lisa,' he said quietly. 'We cannot start looking too far for problems. Other people are watching our outreach workers and they will report them as spies. They are not spies.'

'So can we visit this woman?' I asked.

'I will ask some people first. We must be careful.' Adam Ali knew many people in the community. He was respected and trusted. If he said something was wrong, we listened.

'Does anyone else have news of their work for us?' I turned back to the group.

'Well, I want a T-shirt and we think you should give us all at least five pens each,' said a well-dressed older woman sitting at the front. Her buck teeth gave her a comical grin. Zenub. Always the talker and always with a smile.

'And the expat nurses before you promised us a party with tea and silabiyas (doughnuts) and they told us they would give us all presents.' She looked at me. 'Are you going to give us presents?' she asked, her eyebrows raised.

I looked at her and blinked. Was she for real? I burst out laughing.

'Good morning, Zenub. And how are you today?'

****

Later that morning Adam Ali and I stepped out of the land cruiser beside a ramshackle fence.

'This is the house of Neema's cousin,' he said, reaching in to pick up the radio handset from the dashboard.

'Ahmed, will you wait for us in the car?' I asked. 'We won't be long. Just listen to the radio and call us if there's any trouble.' Ahmed wound down the window and reclined his seat.

'Don't worry. I will wait,' he said, glad of the respite in the heat of the day.

I followed Adam Ali into the family compound.

'Salaam aleikum,' he called as we stood waiting at the front gate.

'Welcome,' called a voice. 'Come in.' When we entered the compound we saw a group of men sitting around a young woman. They sat under the shade of the thatched rakuba, a protective circle around their sister, daughter, niece and aunt.

She stood to welcome us, stiff and slightly bent as she shook hands with each of us. The men stood also, a cloud of white jelabiya gowns and rustling worry beads. We moved through the group, shaking hands, murmuring our greetings and smiling at those we recognised.

Miriam was only 19 and already a widow. Her husband was killed in an attack six months ago. The week before she was nine months pregnant and preparing her home for the birth of her first child. The day we met she had no baby, no home and her body was covered with bruises, a living reminder of the evils of war.

The Janjaweed militia had moved through town a week ago, stirring up trouble, looking for a fight, she told us. We had heard the disturbances from our own compound, heard the gunshots on and off during the day. We still moved to the clinic and pharmacy but made our journeys short and stayed in radio contact every fifteen minutes. Patients still had to be seen.

A group of four or five Janjaweed had come to her compound one afternoon, knocking over tables and kicking open doors. She hid inside one of the tuckuls praying the men would leave without finding her. But in a war there is nowhere safe to hide. She heard their footsteps outside her hiding place and knew she was trapped. The men found her and pulled her out into the daylight. 'What have you got in there?' asked one man, tapping her pregnant belly with his gun.

'I think she's got money inside,' said another, knocking Miriam sideways with his stick.

'I want that money,' said another. 'How do we get it out?'

They didn't cut Miriam and she survived to tell her story. But what those men did was an abomination. They beat her with their guns, pushed her to the ground and kicked, punched and whipped her. They laughed as she rolled, made bets as they joked who would get the money, wondering how much she had inside. When they tired of their game some time later her baby was dead and Miriam went into labour.

She sat in front of me, her eyes on the ground.

'They have taken everything from me now,' she said. 'My husband and now my baby. Now I must leave.'

I looked at Miriam, at the scarring welts healing on her arms, the awkward angle of her left arm as it rested in her lap. My mind was blank. What could I say?

Go to the police? They would arrest her for spreading lies.

Stay in her compound? The Janjaweed militia would surely return.

I am sorry? My sorrow was no use to her.

There was nothing I could do to keep her safe, nothing I could say to make her feel better. I looked at her wounds, listened as she spoke and made notes of her concerns. Her story would become another statistic. 'Woman assaulted in Darfur.' Who would be interested in her? But I couldn't ignore her. She sat in front of me and I could hear her breathe, watch her wince as she moved. I wished that others could have seen her, sitting so quietly on the mat. Maybe then they would feel as angry as I did. As angry and powerless.

So I did what I could as a nurse — I gave her tablets to ease her physical pain. I asked her to visit me at the clinic the following day so I could examine her more carefully. She shook her head as I spoke.

'Mamumkin,' she said quietly. Not possible. 'We leave tonight, my father, my sisters and their families. We are moving far from here, somewhere where we will be safe.'

We never saw Miriam again.

****

The following morning I woke late, my head aching from the brutality of Miriam's story. Babies, sticks, guns, rolling and screaming filled my dreams. I felt heavy as I ducked out of my tuckul, my laces untied and my hair unbrushed.

'Morning, Cinderella,' said Toby 'You look like you need a coffee. Here.' He passed me a plastic mug, filled with hot, strong coffee. 'Don't worry, I washed the sock first.'

It was Toby's standing joke — washing the coffee sock. We had no coffee plunger or filter paper to prepare our coffee. Without coffee the project would grind to a halt. Toby and Steve lived on it. And Sam's morning coffee ritual was a graceful performance, stretching over half an hour and he stirred and brewed the perfect cup of coffee. So Toby had improvised and he made an efficient coffee strainer out of a sock.

It hung on a stick under the rakuba, filling puddles in the sand with cold coffee until the next round. Forgetting to clean the sock after use was a grave offence. Dust, insects and a thick slurry of old coffee grounds in the sock were not a welcome sight first thing in the morning.

I still struggled with Toby, with his laid-back ways and slow drawl. In those days of frenetic activity and crushing need I felt frustrated and impatient with his slow, ponderous ways. The rest of us were working at 110 per cent, but still Toby stopped for his regular coffees and his frequent cigarettes. 'Just relax,' he would say as I rushed back to the compound to update the weekly report. I had started to keep my distance out of a desire to avoid any confrontation with him. I certainly didn't have time for a fight!

I sat clutching my cup and started to plan my day. We still had no permission to return to the displaced groups in the riverbed south of Saleem, and each day I prayed for our return to El Wadi. And so we waited. Today I had my routine work — outreach worker meeting, restock the clinic, write a report on Miriam's injuries and help Sam in the clinic.

'Morning, everyone. We've got a new plan for this week, listen up.' A dishevelled-looking Steve walked over to the kettle and filled the coffee sock with boiling water. He held the sock and watched while the dark coffee started to drip slowly into his mug.

'We're going to El Wadi tomorrow and we'll stay for three days. So start making plans.' He squinted as he drew on his cigarette, holding it between his teeth as he talked.

'We've got Dave coming from HQ in Amsterdam today. He's on a field visit, but he's agreed to hold the fort while we go up to El Wadi. The team will be Toby, Lisa and me with Musa and Ahmed. We'll leave Sam here with Adam Ali to run the clinic. Any questions?'

I sat quietly, my cup of coffee forgotten. We were going back! I could run a clinic and do it properly this time. I could make it up to those women who we had left behind. All of a sudden I couldn't wait to get started. My headache was forgotten.

'This fucking sock isn't working again. Did you forget to clean it again, Toby?' Steve swore as he threw the coffee sock on the table. 'Five minutes of waiting and I get half a cup of coffee. Great!' He scooped up his cup and stalked off to the computer on the far side of the rakuba.

'Don't worry, Toby. He's just stressed,' I said.

'Next time he can clean his own fucking sock,' muttered Toby, kicking the chair as he walked out. 'Now I suppose I'm expected to drop everything and organise you guys for tomorrow. Does no one know how *busy* I am?!'

'I don't appreciate all the swearing,' said Sam softly, his West African accent quiet and careful. 'We should all be working together. It is our sock, our project, our work.' He stood up and lifted his bag from the table. 'We are leaving for the clinic now, Lisa. Have a good day and we will see you at lunch time.' He smiled and bowed slightly. And with grace and good manners he left, ever the gentleman.

****

The following morning we stood beside the vehicles and watched while Toby muttered and stormed around the compound.

'How am I supposed to know what's in these boxes?' he said, kicking one with his boot. 'I told you guys to load the vehicles last night,' he called to the guards. 'Where's the rope? I left it right here. I need a cup of coffee.' On and on he went.

I was impatient. I wanted to get past the security officers in Saleem, through the checkpoints on the edge of town and back to El Wadi. We had *so* much work to do.

'Come on, Toby, let's just go. Don't worry about the rest of the stuff. We've got the drugs and the clinic equipment, I packed them last night. That's all we really need,' I said as I turned towards the door.

But he was gone. The coffee came first.

I sat on the front seat and ground my teeth. This was not a good start. Behind me I heard Adam Ali's voice.

'Put these boxes in the first car and the rest in the second,' as he organised the guards.

Steve, Musa and Ahmed stood together in the shade, planning the day.

'Now have you got everything?' asked Dave, peering in through the window. He had arrived from Nyala the day before, full of smiles and enthusiasm.

'Darfur was my project long before anyone had heard of it,' he'd told me last night. 'We worked sixteen-hour days and every day was harder than the day before. But I loved it.'

Dave had been one of the first coordinators when MSF started its emergency nutrition programme in Darfur in 2003.

'You think it's difficult now, you should have seen it then,' he said, blowing perfect rings from a precious cigar. 'You guys have it easy now, trust me.'

I liked Dave's quiet confidence. I sat smiling as I listened to his stories. He had seen some of the worst fighting and malnutrition in Darfur, but still his belief in change and in goodness were strong. He told stories of disastrous supply problems, endless hours waiting for paperwork to be approved by the authorities and of his love for all things technical. If it could be taken apart then Dave would do it. The spoils of his gift-pack lay on the table — Dutch sweets, Italian coffee and bars of Belgian chocolate. I liked the man. But as I listened to him telling me how 'easy' the situation was now, I started to feel irritated. Sure he had seen a lot, but on no account was our mission 'easy'. Wanting to avoid any arguments I reached for more chocolates.

'Tell me about the hammocks,' I said. And he launched into his favourite tale of a technically perfect hammock, with weight-bearing precision and maximum comfort made from his warehouse leftovers. He talked about his Darfur invention and leaned back in his chair with his eyes closed. 'Ahhhh, the good old days...'

It was after nine o'clock before we left, Toby still muttering and shaking his head.

'I don't know, I just don't know,' I heard him say as he climbed into the front seat. I moved to the back of the second vehicle and sat behind Steve as we drove slowly towards the security office. Steve had negotiated permission to travel while he met with local security leaders the previous day. He had used the satellite phone to make contact with the Commander Ali in El Wadi before our departure. But still I held my breath, not knowing what new form or official stamp would be invented to block our movement for the day.

The checkpoints were unpredictable. The young soldiers spent their days lying idly in the shade and drawing patterns in the sand.

But they were liable to halt our journey with their ignorance or on a whim. That day they waved us through, their machine guns lying quietly on their tripods, the rocket-propelled grenade launchers driven nose first into the sand. I didn't care about the guns or the soldiers. My mind was already in El Wadi; planning, organising and anticipating.

****

I stood under the wide red-roofed verandah and looked out across the medical compound. We had arrived in El Wadi that morning after an exasperating two hours of waiting. With Toby's muttering, Adam Ali's organisation and my seething frustration as the hours passed, the wait had seemed endless. In a cloud of dust and sand, the guards waving us off at the front gate, we roared out of Saleem long after daybreak.

In the morning heat the air shimmered above the corrugated iron roofs. To my right, behind the stone wall, lay the lake. The level started to drop as the dry season advanced. Steve told me that within three months we would be able to cross the lake bed on foot — the dry mud starting to crack in the heat. But for now it looked cool and enticing, too deep even for a camel to cross.

On the far side of the compound lay a second building, identical to the first. Long and narrow, it housed two consultation rooms and a wide verandah. Its walls were low and wide, polished to a smooth shine by generations of waiting patients. The floors were painted red, quietly faded in the harsh sunlight. The paint lay peeling and flaking in the sun. The walls were white in days gone by, the ants' nests and spider webs had claimed them in patterns of spun sand and silky webs.

The walled compound by the lake belonged to the Ministry of

Health. Dr Abaker was the medical officer who ran the clinic. As the Ministry of Health's only representative in town, he tried to provide free healthcare to the town's 20,000 inhabitants. He had qualified in 1973 and worked in El Wadi ever since. He often had no drugs, no equipment or support from the Ministry of Health in Nyala. The weeks stretched into months as he waited for his salary to arrive. It had been fourteen months since the last truck arrived with all his supplies. But each month he stood on the verandah and looked out towards the main road, ever hopeful. That was where we found him when we arrived.

****

'You can use my clinic if you wish, but I would like to help you,' he said as we sat in the echoing consultation room. 'I know these people and my wife and I have been looking after them for a long time.'

His wife, Hawa, was also a medical officer. She was in fact the senior medical officer. I looked across at her. She sat quietly, beautifully wrapped in swathes of white fabric, her imitation Chanel handbag on the table in front of her. I was surprised to find such a highly educated woman working as her husband's superior in this far-flung town. Education and opportunities were obstacles that prevented most women from reaching any level on the ladder of success. What favours or advantages had she needed to reach her top-rung post? I never found the answers. Over the weeks and month that we worked together I did not speak freely to Hawa once. She sat with her face shuttered and her eyes averted. We spoke about patients when the need arose, but nothing else. And she remained as quiet and beautiful as she was on that first day.

We unpacked the vehicles while Steve met with community

leaders to discuss their needs. I organised the clinic, where to triage and where to treat. Musa pulled thick curtains of cobwebs from the ceiling with a stick while I pried the rusting shutters open to let in the light. We stood in the empty, echoing room and looked around at our new home away from home. A thick layer of sand and dust lay on the floor, scuffed tracks left patterns in the sand as hedgehogs explored during the night.

'Well, I wouldn't want to remove an appendix in here,' I said to Musa.

'Inshallah they will keep their appendix,' he replied. 'And we will make this a good place to work.' He smiled his gentle, patient smile and nodded. 'This will be a good place.'

When Musa talked I believed him, I trusted him. My throat felt tight with aching sadness as I pictured the group of women we left behind on our last visit to El Wadi. We were not going to let them down this time.

Steve negotiated time and space from Commander Ali while we swept and made plans. We wanted to see and treat only the sickest in the community. It would give us an idea of their needs and their wounds, both inside and out. Three days were barely enough to touch the surface but we'd try. There were no other agencies in El Wadi at the time, no United Nations or ICRC, no food supplies or protection. The people were alone.

As the guards opened the gates an hour later, the five of us stood, open mouthed, as the crowds flooded in. Four hundred, five hundred, then six hundred people stood, sat and queued around us. Soon the compound was full, the queue of donkeys, horses and camels creating a traffic jam at the front gate. I didn't know whether to laugh or cry.

I turned and walked into the consultation room.

'Come on, Ahmed, let's do some work,' I said. And so we began.

****

Our little table sat at the far end of the dimly lit room. Ahmed and I squeezed onto a wooden box, our only chair. Around us flies buzzed, the metal grills over the four small windows trapping them in a prison of heat and darkness. We had moved through the crowd with Musa, selecting the sickest patients and bringing them into the consultation room. The line of patients lying and sitting on the floor started with the babies and their mothers. Tiny, fevered babies with malaria, diarrhoea, pneumonia and malnutrition. We carried the sickest outside after their first dose of treatment and taught their mothers how to spoon rehydration solution into their unmoving mouths. Musa stopped his triage in the sun now and then to supervise the women, filling their empty green soda bottles with clean, filtered water and more rehydration powder. As if by magic those tiny scraps of life started to stir, their infant tongues moving as the cool water nourished and rehydrated them and the paracetamol broke their fevers.

Back inside, the queue at our table had grown. Sitting beside Ahmed on the wooden box were two children, brother and sister.

'They were shot in an attack two weeks ago,' Ahmed translated. 'Their parents are too afraid to bring them to see us, so they have come alone.' The seven-year-old boy reached out and wrapped his arm protectively around his little sister and he sniffed.

'How were they shot?' I asked, kneeling beside the boy and lifting his jelabiya gown. Around his thigh a dirty brown bandage held a stiff, foetid dressing.

'After the SLA attack the soldiers started firing around the village. They shot into tuckuls and around the market. They said they were looking for SLA soldiers hiding in the tuckuls. These children were in their house when they were shot.'

I fished around in my pocket and pulled out a paracetamol tablet. Then I opened my water bottle and held it up to the little boy's mouth, watching while he swallowed the tablet.

'Tell him I'm going to clean his leg,' I told Ahmed. The little boy let go of his sister and sat still, his back rigid against the wall. I cut away at the dressing and peered at the wound. Entry wound at the back, exit at the front. He had been shot from behind. I cleaned and scraped until pink, bleeding tissue emerged, healthy and strong. He sat there quietly, his eyes squeezed shut and tears streaming down his face. His thigh was hot and tight, the bacteria filling his leg with inflammation and pain. After the thorough cleaning I prepared a syringe of antibiotics and quickly injected it into his other leg. Then I pulled down his gown, covering his leg. He reached out his right hand towards me, wiping his face with his left hand.

'My name is Hussain. Shukran.' Thank you. And he shook my hand, the bravest little boy in Darfur.

I turned to his sister and smiled. She squealed and hid her face behind her brother's shoulder. I could smell her wound before I saw it. She had been shot through the knee, her lower leg hung painful and swollen. The traditional healer had splinted her knee, the grasses and poultice leaving a green smear across her leg. Again I cut away the dressing and started to clean, scrape and inject antibiotics. She whimpered and cried, her brother holding her tightly and whispering in her ear. The hot, swollen knee needed surgery, proper cleaning and a course of intravenous antibiotics. Instead I dressed it carefully and filled a bag with gauze and bandages to give to her parents. I only hoped they knew what to do.

'Why don't they report this to the police?' I asked Ahmed.

'Their mother tried to, but the police said she is SLA and that their father shot them while he was cleaning his gun. Now the police are searching for their father and they will arrest him. They are Zaghawa. That is the problem.' Ahmed reached across and stroked the little girl's cheek.

I handed the boy their prescriptions for antibiotics and paracetamol, and watched as he led his sister slowly out through the crowded room. They hobbled and stopped often, both in pain and their arms supported each other. I sat back and wiped my eyes. The little girl had also been shot from behind.

****

That evening, after the last patient had gone, I walked slowly out of the consultation room. The sun had set, but the sky was lit with an orange light in the dusk. Inside the consultation room we had been treating patients by the light of kerosene lanterns for an hour before we stopped work. I stood on the bare earth behind the consultation room and rested my head against the stone wall. I hadn't been to the toilet all day; there was no toilet in the compound. Besides, I had given most of my water away as I worked, handing out paracetamol from my pocket pharmacy. I must remember to keep a spare water bottle, I told myself. I loosened my trousers and squatted down to wee. There was nothing. My body was dry after the exhausting day.

'Hey, Lisa, we've got another patient out here,' called Toby from the front courtyard. 'Where are you?'

I stood up, pulling up my trousers as I walked back to the verandah.

'Here I am, just give me a second to wash my hands,' I said, walking over to the jerry can resting on the wall. There wasn't time to fetch filtered water from the car for a drink. I sighed.

She lay on a mat at the foot of the tree. The first stars were already out and the heat of the day was fading. But in her world there were no stars or warmth. Her name was Asha and she was dying.

'She has been sick for one week and now she is not passing urine for four days,' translated Musa.

This woman looked as though she had been ill for much longer than a week, but there wasn't time now to untangle her history. We could do that tomorrow. Her breath smelled sweet and her eyes sunken as I knelt beside her. She was severely dehydrated.

It was after 7 p.m. when we started to work on her, Musa holding the lantern beside me. It had been a long, crowded day and my head thundered with a thirsty headache. Beside me Musa's stomach rumbled with hunger.

'You go,' I told him. 'I'll be fine here. Just bring me some water and save me some food, okay?' There was no point in both of us being exhausted. He needed some rest.

The next four hours passed quickly. Intravenous fluids, antibiotics, malaria tests and more. I radioed Sam in Saleem for advice. Standing beside the vehicle I held the radio handset as he told me what to look for, how to examine her more carefully. I watched the evening star, bright and clear in the still night air. I watched the others sitting round the mat, eating their Ramadan meal, the kerosene lantern casting shadows on the sand. And my stomach growled.

By 11 p.m. she was stable, more wakeful and feeling thirsty. Asha's daughter lifted her shoulders and whispered softly as she spooned soup into her mouth. I didn't know what had caused her to become so dehydrated, but we could get to the bottom of it tomorrow.

I gathered my mosquito net and hung it from the tree above her so she and her daughter would have some relief from the flying menace of mosquitoes overnight. It was no use to me. Toby had forgotten to bring the mattresses and blankets. So I crawled into the back of the land cruiser and kicked the empty bottles out onto the sand. Lifting the seats up I tied each one to the wall, making some space on the floor where I could sleep. I lay down on the corrugated floor. The metal buckles dug into my back and my stomach squeezed with hunger. But all I wanted was sleep, precious sleep. And it came quickly.

I was woken a few hours later by voices. Musa and Ahmed were standing beside Asha, their torches playing patterns on the mosquito netting.

'She wants to go to the toilet, Musa said sleepily as I approached. We carried her to the long grass and held her as she cried and groaned.

'She says she needs to go but nothing is happening,' said Musa.

'Let's carry her back to the mat and I will look for a catheter,' I said. 'It's no problem, tell her.' It took an hour in the flickering torchlight to finally get our one and only urinary catheter into her emaciated body. My hands shook with exhaustion, my eyes blinking fast as I concentrated.

'Next time I'll pack one of every size of bloody catheter,' I muttered as I worked. 'This one is made for an elephant.'

By 3.30 a.m. she was asleep, a few drops of dark urine sitting in the catheter tubing. I hung a new bag of intravenous fluid while Asha's daughter played with the torchlight. Musa and Ahmed had fallen asleep on the mat beside us, Ahmed's gentle snoring touching the night air. I walked slowly back to the vehicle and crawled in. It was so cold, and I shivered as I tried to find a spot that was comfortable.

'Damn Toby and his packing,' I thought, sniffing and rubbing my eyes. 'Next time I'll do all the packing and we'll have feather pillows.' With that thought I fell asleep, out cold after my longest day in Darfur.

****

While we worked and worried and slept in the cold, the rest of the world carried on, unaware. Other tragedies and dramas occupied the minds of those living in the affluent west. The Bali bombings had unleashed such terror, leaving people reeling with fear. The earthquake in Kashmir killed 80,000 and winter was about to set in. To draw the public closer to the suffering, Angelina Jolie travelled to Pakistan, to be seen in amongst the rubble and deprivation. When she urged for more aid, people listened and donated. Everyone wanted to see Angelina, and her beauty was a vehicle for their compassion.

Closer to the hearts of many, Hurricane Wilma wrought untold damage as it swept across Florida, Mexico and Central America. Loss and suffering, helplessness and fear were brought closer to home. People's own lives were touched and compassion was given meaning.

Our drama in a small corner of Darfur was one of many, our needs and frustrations just part of living in a chaotic, mad world. But it gave my life meaning, to be part of a solution, no matter how small. Seeing the overwhelming needs and fears in the world we can all be excused for wanting to withdraw. When there is nothing you can do but watch the misery of others' lives it is self-preservation to close your ears and eyes. I know because I have done it often. But stepping forward and participating, allowing yourself to feel and see and reach out, can cure apathy. It's about being part of the chaos and refusing to accept all the madness. It comes down to choice.

****

It was just after 2 p.m. on the second day when we heard an engine roar and the whooping and cheering of soldiers. Women screamed and the consultation room was thrown into panic. I ran to the window. There in the middle of the compound sat a military vehicle, the machine gun mounted on the back and soldiers standing around it, one leg up on the side of the truck, ready to jump down on command. Sitting behind the wheel was Commander Ali — the first commander we had met in the marketplace. Sallow faced and smiling, he sat revving the engine. He had driven twice round the compound, scattering patients and filling them with terror. Now all was still. White patient cards lay on the ground where they had been dropped.

I heard Steve's footsteps, wide and heavy, as he crossed the verandah quickly.

'Hello, Commander,' we heard him say. 'There seems to be a misunderstanding here, sir. No uniforms or weapons are allowed in our clinics.'

The commander laughed. I looked around the crowded consultation room and took a deep breath. Dr Abaker and his wife had a long queue of patients waiting to be seen. The seriously ill patients lay on mats around my table, some groaning or crying.

Which ones can I treat now if we have five minutes to leave, I thought, quickly scanning the mats. Antibiotics and pain relief, dressings and malaria treatment were the fastest and easiest to dispense. If any of these patients had malaria, pneumonia or a wound they were in luck. I could throw some treatment to them. Otherwise we would leave them. And they would come back to haunt my dreams.

I ran to the door with Ahmed, ready to raid our pharmacy stores. We stopped. There stood the commander, his arm on Steve's shoulder, laughing.

I looked at Ahmed. 'What's going on?' I asked. He shrugged.

After a few minutes the commander got back into the vehicle, revved the engine loudly and reversed suddenly into the waiting area. Mothers screamed and scattered, their children stumbling and crying with fright. Then he roared out the front gate, through the crowded chaos of donkeys and camels and out onto the sandy track. The soldiers on the back stumbled and fell as he drove, their comical dance never quite bringing a smile to my face.

'Just a show of power,' Steve said, walking back to us. 'We've talked and I asked him to work with us, not against us. He's gone now, but I have a feeling he'll be back.' He dragged his hand through his hair and sighed. 'We'll have to work faster, guys. We don't know when they'll make us leave.' With that he walked up the steps, past us and into the pharmacy.

Steve puzzled and overwhelmed me. With his aggressive, boiling temper he cowed some of the staff when he found them not doing their best. Apathy and mediocrity were not an acceptable part of his work ethic. But with a breath he could be gentle and insightful, laying his hand on a patient's arm with empathy or sitting cross-legged with the staff listening and smiling while they talked. His temper repelled me, and his compassion and strength drew me in. In those first weeks I already knew that if the bombs started to fall or the soldiers came back for us that I would be safe with Steve. We all would be.

We planned to stay for three days. We had government permission and security permission. We had also confirmed our plans with this same commander only the day before. But what are plans in Darfur? They are ideas and activities to be played with, manipulated and changed at a moment's notice by those with power. Patients are simply a tool to people like him. A way to frighten and intimidate. The compound was nearly empty now. The discarded health cards showed what we had lost. I bent to read several; severe malnutrition, dehydration, partial thickness burns. And who knew whether any of these patients would come back.

I thought of Liz and our evening of music and dance in Nyala. We had stood on the roof of the Spanish Red Crescent house and watched the lights of Nyala flicker and glow in the dark. I wanted so much to be part of this Darfur life, to work and try and press for what I believed in. Safety. Respect. Health. We toasted to Nyala and to life. 'May the party never end,' she laughed as we drank our punch, sucking the juice from chunks of watermelon. Standing in the deserted courtyard of El Wadi clinic my heart felt so heavy, exhausted by the relentless unfairness that kept us from our patients.

'It's okay,' said Musa, standing beside me. 'They will come back tomorrow. Don't worry for them, Lisa. These people are used to the fear and disappointing times.' With his words and his smile Musa smoothed my exhaustion and my sadness. I climbed the stairs with him and we walked back inside to see the sickest of the patients still lying on the floor.

That evening we sat on the sand, outside the clinic wall, and watched the sun set. Back in the compound Toby was preparing dinner, the pots and pans clanging as he worked. Steve and I sat with our backs against the warm stone wall, our eyes closed. If there is a moment of my time in El Wadi that I would slip into my little bag of memories, it would be that one evening. I held my cup of tea in my lap, its warmth reassuring and familiar. The deepening orange of the sky played patterns against my closed eyes. When I looked again the evening star hung just above the horizon, bright and unwavering. All along the water's edge children laughed and shouted as they led their donkeys into the water. Strapped to the side of each donkey hung a pair of animal skins, ready to be filled with water and slowly carried home. Some children carried plastic jerry cans, and they waded out into the cool dark water to fill them. Their silhouettes danced against the orange sky as they sang, splashed, danced and talked. Two donkeys walked further out into the water, their bellies cooled by the waves. The fear and crowding, thirst and exhaustion of the day faded from my memory. I had never been so tired or so content to simply be.

'Do you think they always dance and sing?' I asked Steve sleepily.

'That's what children do best, isn't it?' he replied. 'If only the adults would stop playing these games of war.'

Whump, whump. One of the donkeys was ushered out of the lake, the animal skins full and dripping in the dim light. 'Geeeer, geeeer,' shrilled the boy. The donkey was in no hurry. The boy pushed and cajoled, and finally the donkey stood, dripping and well watered, ready for the trek home. The little boy ran and jumped onto its back, clipping its rump with a sick.

'Wait for me,' shouted a little voice, and out of the water ran another boy. There was no room on the back of the donkey, so he threw his arms around the donkey's neck and hung upside down for the journey home. And off they went, their silhouettes against the fading dusk. One singing as he sat on top, the other shrieking with laughter as he swung, freely and without fear, from below. In the midst of war, children are the future. Their laugher and their joy the only hope.

****

Our second day continued much the same as the first. I ran between the consultation room and the storeroom on the other side of the compound. Asha, the severely dehydrated lady from the night before, lay on her mat on the floor. Despite my questions and palpations I couldn't find the cause of her illness. The history from family members was contradictory and confusing, as happened so often. She lay in the darkened room among boxes and yellowing piles of paper, her eyes closed and her breath quiet in the dark.

Above her hung an empty bag of intravenous fluids. It hung from a nail on the floor, one I'd found that morning and hammered into the plaster with the sole of my boot.

I stood at the door and greeted the women inside.

'Salaam aleikum. Kula tamam?' I asked. Is everyone well?

They all nodded and smiled. The room was full of women now. Her sisters and aunts, friends and neighbours had heard she was in the clinic and they had come to bring her comfort. All around her lay bundles of food, clean clothes and bowls of cool, fresh water. Her daughter stood and shook my hand.

'Any urine?' I asked, gesturing to her mother.

She shook her head.

It had been five days now without urine and surely she was beyond help. She needed blood tests, a CT scan and dialysis at least. But what could I do? Close the door and leave her alone to die? I knelt down and touched her shoulder. My back ached from my night on the cold metal floor and my head felt cloudy with tiredness.

'Hello,' I whispered. 'How are you, Asha?' She opened her eyes and smiled weakly.

'Lisa, we need you inside.' Musa stood at the door. Time. Time. There was never enough time! I reached for another bag of intravenous fluid and hung it from the broken nail.

'Call me when it's finished,' I said to Asha's daughter, pointing at the bag. She smiled and nodded.

'Shukran akeik,' she said, touching her heart. Thank you very much.

I rubbed my eyes and walked out into the bright sunlight.

****

When I walked back into the consultation room, Musa looked up at me.

'Ahmed is working outside now. I will translate for you now,' he said, smiling.

My impatience and bad temper had hurt Ahmed, I knew it. Trapped in a hot, dim room I was ready to burst with frustration. His translations were slow, patient histories confusing and the light was too poor to conduct a proper examination. And all the while people called to me through the grilled windows — please help me, see my child, my baby, please help. In the end I snapped at Ahmed — make them go away, translate faster, what is she saying, make them go *away*!

But now Musa sat beside me, his face ever smiling. I smiled back and resolved to keep my smile for the rest of the day. As it turned out the day was actually not so bad.

****

It was our third and last day and everyone was tired. Toby still ran the malaria-testing area on the verandah. He taught two local women, traditional midwives clothed in white, how to perform the test on their own. It was an impressive achievement given his impatience and their illiteracy. Taught entirely using sign language these women now diagnosed 90 per cent of the malaria presenting in the clinic.

Steve's long legs ached after hours and days spent sitting cross-legged on the floor of our makeshift pharmacy. He filled the prescriptions that Dr Abaker, Dr Hawa and I wrote next door. He had learned some of the common medication and how to match medications with a diagnosis. Both Abaker and Hawa were inordinately fond of antibiotics, prescribing them for headaches, stomach aches and the eternal 'burning feet'. I knew their prescribing was crazy but how else could we work? We were using their clinic, raising the expectations of their community. I couldn't keep them away and there weren't enough hours in any day to train either of them. But with Steve's help, and the MSF bible beside him, *Essential Drugs*, he managed to alter the worst prescriptions to protect the patients from their doctors. He too was a resourceful teacher. He had found a local man, Issa, who taught at the local school. Issa could read and write English and could explain our written instructions to patients. Where would we have been without him?

Musa and Ahmed worked tirelessly triaging, translating and diffusing arguments that broke out among patients, tired of sitting for hours in the hot sun. They spat and toiled through each day, and sank onto their mats at nightfall, exhausted and hungry from their Ramadan fast. But still they rose at sunset, washed their arms and feet, pulled on their clean white jelabiya gowns, before kneeling to pray. Without their prayer mats they knelt in the sand, their foreheads stamped with crystals of sand each time they bowed, giving thanks for life's blessings.

With the end of our last day in sight we still had so much to do. Over three hundred patients crowded into the shade below the verandah.

I looked up at my next patient and smiled. She looked familiar. But her eyes were closed and her head rested against the wall.

'Salaam aleik,' she said, and smiled.

Hanan — the woman with the breast abscesses! She was back! I wanted to run around the table and throw my arms around her. To laugh and cry with thanks that she was alive. But I didn't. Muslim etiquette precludes random acts of hugging with strangers, especially outsiders like me.

'How are you?' I asked, unable to stop smiling.

'Better,' she said. 'But my baby . . .' She turned stiffly and called her mother.

A heavy-boned woman with huge, pendulous breasts came striding over to our table.

'Baby is sick. Here. You have him,' she said loudly and reached over the table to drop the baby in my lap. He was still wrapped in the same foetid green cloth.

I opened the cloth and my heart broke. Inside lay the tiniest, thinnest baby I have ever seen. His skin barely held his bones inside, they jutted out sharply, ribs, pelvis and limbs in aching shadows. His chest barely moved with each breath as his body slowly died from malnutrition. He was less than five weeks old. I held his body to my chest and felt the bones rub against my skin. His head moved slightly as he tried to nuzzle my neck, searching in vain for milk. I closed my eyes.

'I try to feed him but these are nearly empty now,' bellowed his grandmother, beating her breasts with both hands. 'Can he have some of yours?' She reached over and squeezed my breasts. I yelped.

'I have no milk,' I squeaked. 'We'll try something else.' And I raised the baby up to her. 'Take him.' The old woman sighed and reached for the little bundle.

'Musa, can we take a look at her wounds?' I asked

I walked to the windowsill and reached for a pair of gloves. She unbuttoned her shirt and revealed thick grey-and-white gauze pads taped to her chest. The same ones I had given her that day in the market two weeks before.

Under the dressings and layers of drying white cream, her abscesses were healing, their angry red edges fading and the pus drying.

'Fever?' I asked.

She shook her head.

'Eating and drinking?'

She nodded. If nothing else we had saved this young mother. When she arrived in the market that day I was sure of nothing. But seeing her sitting in front of me, smiling, I was sure.

'Musa, would you redress her wounds and give her more supplies?'

Musa's hands were gentle, born of years of experience watching while his father worked in a hospital and treated patients who came to their door at night. All the rules of etiquette were swept away. Musa treated her wounded breasts and I examined patients on a sandy floor while others looked on. In war the boundaries and rules sway and blend with the aching need that fills each day.

Musa led her to a stool in the corner and I left him to work. Walking outside I searched the crowd for Halima, our new cooking lady. She stood at the pharmacy door, a silver tray full of glass tumblers overflowing with hot, sweet tea. Steve's hand emerged through the door and took one.

'Shukran, Halima.' Thank you.

'Alawajip,' she said with a smile. You're welcome. And she turned to me.

'Halima, I need milk. Can you get me milk?' I asked.

She looked at her tray, uncertain, and held it out to me.

'Take tea,' she said. 'Not milk.'

'No, I need a cup of goat's milk for a baby. Quickly. Can you get me some?' It was already 11 o'clock and we had three hours left to run our clinic.

Halima put down her tray, hoisted her dress above her knees and ran across the verandah.

'One cup,' she shouted. 'No problem,' and off she ran.

I picked up the tray and carried it over to Toby. It seemed unfair to be drinking in front of all these people as they fasted for Ramadan. But I was beyond worrying. We needed sustenance.

Toby reached for a glass. He drank it quickly then reached for another. While I waited for him to finish I looked at the long line of people waiting on the floor.

'Why are they waiting here?' I asked.

'They've all got positive malaria tests and they're waiting to get in to see you guys inside,' he said, wiping his mouth. 'She's been waiting for two hours.' He pointed to a young woman, lying unmoving on a mat.

'Toby! You should have called me,' I snapped. 'Seriously ill people do not wait.'

'Lisa, they're all sick. What do you want me to do — send them all in to you at once? We've got a few hours left. We do what we can. Just relax,' he said with a drawl.

I looked out at the sea of faces still waiting to be treated, and felt a headache grip my temples with its steel grip. Which patients would die because we weren't working quickly enough? Which mothers would I have to hold, apologising that there was nothing I could do to save their child after endless hours of waiting? I slammed the tray on the table and reached for a pen. In ten minutes I had written the malaria treatment for every patient lying on the floor and sent them to the pharmacy.

'It's not rocket science, Toby. Just follow the treatment guidelines beside you,' I said. I was in no mood to relax as I walked back into the consultation room.

On any other day, in any other place, a rational understanding would have softened my tone and made me grateful for any help. But standing beside Toby on the sandy verandah, my shirt clinging to my back with sweat, all rational thoughts evaporated. Surely it wasn't Toby's fault for working slowly. And surely he was doing his best, untrained and unprepared for the flood of patients that now depended on him and his white-veiled midwives for their diagnosis.

But with his relaxed, just-do-what-you-can attitude, patients would die. Leaving the sickest patients to lie in their fevered cocoons, covered in torn rags and sheets on the verandah floor, they would die. Waiting while I worked my way through the headaches and runny noses that made their way to my desk with their sharp elbows and persuasive pleading. The crush of need overwhelmed me and I felt afraid. Afraid of failing those people, afraid of the power I had to save or ignore patients. Through my fear of failure, anger snapped at my throat. If only the others would work faster, if only there were more trained health workers, if only . . . I sat back down at my desk and took a deep breath while my anger prowled and goaded me to find fault with others.

Musa had redressed the young woman's abscesses and was holding the baby gently in his arms when I sat down.

'Ah Lisa, what can we do?' he asked. 'He is almost gone.' He pulled back the cloth and revealed the tiny, starving baby inside.

I rummaged in the silver box and pulled out a long thin gastric tube. I vaguely remembered a technique using tube to feed small babies. A picture hovered in my mind, barely there but holding the answer to the baby's life.

'If he's still alive, Musa, then we have to keep trying,' I replied.

I knelt on the ground and started to tape the tube to Hanan's wounded breast. She looked at me strangely.

'For milk,' I said, too tired to explain.

'Musa, could you get me some sugar from Steve next door?' I asked.

He returned a few minutes later with the sugar. Halima, the tea lady, flew through the door behind him, a small jug in her hand.

'Milk!' she shouted. 'I have milk!'

Goat's milk can cause many problems for sick or dehydrated babies. Anaemia, nutrient deficiency and kidney problems to name a few. We saw it all too often in the clinic. Diluting and sweetening the milk made it more palatable and it was safer. I didn't understand why, but time was running out. I was ready to try anything. I poured some milk into an empty tea glass, sprinkled in sugar and added water from my water bottle. Stirring it with my pen I whispered a prayer for the baby's life. My prayers had faded over the weeks as each patient died, or suffered or cried. There were no answers, no solutions to their pain and the prayers went unanswered. Surely this one would bring life.

Hanan sat quietly, saying nothing. I saw the old woman eye the leftover milk in the jug.

'Take it,' I said, gesturing to the jug.

She needed no encouragement and drained the milk in a flash. She smacked her lips and looked around.

'More?' she asked.

'No,' I said. 'This is for the baby not you,' putting my hand over the half-full glass.

She pouted.

Musa held the watery milk in one hand, the tip of the tube in the other. I lifted the baby and gently turned him, his tiny mouth against his mother's breast. But more importantly he was close to the other end of the plastic tube. A drop of milk wavered on the tube and we watched as it fell onto his lips. Musa and I drew a breath. The baby didn't swallow and the milk fell from his lips. And then, so slowly it almost hurt to watch, another drop fell. Milk filled the plastic tube and sat waiting for the tiny mouth to start sucking. If he could suck from his mother's healing breast and draw milk from the tube, there was a chance her breast would start to produce milk again. The baby opened his mouth and his little tongue started to move. As he sucked on the tube the milk was slowly drawn from the cup and into his mouth.

'He's sucking,' whispered Musa.

His pendulous grandmother watched over her daughter's shoulder. She frowned.

'No milk,' she said, pointing at the bandaged breasts.

'No problem,' I said, still holding the baby carefully. 'Lots of milk now,' and I nodded at Musa's cup. No problem. I felt as though I could fly — we were going to save this little life, Musa and me.

I left the three of them and pushed my way out through the crowded room. Outside Toby was still working, his queue shorter than before.

'Thank you, Toby,' I said. 'I just couldn't do it all on my own.' My anger had evaporated with the sight of the tiny baby inside. Of course we couldn't save everyone, I knew that. But in the burning heat of the day, with their hands reaching over the verandah wall towards me and their eyes pleading for help I wanted to save them all. To be able to say 'Yes, you are all important. We will take away your pain and your sadness'. I simply couldn't accept that we would fail them. But as my headache loosened its grip I knew we were doing our best. Even Toby.

'I told you, Lisa. Don't worry so much. Just relax,' he replied with a smile.

I turned and pushed my way through the crowd surging towards the pharmacy door. With sharp elbows and soft babies on their backs the women defended their place, pushing and swaying, chattering and complaining. They didn't know whether we would come back again. Some would be driven into the bush over the coming weeks. Some would lose their children as they succumbed to malaria and dehydration while the village pharmacy lay empty. This could be their only chance for treatment. So they pushed like there was no tomorrow.

I squeezed my way through and climbed over the table that served as a barrier at the pharmacy entrance.

'Hey, don't go giving those women ideas,' said Steve. 'If they start launching themselves over that table we'll be finished.' He chuckled at the thought.

Steve sat on the floor, a little girl of about three resting on his lap. In front of him sat a mug of sweet orange juice. He opened his hand and revealed five tablets.

'I'm trying to make sure every kid gets their first dose of malaria treatment now,' he said. 'The first few screamed and vomited all over me, but now I've figured it out. They *love* the orange juice. So I sweet talk them first with a drink then 1-2-3-4-5. They swallow all the pills. It works but it takes a while.'

He lent forward and picked up the cup. His little charge reached for the handle, wanting more of the sweet drink.

'No, no,' whispered Steve. 'One pill. One drink.' She looked up at him balefully. Then she squeezed her eyes shut and opened her mouth. And in went the first pill.

'You're doing a good job, Steve. Thank you,' I said. It was still hard to believe that the angry, impatient, chain-smoking man who unsettled and frightened me when his temper hit boiling point was the same one sitting before me now. His white shirt was wet with vomit and tears, his hair sticking to his scalp with perspiration. But there in his cross-legged haven the little girl was safe and I'd never seen Steve look so happy.

Cerebral malaria kills an estimated 700,000–900,000 in sub-Saharan Africa every year. Three thousand children a day. But who really knows the true numbers. Their births are often not registered, their deaths unrecorded in remote, hidden villages and river beds. The estimates say little of the reality of malaria. While the malaria parasite ravages their victim's red blood cells, these children shake with fever, their bodies wracked with pain and dehydration. As the parasites win the battle, the victim loses consciousness, their brain starved of oxygen. They start to have seizures and the end is very near. Every day from June to October the malaria parasites win their battle. And it hurts to watch.

I climbed back out onto the verandah and stood with my head resting against the wall. Behind me hundreds of patients still waited. I felt their eyes on me. We were making a difference. There were people going home with life-saving treatment. With my eyes closed I could still hear Steve's voice, soft and low, as he coaxed in the last tablet. At the far end of the verandah I heard Toby laugh as he taught the midwives something new. We were winning one by one. But all around me the aching need pushed in. More. More. More they seemed to whisper. We had two hours left. And I was afraid we would let them down again.

****

At the end of the day we stood at the checkpoint on the edge of town and waited for the commander. Commander Ali had given us clear instructions — finish our work by 2 p.m. and wait here for him to give us permission to leave.

The young soldier stood with his back to us as he watched his colleague disappear along the dusty path. Without a radio or phone they had to walk the 1 km back to the barracks to inform Commander Ail of our presence. On the table the newspaper pulled and tugged in the breeze, his Kalashnikov weighing it down. Here at the edge of town the wind gusted and cooled the air, a welcome relief from the still, hot air down by the lake. The sorghum roof of the rakuba rustled and whispered and I closed my eyes in the peaceful calm.

We turned away two hundred people as we closed the clinic that afternoon. They had minor problems, chronic complaints and the perennial problem of 'burning feet'. None were really sick. I knew we couldn't see them all, but still I worried that I was missing those with real complaints, those too weak or too quiet to push through the crowd to where we stood. A hand on their forehead and a quick feel of their pulse was all we could do in those last, frenetic moments of the day.

'Come on, Lisa. If we are late to see the commander he might refuse permission the next time. We need to go *now!*' Steve had warned.

It was just after two as we stood at the checkpoint watching the sentry as he slowly ambled off to the barracks.

'How long will we have to wait?' I asked Steve.

'As long as the commander wants,' he replied. 'Just relax.'

I squatted in the shade and looked around. All around us spent cartridges lay in the sand, leftovers from target practice. In every direction trees lay broken, felled in an attempt to remove potential enemy cover. The burned-out shells of a village 500 m away was a vivid reminder of a recent battle. Zaghawa townsfolk were slowly but surely being pushed out of town, just as they were in Saleem. In the distance to the east and west sat a long row of rocky hills, the hiding places of the SLA. I caught the young soldier looking at me and then out to the hills. He shook his head.

'Music?' he asked as he reached for a cassette player resting under the table. He stretched up his arm and pulled two cassette tapes from the sorghum roof. He blew on them hard, shooing away the sand and leaves. We stood watching as he opened the heavy black tape player and dropped in the first tape. Craig David's voice crooned through the speakers as the soldier knocked out the rhythm against his rifle.

> 'we were meant to be
> together for eternity
> but now you're gone it's plain to see
> I was living just a fantasy'

We stood waiting for an hour. An hour of Craig David. An hour we could have used to treat more patients. An hour we could have relaxed after the battering three days of non-stop work, backs aching after cold, metal sleep in the back of the vehicles. Instead we stood, our backs in the sun, and we waited.

A little after three Steve dropped his cigarette in the sand and covered it with his boot.

'Stand up, guys. Here he comes,' he said, walking out onto the track. There in the distance we saw a haze of dust and heard the roar of an engine. The young soldier quickly stopped the music and dropped the cassette player under the table.

'Good afternoon, Commander,' said Steve, reaching out to shake his hand when the vehicle arrived. 'We finished at two and we are here to take your permission to leave.'

'I was not ready at two,' replied the commander. 'And now I am.' He looked at each of us with a smile. 'Tell me how the work was?' he asked. 'Did you see any gunshot wounds? Did you treat any SLA soldiers? Tell me everything.' He looked at me.

'No sir, we saw only women and children,' replied Steve. 'And some old men and their aches and pains. You are welcome to visit any time. Just please respect our rule by leaving your uniforms and guns at the gate.'

The commander looked at Steve.

'I need to know everything,' he said, unsmiling. 'Do not hide anything from me.'

Steve returned his stare. 'You are welcome any time,' he repeated. 'You have your rules and we have ours.'

The commander and Steve talked for some time — politics and families, war and its price. The soldiers on the back of the vehicle looked bored as they stood, fingering the machine gun and picking their noses. While the men talked I thought of the patients we had left behind. Asha still lay in the dark, her circle of women singing softly as they massaged her arms and legs, easing her towards death. I had removed her intravenous line and begged her to come to Saleem.

'Mamumkin,' said her daughter. Not possible.

So I left her in the dark, the empty bag of fluid still hanging from its nail.

Hanan and her baby still sat on the consultation room floor, her mother holding the cup as the tiny baby started to suck and drink, his body aching for milk.

'Leben tamam,' said the old woman. Good milk, as she dipped in her finger and licked off the milk.

'It's for the baby, not you,' I told her. 'You are fat.' I grabbed her waist and wrapped my fingers around its folds. She giggled and wriggled as she nodded her head.

'No problem,' she smiled.

When Commander Ali finally allowed us to go it was 3.30 p.m.

'See you next time,' he said as he climbed back into the vehicle. 'It is good to have you.' He smiled. With a roar and a skidding turn in the sand he drove off, the cloud of dust soon hiding them from sight.

'Come on, guys. Let's go home. I need a shower,' said Steve. 'It's been a long week.'

And we slowly walked back to the vehicles. Behind us Craig David started to sing.

'I'm walking away from the troubles in my life'

I wanted to walk away. Caught between pride and failure I didn't know how to help the people of El Wadi. With unlimited time and access to the people, with more staff, vaccinations, clean water, education and food perhaps we could really make a difference. But trapped as they were in a small town, in a place that didn't matter to the world, all we could do was repair some of the most broken and unwell who came to see us. I thought of the tiny baby with his drops of watery milk that fell from the tube as we watched. How many other babies were out there, dying for our help? I can't console myself with the knowledge that we tried, that we made a difference to a few and that it is enough. We can't accept their deaths, their suffering and their pain. Death may be natural, but not for babies, for their older brothers and sisters or their desperate parents who have done no wrong. Looking into their eyes, watching while their children shivered with fever and hunger, I couldn't relax. There simply wasn't time. And I knew we could do more. I rested my head against the window as we drove slowly back to Saleem. Next time we would see more patients, reach further with our care and somehow make a difference in El Wadi. If we didn't do it, no one would.

CHAPTER FIVE

I woke slowly, gently, and listened to the sparrows as they stirred and chattered in the roof beside me. Each night I dragged my bed outside, drawing long troughs through the sand as I dragged it beside my tuckul. The evening heat was too much to bear, the still night air suffocating as I tried to sleep in the mud-brick confines of the tuckul. The two small windows were hidden by the long, overlapping stalks of thatching. Even with my bed by the open door the air was stifling.

Lying under the night sky I could breathe, feel the slight breeze and luxuriate in the softness of my bed. The loosely woven rope hung from the bed frame, the cotton mattress lying like a hammock in its drooping arms. When I climbed into bed at the end of a long, exhausting day I felt safe, enveloped by the mattress around me. Even my aching back each morning was worth it for the bliss of lying beneath the stars at night.

After nine weeks in Darfur I lost myself in the work and need that crowded in every day and night. There was no life outside Darfur. There was only the struggle and scramble to help, treat, listen and save the men, women and children around us. Our workload seemed to increase exponentially. Attacks on locals occurred every day. The injuries brought to us were increasing in number and intensity.

Rape, attempted rape, torture, theft and murder all left their scars. All tribes were affected. SLA incursions into town took prisoners who were as badly treated as any other. There were no rules or clear lines — good and evil, right and wrong. All sides seemed able to inflict punishment and they wailed into the night when their own kin were injured or killed.

In our day-to-day work, though, we cared for the victims of all tribes. Birgit and Zaghawa, Masalit and Fur. Their women were beaten and their men were shot. But the shame of the war is in the tears of the children. Why was no one listening to them? I wondered. Perhaps because they didn't matter outside Darfur. The world wasn't listening. At night I held my pillow and wept.

Our work outside the African Union compound began at the end of November. With Janjaweed militia venturing more confidently into town, and fear and threats shadowing every day, many tribes made a choice; stay in town and beg the African Union for help or leave. Some fled south, towards the SLA stronghold of Muhajariya. Some fled east, taking refuge in the hills with the SLA. There they had access to fresh water in the lake near the ridge, but no food. Many fled to the barbed wire wasteland that circled the African Union's compound on the outskirts of Saleem. There they camped in the scorching heat of the day, hiding under shrubs or building makeshift shelters from scraps of plastic and fabric. Women and children sat together, frightened and helpless, and they waited for help.

We set up a big white tent outside the entrance to the African Union. Close to their front gate we examined and treated endless lines of patients — thirsty, hungry and frightened. And the African Union did not want them there. They refused to supply the crowds with water — claiming that doing so would encourage them to stay. Meanwhile the shining metal pipe that ran through the long, dry grass, from the African Union's compound to the borehole 2 km away, carried clean, fresh water, morning and night, with a flick of their generator switch.

Adam Ali unzipped the tent flaps while Musa and Ahmed carried the drug boxes from the vehicle and laid them gently on the sand.

'Noora has a message for you, Lisa,' called Adam Ali over his shoulder as he tied back the tent. Noora was one of our outreach workers. She was a hard-working girl, always ready to work longer or harder than the others. While Zenub talked and demanded and laughed in our morning meetings, Noora sat quietly copying her patient referrals neatly into a book, ready to present her work from the previous day.

She stood at the entrance to the tent, her dress torn and her hair untidy. She had fled town after being stopped at a security checkpoint three days before.

'They told me I was not allowed to walk on their ground,' she told us before she left, crying as she stood at the gate to our compound. 'They said they would kill me if they saw me walking there again. But the hand pump is on that path. They have beaten women at other hand pumps in town. I have to use this one, this is the last one.'

'They' were local Birgit men. The Birgit were currently the most powerful tribe in the area. In those days of shifting allegiance, power shifted with a handshake. Their power was absolute.

Now Noora stood in the sun, a line of young children behind her.

'I found these children around the camp. They are all sick and they need water,' she said, ushering them into the tent. 'I will go and bring the babies now. Some are dying.' With that she turned and walked quickly away.

I looked at the children. Nine of them stood together, holding hands. The eldest looked about seven years old, the youngest three.

Their clothes were dirty, their noses running. One of the oldest stepped forward.

'Please can we have some water?' she asked. 'My sister needs water.'

Beside her, a little girl stood crying.

'Adam Ali, grab the jerry can from the car, will you? I'll get the cups.' I ran to the metal trunk and pulled out three orange cups. They still smelled of sweet orange juice — a memory of Steve's malaria magic in El Wadi. I instructed the children to sit, their legs outstretched in the sand. I took two cups from Adam Ali and handed them to the smallest children. The little sobbing girl spilled her water as she trembled. I knelt down beside her, one arm round her shoulders, and held the cup to her mouth. Slowly she started to drink, little sips between shuddering sobs. A trickle of water ran down the front of her dress. I gently pinched the skin on the back of her hand, a quick test for dehydration. Her dry skin rose to a ridge and held its shape as I released my fingers. The skin of a three-year-old should snap back with elasticity and vitality. Not shrink like an old woman's.

'My God, Adam Ali. Look at this,' I said.

'This one is the same,' he replied, holding up the arm of a five-year-old beside me. 'He says he has had no water since yesterday.'

I leaned back on my boots and looked along the line of gulping, sobbing children. *That* is the reality of war — not frightening statistics of death, front lines and the changing allegiances of tribes. The reality of war is those children, their dusty feet lying on the sand as they drank and sniffed. Flies gathered on their wet clothes within minutes, greedily sucking away the moisture. Around us the hot wind blew, tugging at the tent and sending whirling eddies of sand into the air. Soon we were all covered in a scratching of sand. And still they drank.

'Here are the babies.' Noora stood again at the entrance. A group of women stood round her, each holding a small baby. Noora held one in her arms. 'This one belongs to my sister,' she said. 'He is not sucking.' He lay in her arms — eighteen days old and severely dehydrated. I reached out for him and put my little finger in his mouth. His tongue didn't move.

'Adam Ali, please get me a syringe and a cup of water.'

'How many cups of water is his mother drinking every day? Is she eating?' I asked Noora.

'She drinks maybe one cup a day,' she replied. 'I give her my food at night so she can eat but it is not enough.'

Her sister was starving and dehydrated, and this baby was dying without her milk.

Adam Ali passed me the syringe of water and I started to trickle drops into the baby's mouth. His little tongue, wooden and hard, rested against my finger. I felt the weight of his body against my knees and looked at the soft blue blanket that surrounded him. It was a blanket from another time, a time of wealth, a time of plenty.

Sometimes the simplest solutions are the best ones — water gave this baby life. His tongue started to move, touching my finger gently at first. More, it asked. Within minutes he was sucking, drawing in the water and swallowing quietly. His tongue started to soften, but still it didn't feel like the tongue of an eighteen-day-old baby.

'Adam Ali, is this baby going to die?' I asked. 'After our syringes of water will he die with his mother?' Adam Ali had seen this all before. I had given up my optimism, my feelings of expertise in nursing faded every day. And each time I turned to Adam Ali.

'Inshallah he will live,' he replied. God willing.

God willing his mother could have more than one cup of water a day. God willing she could find food to eat. God willing she would start to produce milk before this baby died. God willing. Or perhaps God wasn't willing. Perhaps they were all damned to die from hunger and thirst in this godforsaken place. I didn't have any answers these days.

I could lie under the stars outside and sleep because it was my escape from the reality of life. On the island of my narrow bed the tears and pain of the day couldn't touch me. I had spent too many afternoons sitting beside Adam Ali in the dim consultation hut listening to stories of pain and suffering to believe any more in hope, in change and justice. With Adam Ali's shoulder against mine, I recorded their injuries and prescribed tablets to take away their pain. With Musa beside me I leaned on a donkey cart to treat the latest patient, beaten, whipped or shot in the fields for being in the wrong place at the wrong time. And for being from the 'wrong' tribe. While the donkey shifted and snorted in the evening light we washed the blood from torn skin, suturing and repairing what we could. Perhaps there was no end. No one was trying to stop the pain, to stop the killing. There was only us, our feet covered in splashes of blood as it fell through the flat bed of the donkey carts, while we worked. My optimism had gone, my hope for change fading with each passing day.

Kneeling beside Adam Ali I worked with a slowly spreading quietness in my heart. A still, cold quiet that stole my faith in goodness and hope. When the baby had drunk three small syringes filled with water I stopped. We gave Noora five clean syringes and our orange cup for water. The last we saw of her she was walking through the long grass, carrying her nephew to his fate. We never saw Noora again. She fled into the hills after an attack near the African Union several days later. Noora with her long fingers and shy smile. Perhaps she is happy with her people now, safe and protected. Or perhaps she is dead, her fears and her hunger behind her forever. The baby died, that much we knew. He died two days later. His mother said he was still not sucking. His body was buried in a shallow grave on the edge of the African Union compound. Another victim of this unjust war. A silent reminder of their shame and neglect.

****

At the end of each clinic day we returned to our compound. Halima and Selwa still sang while they worked, and they giggled when I spoke to them in Arabic. My patients understood me, but my accent was enough to send Selwa into fits of laughter. There was precious little laughter in those days, so I talked even more to hear her laugh. Then I retreated to the shower to cry.

Each of us withdrew after a day at the African Union, worn and beaten by the heat, thirst and misery. Steve threw his bag on the table and walked straight to the computer while the kettle boiled for yet another cup of coffee. Sam disappeared into the shower and spent an hour washing and scrubbing his frustrations away. Toby just sat and smoked. I dropped my bag on the table, grabbed a can of soda and walked back to the vehicle, ready for the next outreach worker meeting at the clinic. Why were there never enough hours in the day? Our conversation had long since dried up, leaving the compound quiet until each of us was renewed by a shower and food.

None of us wanted to continue working outside the African Union, we shouldn't have to. The people were seeking safety and protection in their barren, wind-torn camp. But the African Union was not there to protect the people — their mandate was to *observe* the peace process, not to protect. So they watched from within their compound while we worked outside.

When we finished work outside the African Union early I escaped to the MSF warehouse in the marketplace. There in the hot brick building I could lose myself among shelves of drugs and equipment, counting and tidying, rearranging and just sitting while

I tried to forget the day. Abdullah, the warehouse guard, sat outside on his wooden box while I worked inside. Every now and then he stood in the entrance and knocked on the thin metal door.

'Do you want tea?' he called, his voice echoing around the room.

'Yes, please,' I always called back. Tea with Abdullah was my reason for being there, my own quiet pleasure without the other expats. Abdullah walked over to the restaurant, a small makeshift shelter that lent haphazardly against a concrete wall. Inside the plastic walls, little wooden stools sat in circles, ready for customers now that Ramadan was over and everyone was back for daytime food. Miriam sat at a low stool in one corner and stirred her pots of stew, macaroni and oily sauce. Abdullah and Miriam invited me across for a meal more times than I could count, not ever charging me for my little plastic bowls of stew and bread. Instead Miriam stood over me while I ate, ready to fill each bowl when she thought it was needed. I didn't like liver stew and normally avoided goat meat at every meal. But with Miriam watching me, a wide smile on her face, and Abdullah nodding beside me while he slurped and sucked on his stew and bones, how could I refuse their hospitality?

'Why are you not married?' Musa asked me often. 'You are too thin to be married, but I can make you fat.'

'If you like I can bring my brother,' Miriam offered one day. 'If you have no family here I can find you a husband. You can be my sister.' She nodded vigorously and turned to talk to Abdullah. I was soon lost in their Arabic, but I caught some words. Fat, happy, many children, new clothes, good husband. They had my future planned. In the fear and unhappiness that surrounded them, through the attacks and insecurity, they still managed to laugh, to plan and to have hope.

The Janjaweed still gathered in the marketplace, sitting in small groups under the shady trees while they smoked. From my sunny porch at the warehouse I felt safe, with Abdullah at my side and Miriam carrying tea across to us on a small silver tray. I knew the Janjaweed were around, but somehow I felt removed from the fear they brought to town. They wouldn't touch us, that much I believed. When we drove past a group in the marketplace I avoided their eyes. I couldn't bear to look at them, to put faces to the men who wrought such damage in my community. I wanted to roll down the window and scream at them, to cry out my frustrations and anger whenever we passed. You rapist, you murderer, you cold-hearted monster. I'd scream until my throat was raw if I thought it would do any good. But I did nothing. It was not my place to judge, to criticise, to take sides. I closed my eyes, held my breath and we drove slowly by, Musa concentrating intently on the track ahead of us.

****

Each time we visited the camp at the African Union, the hot dry wind blew and dust storms rose in sand-whipping fury. The African Union's commander allowed us to leave two large water barrels, each capable of holding 250 litres of water. Steve negotiated with them a water-sustaining compromise. MSF would supply the water barrels and we agreed to not establish a permanent clinic outside their compound. In exchange the African Union would fill the water barrels each day, for as long as the people remained.

But every time we arrived at our tent clinic, the line of empty jerry cans grew longer. I stood on the sandbag steps beside each barrel in turn and lifted the hot, black lid to peer in.

'Mafi moya,' the children would call from their queue each time. No water.

The children crouched in the sun, guarding their jerry cans. They waited every day, hoping that the African Union would bring them water. Their families were still too afraid to return to town and to the hand pumps that waited for them there. Night-time raids, fires and attacks continued unabated. They were not ready to trust anyone.

'Tomorrow,' called one of the children. 'Inshallah.' Tomorrow, always tomorrow.

Already the queue of quiet, dehydrated children and toddlers was waiting at the entrance to our tent. Waiting for our hand-outs of water, orange cups and compassion.

'That's it. I've fucking had enough,' I yelled, kicking an empty barrel. 'Enough!' The children scrambled back, startled.

'Steve, I want water for these children and I want it *now!*' I shouted.

'OK, OK, calm down,' he said, walking over to where I stood. 'They promised me they would fill it yesterday.' He knocked on the barrel and listened as the sound echoed in the empty hollow.

'Adam Ali, come with me. We're off to have a few words with the gentlemen inside,' he called.

I watched as Adam Ali and Steve disappeared in through the heavily guarded front gates of the African Union's compound.

They re-emerged half an hour later.

'The commander says there's a problem with their water truck,' said Steve. 'Says it will be fixed by this afternoon and they'll fill both barrels tonight.'

'And yesterday it was a different problem and the day before that. They're all excuses!' I was so angry I was shaking. Every day I held crying children as they drank away the worst of their dehydration. And every tomorrow they were back, often without a single sip of water between our visits.

'Well, what do you want me to do — drive the water truck myself?' asked Steve. 'There are ways to get things done, Lisa. Negotiation and discussion. Anger and aggression achieves nothing. Just relax.'

I leaned forward, resting my head on the plastic table. Relax. It had been three weeks since we had been to El Wadi and the children were dying there. I spent my days outside the African Union watching children suffer and cry. The outreach workers continued to bring stories of horror and fear from all sectors of the community. And we passed a column of Janjaweed militia each day as we left the African Union's compound. They were making their way into town, their horses in single file, waiting until nightfall to resume their campaign of terror.

I took a deep breath.

'Adam Ali, can you get me a bucket? I think I'm going to be sick,' I said, my head in my hands.

****

The following day we arrived early. Our African Union clinic was now part of our daily routine, despite our promise to not make it a regular occurrence. Still families gathered under trees and shrubs, hoping for protection from the Janjaweed and the flares in tribal violence in town. Still the children gathered in the shade of the tent, desperate for water when we arrived. We couldn't stop our clinic, couldn't sit at home knowing they all waited for our help, our care and our water.

Standing in the shade of the tent stood a group of young boys. They played with a stone, scuffing and kicking the earth as they each vied for their makeshift ball.

'Salaam aleikum,' called one boy. 'We have water today!' All the boys cheered.

I ran to the water barrels and looked at the long line of children waiting in the sun. Each stood smiling, taking their turn to fill their jerry cans from the two taps. I felt tears well up in my eyes. Water!

They finally had water without our pushing and demanding. I wiped my eyes and turned back to the boys. I gave them the thumbs up and they smiled back, giving me a show of thumbs up in return.

After the morning round of water for the weak and thirsty children, Adam Ali and I sat at the little plastic table and started to see patients. Eye infections, diarrhoea, abdominal pain and chest infections were common. Everyone was sleeping out in the open, and at night the temperature plummeted. Even on my cocooned bed I slept with two blankets and a sleeping bag. I shivered in the early-morning dawn. How did they manage, sleeping under the stars with nothing more than a sheet or less? Some had managed to carry supplies of food, bags of grain and cooking pots, when they fled town. Some had returned for a bed or a bundle of thatching during daylight hours, to give them some comfort. But most had left town only with the clothes they were wearing.

Part way through the afternoon I leaned back in my chair, my back aching after hours of sitting as we examined and talked to patients. I turned and looked out through the front entrance of the tent. Sitting on the roof of our land cruiser was Saad, one of the laughing, stone-playing boys we met that morning. Next to him, beyond my sight, sat Steve. Despite the language barrier they sat together, talking and exploring. Saad examined Steve's watch while Steve asked Saad questions to learn about the boy. I watched while Saad talked, his hands moving as he described people and he drew pictures in the air. He talked and smiled, his head to one side as he listened to Steve. He caught my eye for a moment and bent down to smile. He waved and nodded his greeting. Then he turned back to Steve, shouting 'Barcelona!' They were obviously talking the universal language of football. I will always remember that moment — Saad's bright, smiling eyes and his quick wave as he looked my way. Happy, healthy and at peace for a moment.

Then it was back to work. The women crowded the tent, trying to squeeze into the shade afforded by the tent. Talking, asking, babies crying, hands stretching closer and closer. Me, me choose me, they asked. A hand tapped my elbow and I turned. One touched my other shoulder. I turned again. Every face was pleading — please help me.

I pushed back the chair and growled — 'Adam Ali, I can't work when people are so close, crowding me, pulling at me. Please, I need some space!'

He translated for me, patiently moving them further away, then he sat down. And the women started to edge forward. I knew they needed me, knew of their exhaustion and fear. I had seen some of them in the marketplace, weeks before, as they passed the warehouse where I sat with Abdullah and a steaming cup of tea. We had smiled and waved in days gone by, shared worried moments in the clinic while their children were treated for a kaleidoscope of problems. They were my neighbours and my patients. But there in the heat and crush of our sandy, white tent I couldn't smile and laugh. I felt bowed and nearly broken by all that they needed, by the sheer desperation of their lives. It was all I could do to keep up with the patients in front of me. When they pulled and tugged, whispered and shouted for my attention I snapped. But how can you shout at a desperate, frightened woman, I could hear people at home ask me in the years to come. All I knew was that they were dying, the machine of war was slowly crushing them all and there was little we could do to help them. There was me, Adam Ali and our little plastic table. It was wrong and unfair and part of some game of war that I didn't understand. And my heart broke at the utter helplessness of it all.

As we drove away that afternoon the group of boys laughed as they chased our vehicles. Saad ran in front. Cheeky, smiling, normal boys. They had asked Steve for food, me for water and the African Union for protection. Behind their laughter they were hurting, their families hunted and driven out of town. But children accept and adapt to situations that defeat adults like us.

'See you tomorrow,' they called. Two of them turned cartwheels in the sand, showing off to their new friends in the flash white land cruisers.

'Maybe we have water tomorrow,' Saad sang.

Inshallah, I whispered. God willing.

That night we heard vollies of gunfire to the east, in the direction of the African Union. Please let them be there in the morning, I prayed. I looked up at the stars, aching with desperation and fear for their lives. Please.

****

The heat in Khartoum was unbearable. I lay on my bed, the ceiling fan clunking and shuddering above me. I covered my eyes with my arm and hid my tears as they fell. After only nine weeks in the field my spirit was broken. And I had left in tears.

Steve had seen my tears every day and had made the decision to send me out of the project for a week. Out of Saleem. Out of Darfur. All expats were given a week for rest and relaxation in Nyala or Khartoum regularly. It gave them time to eat, rest and recover before heading back to the field. But to me it felt like failure and shame. With my tears and exhaustion I had shown the others that I wasn't strong enough. Each Friday, our one day off, I lay in my tuckul from dawn till dusk, my body craving sleep and escape. But each Saturday morning I sat with my head in my hands, wondering how I would make it through the new week. Gunfire, screams and endless lines of patients slowly pushing filled my days.

The team still operated at a skeleton level, the minimum number needed to keep the programme open and to allow a fast evacuation. The reality was that there simply weren't enough of us to do the work, and I worried that the patients were suffering.

Still Musa prayed, kneeling in the pre-dawn light, and gave his thanks for life's blessings. I had stopped praying. My pleas for a respite in the conflict, for the safety of those around me and for someone to hear our story had fallen on deaf ears. Still they suffered. Still they died. Still the children sat, dehydrated and crying in the sand.

Hiding in Khartoum I was told to forget about it.

'Relax, Lisa,' said Toby as I left. 'We will take care of everything.'

'You need to unwind and forget about this place,' instructed Steve over dinner the night before my departure. 'You're not doing anyone any good running yourself into the ground.'

I heard their words and I knew them to be true. I couldn't save the people of Darfur single-handedly. I needed a rest. But lying there on my bed in Khartoum I felt the weight of failure crushing in on me. Who would give the children their water outside the African Union? Sam was busy with the clinic in town. Who would run the clinic in El Wadi, to see young Hanan with her abscesses and care for her baby? Who would be there when Commander Ali returned with his soldiers to frighten and intimidate? If not me, then who?

The night before I left I lay on my bed, my hands over my ears, blocking out the sound of gunfire. Armed militia moved through town every night now, shooting and burning as they went. A man had been killed in his home three days before. The SLA was blamed for his death. The wave of violence that followed was retribution, a hammer that pounded the innocent as it searched for the guilty.

I spent my first day in Khartoum hiding in my room. I couldn't face the others in the house, laughing, talking and relaxing. The expat house sat on a quiet, dusty corner in a suburban part of the city. It was always full of visitors and travellers, people coming from and going to various projects in Darfur. None were from Saleem.

When I emerged on the second day, I padded downstairs to the kitchen. It was still early and the stone floors were cool. I pulled open the fridge door and stood looking at its overflowing shelves of fresh fruit and vegetables, rows of neatly labelled soda bottles, icy cold and heaven sent. Plastic bags filled the lower shelves, gifts of chocolate and cheese brought by visitors to take to the field. 'Do not eat' read one in black ink. 'Eat this and I will find you' read another. It was a well-respected rule that cheese and chocolate, craved by every isolated project site, were sacred. But still thieving fingers would sneak into bags unseen. I closed the fridge door.

We had little fresh food in Saleem and our cool box held a block of butter and several lukewarm cans of soda on a good day. The sight of all the food now was overwhelming.

I filled the kettle and stood with my back to the counter while it boiled. Carrying the cup of tea out onto the verandah I curled up on the soft wicker sofa and sat quietly. It was still early and the others were sleeping upstairs. I sat breathing in the still cool dawn air, grateful for the peace.

Across the lawn sat an aviary, the brightly coloured birds starting to fill the morning air with their song. Behind the high walls Khartoum started to stir. A thick coil of barbed wire ran across the top of each wall, a warning to others. Keep out. In the corner sat our guard, Michael. The iron gate was kept shut at all times, Michael held the only key. Beside his chair stood the whiteboard. Anyone entering or leaving the house was instructed to write their name, destination and expected time of return. Even in the early-morning calm of the garden, the house was a prison.

****

Gertrude and I had travelled from Darfur together, sharing the five-hour-long flight and endless wait at the airport together. She was also coming out for her R&R, from her project south of Saleem.

'Why don't we go for a swim later?' she asked that morning. 'I can't sit here all day — it will drive me mad!'

So we walked together, through crowded streets and along the wide pot-holed roads to the German Club after lunch.

Gertrude was Dutch, a large, smiling woman in her fifties. She was full of common sense and had no time for fools. With my spirit broken and my body aching, her quiet manner and unhurried stride was a blessing. She didn't probe for answers and was content to walk in silence, her bathing costume swinging in her hand.

'I wonder if they'll let us in,' she said as we walked up the front path to the club. 'It looks like they have a dress code here.'

We both looked down at our dusty feet and grey, torn MSF T-shirts and burst out laughing.

'We'll soon find out!'

We pushed through the dark glass doorway and found ourselves standing in a cool, white-tiled room. A leather sofa sat in the corner.

'MSF?' asked the security guard, looking at our T-shirts. 'ID cards.' He put out his hand and looked at us carefully.

We handed over our cards and stood watching him silently. My weeks of living in the shadow of the military in Saleem had me standing rigidly in front of this uniformed man. I waited for him to speak, to give us permission to move. He stared back.

'You can swim now,' he said, smiling suddenly. 'Have a nice day.'

And the tears started to well up in my eyes.

'Come on, let's go,' whispered Gertrude. 'Don't worry, he's on our side.' And I followed her out into the sunshine.

We spent the rest of the day in the water, swimming, diving and floating in the most beautiful pool I had ever seen. The German Club of Sudan was established in the colonial days by German expats looking for an escape from the noise and rabble of the city. Behind barbed walls lay neatly manicured lawns, flowerbeds and walkways. Around the pool sat rows of sun loungers in the afternoon sunshine. The clientele of the German Club were the wealthy elite of Khartoum; local businessmen, diplomats and their families and the vast UN expat community. Anyone with money. We had discounted passes, a limited number of cards given out for our 'mental wellbeing'.

In between dips I lay in the shade and watched the other guests behind my sunglasses. Sitting at a table not far from us was a group of Arab women, beautiful pale-skinned women in their thirties, at a guess. Their hands were richly stained with henna, a flattering sign of beauty. Their heads were covered with silken scarves, accentuating their carefully painted mouths and wide, black-lined eyes. Around them lay bags and towels, sunscreen and diving goggles. Their children splashed and dived in the deep end, shrieking and laughing as they played. I thought of the children in El Wadi and sighed.

One of the mothers lifted her heavy arm and clicked her fingers impatiently. A waiter ran over and pulled a notebook from his apron pocket.

'Four cokes, four fanta, three burgers, five hot chips and some water,' she said quickly in English.

'Maam, I want ice cream too,' shouted her daughter, standing waist deep in the water. 'Ice cream, ice cream, ice cream,' she chanted.

'Me too,' wailed a smaller child beside her. 'I never get ice cream.'

They splashed their way to the water ladder and ran across the tiles to their mother. I looked at them. Looked at their fat, shining wet legs and round bellies. They were very well-fed five- and seven-year-olds. They stood dripping in the sun and the little one stamped her foot.

Aerial photograph of Darfur; vast expanses of sand and scrub that millions call home.

Camp for the internally displaced: 80,000 people sheltering along a thin strip of land.

The main street of Muhajariya, calm in the evening light.

Children from a community of displaced families, wandering in the dust.

Karen meeting a local leader while patients wait for transport to Muhajariya.

Men on the way to the market, midday wind and dust tugging at their jelabiyia gowns.

Women waiting outside the mobile clinic in Angabo. Some walked for 6 hours to get there.

Seeing patients in the mobile clinic in Angabo.

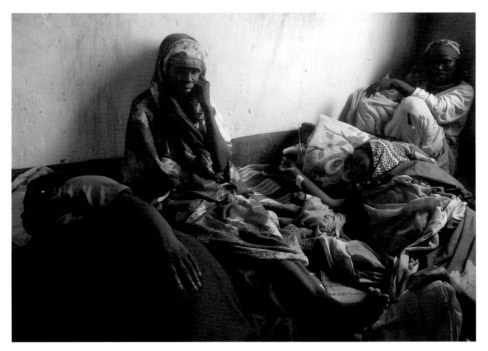

Pregnant women with complications of labour lie waiting for transport to Muhajariya.

Karen treating a woman with eclampsia; she spent hours kneeling on the floor while the woman succumbed to seizures.

Me treating a patient in the back of the vehicle on the way to Muhajariya.

Patients crowd around the vehicle as it is turned into an impromptu mobile clinic in the bush.

Children wait to be seen at a Bilharzia clinic — the blood in their urine samples clearly show the effects of the disease.

A young girl waiting to be seen at a mobile clinic; she spent hours sitting patiently before the 3-hour walk home.

The sorrow and exhaustion of a young woman's life; waiting while her infant is treated for pneumonia.

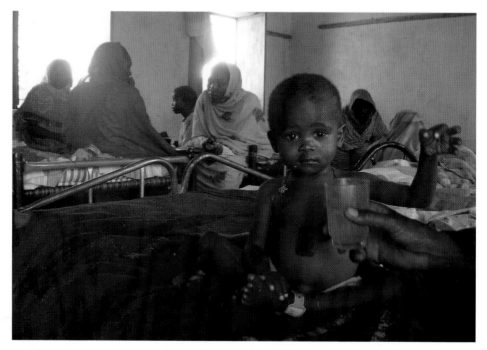

A child with malnutrition finishes a glass of fortified milk in the paediatric ward.

'I want ice cream now,' she shouted at the African waiter.

I felt my stomach lurch and my eyes filled with tears. Those fat, healthy children didn't know how lucky they were. Safe. Protected. Nourished. Shame and anger roared around me. How dare they. I looked away.

For the rest of my R&R I hid in the house, too ashamed to step out into the noise and chaos of Khartoum. UN land cruisers threw up great clouds of dust as they roared along the boulevard. Beggars and lepers sat and crawled along the footpath, their bent and weary limbs reaching up when people passed. It was all so overwhelming and my heart ached with their need and worry. I knew I couldn't save the world. So I closed my eyes to it all.

I slept away each afternoon and emerged at dusk to breathe in the warm air on the verandah as I listened to the birds. I avoided the new arrivals to the expat house, with their cheerful chatter and casual questions asking about life in Darfur. I didn't want to tell them. Instead I watched the guard as he watered the garden, humming as he dragged the hose behind him. Three of the guards were from South Sudan, long displaced by the twenty-three-year-long war but glad to have found work. The cooks were Ethiopian, the washerwoman was Dinka.

Khartoum really is a multicultural society. One culture dominates, though. The Arabs. Their language, their dress, their government. And in the barren desert on the outskirts of the city live many others, in treeless slums, earthen huts and under plastic sheets that bake in the harsh desert sun. From those slums the city draws its workers. Into the slums bleed the refugees and displaced people running from war and ruin in its wake. Somalis, Ethiopians, Dinka, Nuer and Nuba tribes from South Sudan, Chadians and Congolese, all hoping and waiting for a better life when peace returns. Many will be waiting a long time to come.

After five days of rest it was time to go back to Darfur. Gertrude and I stood in the dark at the front gate and waited for the car to take us to the airport. It was 5.30 a.m.

'Are you ready to go back?' she asked.

'I want to go back and try again,' I said, lifting my bag to my shoulder. 'At least there we're part of a solution, helping, listening, caring. I feel so guilty being here, knowing they are there hurting. It's hard to close my eyes now I've seen theirs.'

I tried to shake off the image of the surging crowds in El Wadi, and of the aching suffering in the riverbed as the Zaghawa waited for help. I felt the weight of Hanan's baby in my arms as his pendulous grandmother dropped him. Felt his bones as they shifted and rubbed together as I lifted him to my chest. How could I not take it personally? I nodded as she looked at me, too weary to face a disagreement about responsibility and guilt.

'Let's go back,' I said, as the car hooted outside the gate. 'Let's go back to their war.'

CHAPTER SIX

During my week of escape, little had changed in Saleem. I sat listening as Steve and Toby filled me in on the week's tragedy. Still more families flooded to the African Union, asking for protection from the Janjaweed militia, from the drunken soldiers and local tribes who fomented unrest. Most families had left their possessions in town and they joined the growing crowds around the African Union's compound.

There were no clinics to El Wadi in my absence. Night-time attacks in and around Saleem happened regularly as the government troops and SLA fought. Unprotected and isolated, the team couldn't venture into El Wadi alone.

The long-forgotten groups hiding in the river bed far south of Saleem were still waiting for us. Our supplies of jerry cans and blankets sat locked in our warehouse. With only a small team and being preoccupied with families outside the African Union compound and intermittent gun battles, Steve and Toby had been unable to venture south either.

The daily battle to provide water to the families outside the African Union continued.

'Every day they have a different excuse,' said Toby. 'No truck, no petrol, no driver. Last time it was three days before they filled the water barrels and we hounded them every day. The African Union keeps hoping that the people will just go home.'

'But we have a warehouse full of non-food items now,' said Steve. 'We can give them blankets, jerry cans and plastic sheeting if management gives us the okay.'

'I thought we agreed with the African Union to not make our clinic a permanent fixture,' I said. 'If we start handing out plastic sheets and blankets they'll accuse us of building a community and moving in.'

'So we're damned if we do and we're damned if we don't,' replied Steve. 'We're supposed to keep our mouths shut and count the dead. Fuck that, I've had enough!' He hit the table with his hand and looked up. 'Tomorrow we start distributing, whether they like it or not.'

Steve still unsettled me. With his fist crashing down I felt every muscle tense and the blade of a headache start to twist. Anger is natural and expressing our feelings is an important part of living. But each time he lashed out, shouting, striding across the compound in anger or hitting the table with a sudden rage, I felt so small. As though I could shrink away and hide from his waves of anger, invisible in the dark. With the echoes of night-time gunfire and the sound of quiet sobbing as another woman sat in front of me, my own strength and resilience were shaken. Surrounded by such a harsh world I craved a respite, some kindness and hope to help me stand tall. I am not a soldier, not hardened to the aching misery. Steve wanted to help, to fight for change as much as anyone. But when his anger snapped I felt my own heart shrink. My days of rest and calm in Khartoum vanished as his fist hit the table.

****

After ten weeks without a break, Sam had left Saleem the day before I arrived. He was exhausted by the heat and the workload.

He was the only medic while I was resting in Khartoum and he had been running the clinic in Saleem single-handedly for months. He deserved a break. As we said goodbye in Tala he stood smiling in the shade.

'We keep doing the best we can, Lisa. That is all we can do,' he said. 'Don't take on too much. And I'll be back soon.'

With Sam away I would be responsible for running the local clinic, supervising its two local health workers, managing the outreach workers and following up on their referrals, consulting in the African Union's clinic with Adam Ali and asking every day to return to the river-bed community and El Wadi as soon as possible. My head started to ache at the thought of it all.

'Don't worry, Sam. I'll do what I can and wait for you,' I said, my fingers crossed behind my back. I was going to do everything and I'd do it well, I thought to myself. Even if it killed me.

****

Abdallah and Matthew had arrived in Saleem while I was in Khartoum. Both were experienced MSF medics — trained Sudanese nurses with years of experience in Darfur. Abdallah with his broad shoulders and quiet nature was the boss — the grandfather of our team. He had seen and survived the best and worst of Darfur. His sad eyes and slow smile held stories he wasn't ready to share. Matthew was from South Sudan, a Dinka with the widest eyes and cheekiest grin I'd ever seen. With Matthew in the group there was always laughter as he teased and joked to make us smile. He woke with a twinkle in his eye each day.

Abdallah and Matthew ran the clinic in town while we headed out to the African Union each morning to help save the lives that clung to the edge of town.

****

Toby and Musa started the distribution of blankets and plastic sheeting soon after breakfast. They stood in the back of the covered truck, with its doors anchored wide so they could throw out the goods. Ahmed stood below them, a sheet of paper neatly clipped to his folder as he recorded names and number of people in each family. In the heat and misery of their long, waiting days these women would take all they could, and more. Some changed scarves or borrowed a dress so they could return a second time, pretending to be a sister or aunt as they asked for more plastic or another blanket. But Ahmed was vigilant. No one could fool him, despite their wails and pleas. We had barely enough for one of everything per family, so he had to be fair.

Adam Ali and I sat in the tent, the queue of waiting patients longer than ever. Water-related diseases were still the most common, diarrhoea and dehydration was our daily routine. I paused after an hour and looked out of the tent.

'When will they go home, Adam Ali?' I asked.

'I think they will not go home, Lisa,' he replied. 'If they go home they will die. That is why they stay.' He shook his head. 'This is Darfur. This is how the life goes.'

There was a noise, shouting and movement behind us and we turned. An older woman, perhaps fifty years old, was pushing her way into the tent. The younger women tried to block her path. 'You have to wait,' they called. 'We were here first.'

'I need the doctor,' she called. 'My daughter has a new baby and she is sick.' She pointed into the distance to where her daughter lay.

I looked at the queue of waiting women around me and then followed the line of her finger. Stay or go?

'What do you think, Adam Ali?' I asked, turning to him in my indecision. They all needed us.

'We go,' he said standing up. 'These women are not dying. They can wait.'

So we pushed back our chairs, and amongst the protesting wails from the women around us, we walked out of the tent.

I called out to Toby and Musa as we left, pointing out the direction of our patient and we set off with the older woman. Adam Ali carried the heavy silver box, our portable hospital. I carried a radio handset and 10 litres of water in a jerry can.

'She says her daughter had a baby two days ago,' Adam Ali translated. 'She has no milk and the baby is not sucking. She has a headache and she is vomiting. And the baby cries.'

The jerry can knocked against my leg as we walked, water leaking through my jeans as the plastic lid leaked. And my heart sank. Another case of dehydration that would cost the life of a baby, I just knew it.

We walked for what seemed an eternity, following the outer fence of the African Union. In African time every distance is described as 'not far'. The sun burnt my skin and my head started to ache in the heat. I wondered how long we would be walking. The chain-link fence shone in the sun, the barbed wire glinting from above. We passed the back entrance of the compound, with white sandbags piled high beside the gate. Through the sandbags poked the barrel of two rifles. They pointed low and straight, towards the huddled families.

'Why are their guns out?' I asked, stopping to stare as we crossed the track.

'Don't stop,' replied Adam Ali. 'Keep walking.'

I walked faster to keep up, the jerry can starting to feel heavy as my hand and shoulder ached in the sun.

'They are afraid,' he said once we had passed. 'Afraid of what might happen. The SLA may come to look for their families, to take them into the hills for safety. And the Janjaweed and local tribes would come to fight the SLA if they come into town. The African Union does not want this around their compound. So they hide inside and wait.'

After fifteen minutes we approached a sprawling acacia tree, the only one in sight. My fingers ached with the weight of the jerry can, and I cursed myself for forgetting my hat. In the shade of the tree lay a bed, covered with a bright red scarf. Torn sheets hung in the branches, threaded through the thorns to give some shade and protection from the heat. Around the bed lay pots and bowls, a pair of shoes and a torn mat.

'What's that awful smell?' I asked, covering my nose as a hot wind blew as we approached.

'The African Union have dug some latrines for the people,' said Adam Ali, pointing to a blue plastic wall upwind of the tree. 'The women were talking of them this morning. The latrines are full now, after one week, so the people have stopped using them. The flies are everywhere and every day the smell is worse.'

I shook my head. For certain our workload would start to increase as the flies spread diseases from the overflowing latrines. We were barely coping with dehydration and malnutrition that arose from a lack of water for the children.

I followed as Adam Ali ducked under the branches, my nose still hidden in my sleeve. We knelt beside the bed and called our greetings to the woman beneath the sheets. Silence. I pulled back the sheet and saw the young woman sleeping. Her lips were cracked and her skin dry. Around us a hot wind blew in the 40° heat. She should have been sweating.

'Hello,' I said, shaking her shoulder gently. 'We have come to see you and your baby.'

She opened her eyes slowly and looked at us. She reached down to pull away a second sheet at her side. Lying beside her was her two-day-old baby. His thick dark hair and long fingers were beautiful, the way a healthy baby should look. He sniffled and shifted in the bright light.

'He has passed urine one time since he was born,' said the grandmother. 'And now he is not sucking.'

I lifted the baby and rested him on my lap as I sat on the edge of the bed. His baby fat was soft, his skin silky. I opened his mouth gently and felt his tongue. It was dry and hard, surely a whisper of death for a new baby.

'Adam Ali, can I have the syringe and water again?' I asked. 'He just needs water.'

'She says she wants some pills to stop the vomiting,' translated Adam Ali as he opened the silver box. 'She doesn't want water.'

'Tell her to drink. She is vomiting because she is dehydrated,' I said, exasperated. 'Why does everyone think a pill will fix everything?'

He smiled and shrugged. 'This is Darfur,' he said. 'People like pills.'

As I drizzled water into the baby's mouth Adam Ali prepared a bottle of rehydration solution in an empty green soda bottle.

'Give them my water too,' I said, nodding at my backpack. 'We may as well give them all we have.'

He shook the bottle, mixing the water and white powder vigorously. Then he sat on the edge of the bed and lifted the young woman's shoulders onto his lap. She drank slowly, her eyes closed and her lips open as he poured in the water. He murmured and whispered as he encouraged her to drink. 'Just a little bit more.'

On my lap the newborn baby lapped up the water, his little hands clutching and kneading the air like a kitten.

'There is nothing wrong with him,' I said, touching his soft cheek. 'He's just thirsty.'

'They say they have had no water for two days,' Adam Ali

translated again. 'Her sister tried to go to the hand pump near town but the militia chased her away. No one is going to town now.'

They had no water and this baby would die because of it. I closed my eyes and listened to the baby drink, feeling him move as he came back to life. How simple it would be to save his life, I thought. To give him a chance to be someone, to smile and laugh and make his parents proud. But he was an African baby, even worse for him he was a Darfur baby. He had no chance. And I couldn't stop the madness around him to save his life. When the baby had finished the cup of water I lifted him back onto the bed and sighed.

'We'd better go. There are others waiting in the tent.' I knew there was no point in asking them to come back to town with us. This baby needed more fluids in our clinic and a lot of care. But the answer would be no. Every mother I asked in our little white tent said no. They were too scared to come back into town.

We left them our water, a bag filled with paracetamol and the young woman waved from her bed as we left.

'Shukran,' called her mother, touching her heart. Thank you for helping.

I waved back, but I couldn't smile. Inside I was angry, furious with this madness that allowed these people to watch their children die. As we walked past the guns of the African Union it took all my strength to keep walking.

'Do you feel like men now?!' I wanted to shout. 'There are babies dying out here while you hide behind your walls. Does that frighten you?' But I kept on walking, my eyes on Adam Ali's back. It was hopeless, no one could help them now. The war was too big, too complicated and out of control.

When we returned to the tent I sat down heavily on my chair. I'd had enough of it all. We were out of water and it was only 10 a.m. My headache pounded against my temples.

'What is that man doing, Adam Ali?' I asked, pointing to a solitary man beside a nearby shelter. He looked tall and his girth was substantial. He appeared to be wearing a green uniform and his epaulettes shone in the sun.

Adam Ali turned to the women sitting on the sand around us. He spoke to them briefly, pointing to the man. 'He's from the African Union,' he said. 'They say the African Union come every day, talking to the women and telling them to go home. This man says there will be no more water from today, so they must leave.'

'They *what?!*' I roared. 'Like fuck they will!' I ran out of the tent and reached into the vehicle for the radio. My powers of negotiation and discussion evaporated. If I talked to the lone commander I would scream and swear and cry, achieving nothing for the women with my anger. I'd probably make things worse.

'Steve, you have to come here now. The African Union's threatening to withhold water. They are going from shelter to shelter right now.' My hand was shaking as I held the handset.

'Calm down, Lisa. I'll be right there.'

I am a pacifist at heart. I only want to help and care for the people around me. But standing in the sun that day I felt murderous. My hands were shaking and my body was rigid with anger. The babies were dying, that much I knew. How *dare* they threaten these women as well. How dare they try to force them to their deaths in town. A meeting of local tribal elders was held two days before. The result was an announcement — those living around the African Union compound were instructed to return to their homes. They were accused of making a scene, creating a 'situation' were there was no need. All was forgiven and their safety was assured. But none of those families outside the African Union believed it. The flow of families away from the African Union continued as women headed into the hills, their donkeys loaded with their few possessions, their

children following behind them. Their choices remained few —
stay at the African Union and hope for protection, food and water.
Or head for the hills, looking for the safety of the SLA. But even
in the hills life would be hard. Without food, shelter or medicine,
living on the run at night, their children would suffer. Some women
had no men to look after them. They couldn't wander around the
hills alone. Should they stay or go? The women around us that day
had chosen to stay; waiting, hoping and praying that things would
get better.

****

Steve arrived minutes later and he disappeared into the African
Union compound with Adam Ali. They talked, challenged and
listened for what seemed an age. Promises were made, assurances
given. The women were not being made to leave, Steve was told. It
was all a misunderstanding. But the commander promised to make
sure the women were safe. I believed none of it by now.

When we left at the end of the day I climbed up on the
sandbags and looked into the plastic water barrels, kicking the side
with my boot. Empty. The children watched me in silence. Another
promise broken.

****

That night we all stood at the top of our compound and watched
the sky burn. In the east a huge fire raged, casting a thick pall of
smoke and lighting the night sky. No one spoke. We knew what
was burning — the remaining Zaghawa sectors in town. We could
hear the flames, smell the burning in the air. This was real — there
were no other agencies in town to watch, to hear their screams. But

we were. And there was nothing we could do. I stood beside Steve in the dark. His raging fury forgotten, his shoulders stooped with tiredness. In brief glimpses I saw his sadness and his exhaustion. I wanted to reach out to him, to the compassionate person who could tempt frightened children with tablets in the safety of his arms, the man who could argue and negotiate with the worst of commanders. Through my own tiredness and defeat I wanted to show him I saw his sadness.

All of a sudden gunfire shattered my reverie. Twenty minutes of heavy fighting followed as the SLA took on the government and heavy gunfire blasted the town. We ran and scrambled towards the bomb shelter, familiar with the routine by now. I stumbled down the sandbag stairs of the bomb shelter, Adam Ali's hands reaching up from the darkness to steady me and guide me down. We all sat in silence and listened. Dull, heavy thuds sent vibrations through the earth, the rattle of gunfire filled the air. I buried my head in my arms and closed my eyes. We sat in silence for what seemed an age.

'I need to pee,' announced Matthew in the darkness. 'And I need to pee now.'

Adam Ali turned on his torch and we all turned to look at Matthew.

'My bladder doesn't know that it is war,' he said. 'And it's full now. Really full!' He stood up and danced, wriggled and hopped about in the torchlight.

Adam Ali dropped his torch as he roared with laughter. 'You are a crazy Dinka,' he said as he slapped his knee. 'No one pees in a bomb shelter!'

'Well I'm a Dinka man and I gotta pee,' said Matthew, hopping more urgently from foot to foot. 'You telling me that in three years of war you never had to pee in the fighting?' he asked as he looked around the shelter.

'Never!' shouted everyone in unison, even Abdallah, so reserved and measured in the daylight.

'Go on, Matthew,' said Steve, shifting from his seat on a sandbag near the entrance. 'You go and pee, but stay low. I'm not telling anyone in Nyala how you got shot tonight.'

Matthew stumbled and whispered to himself as he climbed the sandbag stairs. Just outside the entrance we heard him sigh and giggle in the darkness. The fighting continued, unabated, all around us.

****

I stood in the middle of a crowd of women, all pulling, calling and asking for attention. Frustration flared in my heart. They complained of side pain, head pain, back pain and joint pain. Their bodies were aching from the months and years of fear, fighting and surviving. They were thirsty and hungry and aching for peace. Our pills couldn't heal all their aches. But still they called me.

It was our last clinic in El Wadi before Christmas. My last chance to help before I left Darfur for a three-week holiday. Three weeks of guilt. I wanted to help them but they had to help themselves. Drink more water and rest in the heat of the day, I told them. Paracetamol could only do so much. But still they held out their hands asking for more.

Anger suddenly flared as a woman pulled my shirt.

'No!' I shouted. 'I've had enough.' And I pushed through the crowd, struggling to get out, to get away. A pair of hands touched my back gently. I heard a quiet voice behind me speaking in Arabic.

'No. Please. Come back,' she said. 'We need you.'

I stopped and my anger melted with her touch.

'I can't do it,' I whispered.

'Yes. We need you,' she replied.

And I turned back, walking back to the tree and back to my work. Past the women to the children who really needed me. I never saw her face, the one who called me back. But I can still feel her hands on my back, calming and reassuring. Asking to not be forgotten.

Lying on the ground were three little bundles, all fevered children hidden by heavy, wet towels. They had come in together two hours before. Musa led their parents into the crowded consultation room.

'Lisa, this is an emergency,' he called.

I threw down my pen and stepped over the patients lying on the floor around my table. I ran to the door. The first child looked about four, her eyes closed and her head rolled unconsciously in her father's arms. Her temperature was 41°C, dangerously high. The second child looked similar, but she groaned as she moved in her mother's arms. The third child was a boy, perhaps six years old. His temperature was 42°C and his mother looked desperate.

'He doesn't stop shaking,' she cried. He started to convulse in her arms, spasms clawing at his muscles as his overheated brain gave in to the fever. Musa held up the three plastic tests he had done on the children. They were positive — all the children had cerebral malaria.

All around us the patients drew nearer, curious at the spectacle in the doorway. In their lives of fear and survival a day in the clinic gave many of the patients a change of routine. It was a chance to gather together in groups, safely, and talk and rest while they watched the life of the clinic around them. In a crisis I didn't appreciate their curiosity.

'Musa, you get paracetamol and wet towels for all of them. You lot, bring your children outside.' We pushed our way out and into the fresh air. The three children were lowered onto the sand beneath the tree. I pulled a Diazepam tablet from my bag from my pocket

— I had learned to carry a mini pharmacy while I worked to save me time. Quickly dissolving it in a syringe I turned the convulsing boy over and rested him on my knee. Rectal diazepam is one way to break a child's fitting in this situation. I only hoped it would work as he shook and trembled on my lap.

Iglam knelt beside me. She was the oldest of the midwives, and an experienced mother of ten. She and Musa dipped towels in a basin of water and carefully covered each child in a cloak of cooling linen. Iglam couldn't read or write, and our strange-looking mercury thermometers were beyond her. But she was a mother and she knew how to cool and soothe these children. Beside me the little boy lay still, his breaths coming in grunts as his body was released from the convulsions. I emptied the paracetamol from my pocket and started to dissolve them in syringes for each child.

I scribbled a note on an empty health card, asking Steve for three packets of malaria treatment, injections and tablets and a mountain of paracetamol. If the commander returned, these parents would flee. If the fighting resumed, we would all flee. And if I was distracted in my haze of frantic consultations and forgot to return, they might all leave without treatment. I had learned to be prepared. 'Expect the worst' had become my new motto.

I moved from child to child, injecting them with the first dose in their course of malaria treatments when Steve had filled my order. I hoped that they would find Dr Abaker or a traditional healer in the days to come, someone to administer the last two injections.

Musa and I stood and looked at each other when I had finished. Our clothes were soaked with water, streaks of sand and mud on our trousers. My fear for the children's lives and my frustration with our sandy, inadequate treatment area beneath the tree evaporated.

'You look a mess,' I said, smiling.

'So do you,' he replied. And we laughed.

We left Iglam and her little febrile angels and climbed the stairs to the verandah. We would come back to them later.

Sitting at our table with the brightest smile on her face, was a new patient. It was Hanan. When I thought back to our first day in the market, her abscesses open and her baby slowly dying, I thought she would die. Now she sat in front of me, alive and smiling.

'How are you?' I asked.

She unbuttoned her shirt and shyly she showed us her healing breasts. In this reserved, proud culture such a display would be unheard of. But in that crowded room Musa and I leaned forward and clapped with joy at the sight of her healed skin. The skin was pink and shiny as it stretched and puckered over the slowly healing wounds. Under each breast the skin still fought to heal, but the open wounds were gone. To us it was a miracle, one we had fought hard for.

Along the side of her left breast still sat the feeding tube, taped with Musa's white elastoplast. It lay dirty and peeling against her skin. But it was still there.

'How is your baby?' I asked, almost afraid to hear the answer.

'He's getting fat,' thundered his grandmother and she reached for the baby on her back. 'Drinks every five minutes and I can't get enough goat milk or sugar. But her milk is coming back now,' she said, pointing to her daughter.

I reached out and took the little bundle in my arms. Pulling back the blanket I gazed down at the most beautiful baby in Africa. He lay sleeping in my arms and I couldn't hold back the tears. This little baby was a whisper away from death when we met. His bones stuck out sharply, rubbing wounds as the dry skin stretched across the width of his pelvis. He was literally a bag of bones. I thought there was no hope then. And now? Now he was alive and breathing, his bones hidden beneath silky soft skin.

To read about famine one can lose oneself in the horror and bare-bones aching and need. Often it hurts too much to read about. So you turn the page or close the book.

Imagine holding this baby in your arms, his sweet soft skin against your cheek. Hear his gentle breath as he sleeps and watch his lashes quiver as he dreams. That is the reality of starvation and compassion. With time, energy and compassion we saved his life. It was quite simple. And now he had a chance. Remember him the next time you read of famine and hunger. Remember the children who can be saved and stop to listen to them breathe. It's not so hard to do.

****

And so the day passed. Moments of clarity and success. Moments of failure and frustration. Every hour or two I stopped seeing new patients and Adam Ali and I pushed our way out of the room to visit the fevered children outside. We needed the break and fresh air. Inside it was hot, flies sat on every surface and the crowded room echoed with voices, all talking and shouting. It felt like a prison. Outside, beneath the tree, the air felt cooler and the breeze cooled my back as it lifted my wet shirt.

Our first visit outside was not reassuring. All three children lay quietly, their temperatures still over 40°C, their breaths fast and gasping.

'Keep wetting the towels,' I told Iglam. She nodded.

By 3 o'clock they were starting to stir. The two little girls sobbed and sniffed as Iglam gently drizzled their towels with cold water. Their mothers lay beside them, dresses soaked with brown muddy water, and they whispered encouragement under the heavy towels. The boy remained quiet, but his eyes opened as I lifted the towel. He looked at me with big, sad eyes, then closed them and went back to sleep. Their fevers had broken. The malaria parasites were at bay. I sat down on the mat, my hands rough with wet sand and mud, and breathed a sigh of relief. Maybe we would win this time.

****

An hour before sunset, with the consultation room still full, I rubbed my eyes with tiredness.

Beside me sat Adam Ali, his shirt still unwrinkled and his trousers neatly pressed. He sat tall on his little wooden chair, shoulders back and he fingered the pens in his top pocket. Even after a day of consulting, standing and crouching in the sun he looked at peace.

'I'm just going to stop for a moment,' I said, putting down my pen.

'No problem, Lisa,' he replied. 'I can still work.'

He reached for the health card lying on the table.

'What is the problem?' he asked the young woman. She answered quietly and pushed her daughter forward. The little girl looked perhaps four years old. She stood beside Adam Ali's knee with her hands behind her back, her eyes on the floor. Her feet were bare, her dress torn. A cloth bracelet around her wrist hung loosely.

I watched as his face softened and he leant forward, murmuring quietly to her, inviting her to trust him. Adam Ali was a father and he was away from his daughter so often. He adored children and he drew this little girl into his arms like a father. She leaned against him further and further as he spoke, her little hands resting on his leg. Trusting but silent. Still he talked, bringing his arms around her until she stood with her head against his chest, enveloped in his arms. She hadn't said a word. And then she smiled. She looked so safe, so content. There in his arms, with her eyes closed, the chaos and noise around her faded and in my eyes she was an oasis of perfection. If the war escalated and we were chased from this place, my heart would break. Deeply and forever. But whatever happened I would remember her face. Safe in Adam Ali's arms, trusting and at peace. She was happy.

As the sun sank lower and the consultation room started to empty I ached to be outside. Through the metal grill I could see the light change, sunset colours lighting the verandah walls.

'Come on, Adam Ali. Why don't we see the last patients outside?' I said, stretching with tiredness, exhaustion drawing my lids lower with every breath.

We walked outside to the verandah and down the steps to the dusty courtyard. Across the lake the sun was setting, a giant red glow over the lake. I looked around at the waiting patients. The light reflected on their dark skin, their sleepy eyes peaceful. Gone were the desperate women, their fevered children and aching need.

'Come and sit with us,' called an old woman. She shifted on her mat and patted a spot beside her. I walked over, kicked off my boots and sank down beside her.

'Shukran,' she said, touching her heart. She was thanking me for sitting with her.

'Alawajip,' I replied. You're welcome. And I touched my heart, grateful for her thanks, grateful for the respite. After the unrelenting crush and demands of the day I was grateful for her gentleness.

Behind us the fevered children's mat lay empty. Piles of wet towels were strewn on the sand. The basin sat on the mat, filled with brown, sandy water at the end of the day. The children had gone, their fevers down and their mothers smiling. I had watched through the wire grill of the consultation room before sunset as all three women left. They sang as they walked, one hand waving, their voices dancing with thanks. Another success, small but real.

We worked for a while on the mat, half-heartedly as we relaxed and sank lower onto the sand. When the mat was empty, the patients gone, I lay on my back and looked up at the darkening sky. Adam Ali sat on the mat beside me, his arms around his knees.

'Do you like being here?' I asked, wanting to be lulled by his stories. When he spun his tales grown men would become like children, lying peacefully as he spoke of faraway places and people he had seen. He could make them laugh, he could make them cry. He could take them away from the fear and the fighting.

He lay back on the mat, his head resting on his arms and he sighed.

'I like this place. I have to. Darfur is my home,' he said. 'Many years ago I wanted to escape my home, to live a better life. I had great dreams. I was born in Darfur. Not many good things happen to a person born in Darfur, so I studied well and made good results.

'At the time my studies were completed, there were many students looking for opportunities in Iraq. Universities were good, the faithful were honest and life was good there. I borrowed money from my father and I made plans. In 1990 I started my new life in Iraq.

'There were many of us living together in Baghdad. We all came from Sudan. In the day we went to university, we worked hard and learned much. We wanted to grow in our minds and every day was a gift. In the evening time we walked through the city, learning about this new place, meeting good people and eating in fine restaurants. Everything about this life was good. My life was full of opportunities and friendship. For a student from Darfur this was a blessing.

'In 1991 everything changed.' Adam Ali closed his eyes and rubbed them with his fingers. Shaking his head, he sighed. 'In 1991 I lost my opportunities and my dreams, and my life turned to sand.

'During the invasion (of Iraq by the United States) we survived. Life was hard and our studies stopped, but we survived. There were now six of us in the apartment and we took care of each other.

When the fighting stopped and the Americans left we thought we would be safe. We were wrong.

'Saddam Hussein punished the people when the Americans left. He punished the guilty and he punished the innocent. During the day people were taken from their homes and they were killed in the street. I can still hear the sound of the guns. In every street, behind every house. Killing, killing. At night it was worse. In the dark, when it was still hot and we were hungry, people went outside. They went out quietly, perhaps one from each family to search for food and water. The police always found them. Sometimes the people were beaten, sometimes they were shot. But sometimes they were put in a van and taken away to the prison. That was the worst punishment. In prison the punishment was worse than death.'

I watched Adam Ali as he spoke. His words were of a horror I couldn't imagine. His mind was alive with the memories of his old life. I looked at his unwrinkled shirt, at the sharp crease down the front of each trouser leg. His shirt was open at the collar, the first button open to allow in a breath of air. Were it not for the heat I imagine he would have worn a tie, this gentleman trapped in a war. When the breeze blew I caught a breath of his aftershave. His shoes were scuffed and sandy, one shoelace lay untied and loose in the sand. Adam Ali was never untidy. But now he lay lost in his thoughts.

'We survived by staying inside for weeks. We moved around the apartment on our knees, never standing up. In the kitchen we had water from the tap. It was brown water and some days the tap stopped running. Those were bad days. I remember there was a big bag of potatoes in the kitchen. We ate potatoes every day. I brushed off the earth and we had to eat them without cooking. What else can a man do, living like an animal? But we had no choice. I am alive because of those potatoes. Many people died because they had none.

'Sometimes I crawled to the window and looked out onto the street while the sun was low. Every day there were more bodies. In some places they were pushed into piles. And they started to smell. The days were hot and the flies were terrible. The dogs ate the people lying in the street. These people were my neighbours and my friends. And now they were lying in the sun turning black and I could not help them.

'One day I saw the police kill a girl. She was about thirteen years old. For this girl I had to do something. I waited until night and then I went outside. After three weeks on my knees, with only potatoes for nourishment, I was very weak. But I had to help her.

'I wanted to move her body so that the next day she would not be in the sun. She was only a child and she deserved that respect. When I touched her arm the police came.

'"What are you doing?" they asked. "Did you kill this girl? What are you doing here? Where is your identity card?"

'They had many questions but I had no answers. I just wanted to move her body for respect. 'They took me and put me into a van. I knew this was very bad. I thought I would die. That night I stayed in a cell at the police station. I could not sleep. In the morning they came for me, to start questioning me about the girl. I tried to explain that I was only trying to help, and that I was hungry after staying inside for so many weeks. They wouldn't listen. One policeman sat behind the desk, another stood beside me. My chair was small and one leg was short, so when I moved the chair rocked. I tried to sit very still.

'They questioned me and shouted at me the whole day. Sometimes they hit me with a stick. By afternoon time I knew that they wanted money. If I gave them money they would let me go. I was taken back to my cell while the police talked about my money. My father's money was at the apartment and if it bought me freedom then I would leave Baghdad that night.

'After one hour a policeman came for me and took me to a different room. He told me to wait. I sat on the chair and prayed that they had accepted my money. When a man has no power and no voice he is lost. But with faith and money he has hope.

'As I sat on my chair I was praying. Praying for my life, praying for my family. I heard something dripping on the floor, like water. Then I felt something dripping on my shirt. I looked at my shoulder and my shirt was red. I looked up to the ceiling and I saw a man. He was hanging by his ankles with a rope, and it was tied to a hook in the roof. The blood was dripping from his nose, from his mouth and all over his face. He was dead.

'I closed my eyes and my hands were holding the chair. "Please, no, please, no," I was praying. "Please do not do this to me." I was sitting very still and my body felt very cold. The two policemen came into the room. They looked at me and they laughed. "Your money is small but today it is enough," the old one said. "Bring us your money before sunset and you are free. If you do not return, then we will find you and you will wish for his death," he said, pointing his stick at the dead man. They were laughing at me when I walked out of the police station. My legs were weak and I had to stop many times.

'I returned to my apartment, collected my money and paid it to the policemen. I left Baghdad that night and I have never been back. The little girl was still lying on the street when I left, her face looking at the sky. I could not help her. I pray for her still.'

Adam Ali stopped talking and looked at me. 'I have many stories,' he said. 'I am trying to have a good life and to help my brothers and sisters in Darfur. I love this country because it is my home. It is my duty to help.'

When he finished talking we lay in silence. I watched the evening star and listened to the children laughing and splashing at the water's edge. Sometimes there is nothing more to say.

****

The nights were so cold. The waning moon gave no light and the stars glittered in the icy darkness. Two blankets were barely enough to keep me warm till morning. I'd wake at first light, aching as I stretched out my tightly curled, warmth-hidden body. We all stood around the kettle in the early-morning light, stamping our feet and hugging a cup of sweet coffee, collars up, skin shivering.

'I wish it wasn't so bloody cold,' said Toby most mornings.

We all longed for the sun to rise and ease our aching fingers and toes. By 10 a.m. it would be hot. Too hot. And we would stand in the shade of a rakuba or tree, shirts clinging to wet skin, and long for the cool. Human nature demands that we remain unsatisfied.

It was two days before Christmas and I sat on a chair watching Halima and Selwa as they hung the washing on the line. Every morning they foamed and soaped our clothes and sheets in basins of brown water. The sheets fluttered in the breeze, still stiff with soap, and were dry in hours. Socks often went missing. I found some in the bomb shelter and some in the shower, carried on a hot gust of wind that often whipped through the compound. Hawa matched the brown socks with the blue, long ones with short and stacked them neatly in our laundry cupboard at the end of each day.

Sarah had arrived in Saleem to look at our project, to review the programme and evaluate our work. I had seen little of her since my first day in Darfur, when Matthew, Sarah and I fought our way through the chaos of Khartoum airport. With her long, blonde hair and beautiful smile she looked out of place in Saleem. She wore a green silk scarf in her hair and whenever she walked past I caught a hint of perfume. I hadn't even thought of bringing perfume to Darfur. But Sarah was experienced in humanitarian work. And she knew that a woman needs her comforts around her, especially in war.

'What are you all doing to celebrate Christmas?' she asked that afternoon. It was only three days away.

We all shrugged. None of us felt like celebrating Christmas. The community around us would not be celebrating and there was no festive feel in the air. Instead we heard gunshots and the sound of roaring vehicles in the distance.

'Thought we'd give it a miss this year,' said Toby, rocking on his chair. 'There's too much work to do anyway.'

'You can't miss Christmas,' she said, looking at each of us. 'What will I do with all the presents I brought?'

And so it was decided — we would celebrate Christmas after all. We started with the decorations that afternoon. Toby disappeared into his tuckul and emerged a while later clutching a dozen bars of soap.

'I'm just off to the warehouse,' he said. 'I'll be back with my contribution soon.'

I looked around and wondered what I could make. I watched as Selwa unpacked a food box in the kitchen. Cornflakes and tinfoil. I could make Christmas decorations and hang them from the tree! I spent the afternoon cutting stars and moons from cornflake packets, fat and round and easy to wrap with foil. By evening I had a pile shining beside me. Each one was pierced top and bottom with a length of suture material, a lucky find in the expired drug box. Soon we set to work decorating the tree.

Soon the tree stood glittering in the lamplight. It looked rather embarrassed. Toby hung each bar of hospital-issue pink soap from a branch. They turned on their length of blue twine in the darkness. He had spent hours drilling the perfect holes through the brittle soap. Dozens more lay on the warehouse floor, broken and splintered. My cardboard moons and stars turned and twinkled on their thin lines of thread. For all its simplicity the tree looked beautiful. I still jumped whenever the sound of gunfire shook the night. But standing by the tree it felt like Christmas. And no one could take that away.

On Christmas Eve Sarah emerged from our spare tuckul with a box of goodies and set them out on the table. She hung tiny crackers on the tree, little flashes of luxury courtesy of Marks & Spencer. There was Christmas cake with marzipan icing, toffees wrapped in gold and little jars of fruit chutney. Under the tree there was a surprise gift for each of us. A rabbit fur handbag. A set of plastic clothes pegs. A tube of sticky, pink lipstick. The assortment of goodies available in the market was extraordinary. Who would have thought it — lipstick in Darfur? Hawa and Selwa had prepared us a feast, leaving little coloured saucepans all over the kitchen table.

'Happy celebrations,' called Halima as she left.

Chaos and misery still surrounded us. The families still huddled outside the African Union, water was still scarce. Sam and I spent hours in the clinic every day, trying to heal and treat the endless queues of patients. Reports of assaults and torture filled my notebook and needed to be written in reports while they were fresh in my mind. But for one night we needed to escape. To hide in our tradition and forget about the world around us.

Steve still sat at his computer, his back turned to our festivities, a pile of cigarette butts on a dish beside him. Perhaps there would be no Christmas for him. Sam splashed in the shower for an age, humming and scrubbing the day away. I sat on the edge of my bed, eyes closed as I thought of Christmases gone by. My family is small and our Christmas celebrations are brief. Presents, cards, food and then home. But still I missed them, and our quiet evenings round the tree, lights flashing in the artificial green branches. I missed Melanya and Jette, my surrogate family and soulmates in our tumbling bungalow in the Auckland suburbs. I thought of our Danish Christmas parties, hands clutching hands in a long, chaotic line as we sang Danish carols. We danced and ran through the garden and house, frightening the cat and filling the house with laughter. Friends, family and neighbours joined in our evening of noise and celebration. Blessing our home with the love and friendship of a real Danish Christmas.

I worked my feet into the sand as I pictured them all, laughing and dancing without me. Lisa the wanderer, Lisa the wind-blown gypsy. I was never anywhere long enough to be part of a family. Sitting in the dark, my feet covered in warm, powdery sand, I drew a deep breath. I had wanted so much to be part of a family, to be part of something important and good. Steve, Sam and Toby were my family for now. And we were doing something good. At least we were trying. So why did my heart ache, and my weary body long for something more? To laugh and sing and dance perhaps. To believe in goodness and faith and beauty again. But it all seemed so impossibly far in this forgotten, damaged place.

After a while, my sad thoughts winding round me in the growing dark, I heard Steve call my name. I ran my hands through my hair, stood up and walked out to see what he wanted.

'Are you ready for some food?' he called from the shadows. 'Take a seat, I'll be with you all in a minute.'

Beside the tree a table had been set, plastic plates, real paper napkins, cutlery and glasses. The table was overflowing with food, pots and plates and boxes. Sarah had carried our Christmas parcel from Nyala, a box of treats carried lovingly from London by Liz.

I sat down on a plastic chair, and looked at the feast.

'You have to pull a cracker,' said Toby. 'A big one for a silly, paper hat and a small one for a piece of plastic junk, some trinket you can throw away tomorrow. Here, take this one.'

He held out a huge, gold-coloured cracker, grand enough to grace any dinner table in London.

Bang! The gunpowder crack sent shivers down my spine — there were too many sounds like that every day that made my blood run cold. Toby reached down and brushed the sand off a green paper hat.

'There you go,' he said. 'Put that on and see if it feels like Christmas.'

'Are you guys ready for entrees?' asked Steve as he walked over to the table, a heavy pot in both hands. 'I've made cranberry sauce and softened the chutney for your crackers and cheese.' He bent down and rested the two dishes on the table. 'Merry Christmas, guys,' he said with a smile.

I looked up at Steve, his face smiling with his proud Christmas contribution. Gone was the Steve that made me nervous, gone was his anger and tired eyes. Instead he smiled and joked, reaching for a cracker as he sat down beside me.

'Grab the other end,' he said, holding the cracker out to me. 'Let's see what horrendous joke they've stuck in this one.' The cracker went bang and my stomach jumped. Steve reached for the paper hat that fell out, yellow and crumpled after its marathon journey.

'Merry Christmas, everyone,' he said, his hat sitting tightly, and somewhat awkwardly on his head. He raised his glass, a warm soda our Christmas toast. 'Here's to Darfur. To the people and their lives and the future they deserve. Here's to peace.' We all raised our glasses and drank slowly, quietly asking for peace in the glow of the kerosene lanterns.

We ate our bean stew and rice, savoured the thin wedges of cheese and spread Steve's cranberry sauce on Marks and Spencer biscuits. We chose Christmas chocolates from the little dimpled tray with great care. Truffles and pralines are rare in Darfur! Sam told jokes while Sarah talked of home, and the noisy, family-filled Christmases she loved. Afterwards we lifted the tiny silver crackers from the tree and read out the tired old jokes that fell to the sand as we tore the crackers open. I pulled five crackers but got the losing end every time. Steve handed me one of his prizes, a plastic sun on a small plastic key ring.

'Merry Christmas, Lisa,' he said. 'And here's to the New Year.' I smiled back, ready to believe in the spirit of the season and hope for better things, even if only for one night.

Toby sat across the table, his pink paper hat torn and wrinkled but beautiful in its own way. He told stories of Canadian Christmases, of snow and turkey and silver boats of gravy.

We sang carols, reminisced about Christmases gone by and laughed at the absurdity of our celebrations in the desert. I sat back in my chair, watching the others sing and talk. With my toes in the sand and a green hat on my head Christmas felt real but far away. But I looked round at the faces in the light of the kerosene lanterns and thought how lucky I was. Despite the gunfire. Despite Steve's temper that still left me feeling raw. Despite Toby's procrastination in the face of my frustration. And despite the aching hours of work that needed to be done while we talked and laughed and sang. But what greater gift can there be than being present and content with now. Listening to old jokes, relishing Christmas treats and watching the soap as it gently turned on its blue twine. It wasn't perfect but it was enough. And it's a Christmas I'll always remember.

****

We left for El Wadi the following day, on Christmas morning. It was to be my last trip and the hardest. We left after breakfast, Steve, Sarah and I. Toby and Sam stayed in Saleem, our anchors while we travelled. No one talked or smiled as we approached the security office. After the singing and laughter the night before we had returned to reality with a crash. And there was no room for laughter now.

We drove past the burned sector of town, with its blackened tuckuls and scorched thatch walls. We drove past the water pumps, normally crowded in the early-morning light. Now they were deserted, one lay broken where the Janjaweed militia had shot it beyond repair. We stopped outside the security office and walked towards the waiting men. They sat in their chairs, dismantled weapons lying around them. We all shook hands and murmured our greetings, the usual routine. I stood back, too tired to smile and talk. Too tired to pretend that everything was all right and that life was normal. Nothing was right and the joy of Christmas was gone as we stood in the sunlight and waited for their permission to travel.

With our paper signed, the second and third copy taken by them to be filed in a room without shelves, we left for El Wadi. I kept my eyes on the road as we passed the track to the African Union on our right. Despite our negotiations in Nyala and the input of the United Nations the families still waited, thirsty and cold each morning in the dust. There were fewer families now, many had given up on anyone keeping them safe from the Janjaweed militia and other tribesmen with guns. Those left behind simply sat and waited, the way people in Darfur know how to do endlessly. And they prayed. Some were too tired to run further, some had no donkeys or no food to take with them. So they waited for help and protection. But still each day passed the same as the one before.

The checkpoint in El Wadi was still a pleasure to visit. The cool wind blew gently on the edge of town. A new sentry stood to meet us as our vehicles approached the rakuba. We drove slowly, headlights on and hazard lights flashing to make us well seen. The fallen trees around us had died, a shower of dry leaves blowing in the wind. The deserted landscape was eerie at first. But anything can become familiar in life. I knew the trees and their broken trunks, the burned-out village with its empty homes. And I recognised the barracks in the distance, with its straight strong walls and groups of workers at every corner.

'You can go,' the sentry had told us as we stood waiting in the sun. 'Commander Ali says he will see you today when he comes to the clinic.' I didn't know whether that was a good sign or bad, but it meant we could start work early. And that was all that mattered.

Driving into the compound we saw the patients waiting in ordered lines — the clinic guards had obviously been at work. Outside the front gate even the donkeys, camels and horses waited in line. We had sent them a message days before to tell them we were returning.

On the stairs of the verandah stood the midwives, Dr Abaker and Dr Hawa. I smiled as I looked around and marvelled at the order. It was only ten weeks before that we had pushed our way through the crowded compound and fought to manage the eight hundred people who wanted our care. And now they smiled. The patients knew we were coming and knew we would stay. They trusted us. And I smiled back at them with pride.

When the vehicles stopped we all climbed out, the hand shaking and greetings a pleasure as we reacquainted with each other after our weeks apart. Iglam, the old midwife, came forward and clutched my hands between hers.

'Welcome, my sister,' she said with a smile. 'We have missed you.' She reached up with her right hand, and placed it over my heart. It was a real greeting, a heartfelt greeting of people who are more than colleagues. I reached out and touched her heart with my hand.

'Shukran, my sister,' I said, my eyes welling with tears. Thank you for your kindness.

My first journey to Tala, nearly three months before, started in the dawn light outside our office in Nyala. Musa and Adam Ali had been standing, shaking hands and touching hearts with all the guards and drivers who were their friends. I remembered standing on the edge of the group, watching them and envying their friendship and family. Now I was that person, touching, bowing, reaching out to my friends and my new family.

We had been working for two hours when I heard a commotion outside. I had just finished dressing the healing wounds of the brother and sister shot all those weeks ago. They came every week, and stood in line as they waited to be seen. Their wounds slowly healed, the bullets long gone but the damage leaving their limbs weak. They smiled and shook our hands before they turned to leave, slowly walking to the pharmacy for their last course of antibiotics. Two more successes, two more people who trusted us to keep them safe.

Adam Ali stood up with the noise and looked out the window. 'It's Commander Ali and he is coming in here!'

Commander Ali had told us not to treat anyone with a gunshot wound and to report all cases, new or old, to him immediately. I watched as the two children limped towards the pharmacy and I turned to Adam Ali in a panic.

'What if he sees them outside? What if he finds out they have been shot? He will take them!' I pushed past Adam Ali and out to the verandah.

Commander Ali strode across the compound, a wide smile on his face. There at the front gate stood his vehicle, the soldiers and their weapons waiting outside as Steve had requested.

'Welcome,' I said, standing aside as he walked past the patients and into the consultation room. I turned my head and watched as the two children disappeared into the crowd of waiting patients at the pharmacy door. Please let them get out of here quickly, I thought.

Inside the Commander was friendly, talking to patients, stopping to sit on Dr Abaker's table as he worked. Beside him stood a young soldier, following the Commander as he walked; a bodyguard. He wore civilian clothes, as our rules required, and his big leather boots scuffed the floor as he walked. Beneath his brown jacket I saw the barrel of an AK47. I looked at him aghast. We had two military men in the midst of a crowded clinic full of women and children. Who knew what wounds and complaints sat and lay around them? If they found patients they disapproved of, they would take them away. I walked backwards to the door and pushed my way through to the pharmacy.

'Steve,' I hissed. 'The commander is next door and his bodyguard has an AK47. Come now!'

Steve jumped up from the floor and leapt over the table. He didn't say a word.

I stood at the pharmacy door. I didn't want to be next door if anything happened with Commander Ali. Instead I reached down and took the prescription card from the little brother and sister, still waiting at the back of the queue and passed them into the pharmacy.

'Can you give me these medications, Idriss?' I asked. 'I need them urgently.'

When the children had their medications I stood on the top step and watched as they hopped and limped towards the front gate. They walked past the soldiers, past the machine gun mounted in the sun and disappeared down the dusty track. I sighed with relief. They were gone and they were safe. Their gunshot wounds had almost healed. Neither would walk properly again but they were alive and that was the best we could ask for. They wouldn't come back to us again. And the Commander hadn't seen them.

One of the guards stopped me as I walked back to the verandah.

'Problem?' he asked, pointing to the soldiers and then to the consultation room.

'No,' I said. 'No problem, he is just talking today.' I put my hand on the old man's arm and smiled. 'No problem.'

I walked back to my table and sat watching the commander.

'Is everything all right?' I asked Adam Ali. I kept my eyes down and reached for a new health card.

'He wants to know what problems people have and how we are treating them,' he said. 'There has been no trouble so far.'

I looked around the room. All the waiting patients were women, most carried babies. The commander would find little of interest here. I breathed a word of thanks. Soon Steve ushered Commander Ali to the door.

'As I told you,' we heard Steve say. 'Women and children and a few old men. It's the same every day.' They both smiled as they shook hands and I watched through the window as the commander and his bodyguard walked slowly through the crowd and out to the waiting vehicle. He had broken our rules and brought a weapon into the clinic. The commander had made a point — he could go where he wanted. And there was nothing we could do about it. I sighed and went back to work.

The rest of the day passed smoothly. Malaria and pneumonia filled our day, with malnutrition starting to increase in the weekly weighing sessions. All morning thin, screaming babies swung slowly from a soft, black harness as the midwives weighed them outside on the verandah. These were all problems we could manage for now. For the rest of the afternoon life felt good and we worked well.

****

We lay on the mats eating dinner together that evening. Adam Ali, always the talker, had everyone in stitches as he spun a tale. Even as he talked in Arabic we laughed as he mimed and played in the lamplight. First he was an Arab, fat and disgruntled. Then a farmer, backward and outwitted by his camel.

'If we don't laugh then our heart dies,' he said earlier, in a quiet moment. 'My heart will fight to stay alive and so I keep laughing.' His eyes weren't smiling as he talked.

Asha returned, the dehydrated woman we had fought to save each time we came to El Wadi. Her family carried her to the clinic to ask for help every time, to save their mother, sister and aunt. And each time I asked them to come to Saleem and on to the hospital in Nyala. But they stood, their hands folded, and shook their heads. 'Mamumkin,' they always said. Not possible. They would not be allowed to travel. They had no money, no travel permits and they were from the 'wrong' tribe.

That afternoon she arrived in a terrible state, dehydrated and malnourished far worse than before. Again I asked them to bring her to Saleem.

'We have no money,' said her husband. 'We have no permission.'

I talked with Steve and we agreed to transport her to Saleem and on to Nyala with her daughter the next time we planned a trip.

'Carry her into there,' I instructed her daughter, pointing across the compound. I followed them into the storeroom and stood in the musty dim light. We had given her intravenous fluid on our last visit weeks before, and the empty bag still hung on the nail, the plastic tubing hung limply beneath it. Spider webs spun around the nail, slowly embracing the empty bag in our absence.

'I'll go and get the silver box,' I said to Adam Ali. 'She and her daughter will leave with us tomorrow at the end of the clinic, if that's what they want. Will you explain to them what will happen when we get her to Nyala?'

An hour later we were finished. Asha lay on the floor with her new bag of intravenous fluids running freely into her arm. There was something very wrong with her and in my dusty, dark clinic there was nothing I could think of to help her. I felt a wave of helplessness and closed my eyes. Her whole family looked to me to save her. And I had a feeling I was going to fail.

****

It was after 10 p.m. when Steve and I stood quietly in the dark, watching the stars.

'It's been a hell of a day with the Commander's visit,' he said sighing. 'I wonder if he'll be back tomorrow.'

I told him about the two children and my relief as they slipped out the front gate past the soldiers.

'I couldn't cope with too many more visits like that,' I laughed. 'Or I'll need to sneak diazepam tablets from the pharmacy to calm my nerves!' We had no alcohol, little time out and endless days of work. To add to the injustice I didn't even smoke — no vices and few ways to escape the stress. I'd heard stories of people, humanitarian workers under huge stress, who gave in to alcohol, drugs or sex. Mad bursts of escapism in a world gone crazy in a bid to keep their sanity. I needed a vice, but I was too brittle to take any on. If I tried I would surely crumble. Above us stretched the endless heavens, the stars glittering in the darkness. They touched the horizon to the west, almost inviting us to touch them. Perhaps stars could be my vice — losing myself in their ageless light.

'What's that?!' I jumped, pointing to the western horizon. Flashes of light and arcs of red seemed to cut the night sky. But still it was silent.

'Tracer light,' said Steve, turning to look in every direction. 'They've found something, or someone, and they're preparing to attack. My God, it never ends.' He rubbed his face with both hands.

'Come on, let's get some sleep. They're far away now. We'll need our wits about us if they come to town. Rest now.'

I stood a moment longer, watching as the sky flashed and glowed in the distance. What are we doing here? I wondered. Shoring up the dam in this place, saving a life here and there, so they can be killed tomorrow. Shot from behind in their homes or chased by night with lasers of light. This was no game. It was their lives. Their painful, miserable lives, dragged out in a place too far away for anyone to care. It was their deaths that made up the statistics in reports far away. So that people could sit reading the morning newspaper and shudder. 'They're fighting again in Darfur,' they'd say. And turn the page.

I thought of the old guard, standing beside me in his old, grey jelabiya gown. No problem, I'd told him with my hand on his arm. But it was a lie. In El Wadi there were problems. Every day and every night, slowly closing in on them as they struggled to survive. And no one was coming to save them.

****

The following morning our clinic started normally. I woke before dawn, and sat on the edge of the stretcher in the pharmacy. All around me empty plastic bottles of pills, sachets of rehydration powder and prescription papers littered the floor. I reached for my clothes, the same ones as the day before and pulled them on with aching arms. Outside I heard Musa and Ahmed, their quiet prayers murmured in the half light.

I leaned out the window and poured water into my hand. With a splash and a rub my face was clean, the sand pushed back into my hair and my eyes open and ready for a new day.

I watched as the tea lady knelt in the sand, a piece of cardboard in one hand as she fanned the fire for our breakfast.

Click, clack, click, clack went the cardboard. Soon the embers were glowing. She reached for the kettle and balanced it carefully on her wobbly metal stove. Then she stood, hands on her back and stretched her aches to the dawn sky. These women who carry and fetch, lift and push every day of their lives. How their bodies must cry out for rest, waiting for the stillness that comes only briefly in the calm of night.

I poured the rest of my water through my hair, then stood shivering and dripping on the pharmacy floor. Time for a new day, a new challenge. In the room beside me I heard Sarah stir, coughing the sand and dust away.

We stood together a little while later, Steve, Sarah and I, and cradled our morning cups of tea. Steve looked tired, his hair ruffled and shoulders stooped. His twelve months in Darfur were drawing to a close — he looked exhausted. In three days' time he and I would both be leaving. I would have a holiday, he would be heading home.

But there was still work to do. Outside the clinic walls donkeys and camels waited, their nose-bags full of food. Patients already waited quietly, the guards taking care of any queue jumpers as they took control of the gathering crowd. In the storeroom across the compound, Asha slowly filled up with fluid again, our bags of intravenous fluid keeping her dehydration at bay.

As I stood with my tea I could see over the stone wall to the soldiers collecting water from the lake. They came at dawn each day, twenty or thirty soldiers piled onto the back of a huge commercial truck. They whooped and shouted, banged their jerry cans and made a scene each morning in the dawn quiet. I asked Musa why they came all the way into town to collect their water, when the lake stretched north towards their barracks as well.

'This end of town belongs to one tribe,' he told me. 'The far end, near their barracks, belongs to another. They are afraid to go to the far end, afraid that the people there will hit back at them after the clearances. The soldiers target their people often. So they come to the "safe" side of town and tell everyone they are strong and not afraid. That is why they make noise.'

I listened to the soldiers and their bravado. Their big group huddling together at the water's edge while they took water, normally women's work. Without their weapons they weren't so brave.

It was almost 1 o'clock when we again heard a commotion in the compound. I rose from my seat and peered out the window. Commander Ali sat in his vehicle and shouted as Steve talked. He had driven into the compound and his soldiers stood on the back, holding weapons in their hands. Something was very wrong. This was different to other visits. We heard more shouting and then silence. Steve stood back from the vehicle and shook his head. The engine revved and the soldiers stumbled as the commander suddenly drove towards the gate. His dramatic exit was blocked by a herd of cows, slowly making their way down to the lake in a swirling cloud of dust.

'What's going on?' I called to Steve through the window.

'He has given us one hour to leave,' said Steve, walking back to the stairs. 'One hour and we are not welcome back. Someone told him those two children were here with gunshot wounds yesterday. He wanted to know which staff member treated them and threatened to take that person back to the barracks.' He stopped outside my window and looked at me through the metal grill. 'That person would be you.'

We stood looking at each other.

'One hour, Lisa. Clear this place and we are out of here. We can talk and negotiate later.'

I looked around the consultation room and out to the compound. It was full of people waiting to be seen. A lot of people trusted us now — most had stayed even with the Commander's presence in the clinic. They knew they were safe with us and no longer ran away so easily. And we were about to leave them again.

'Adam Ali, you prescribe the malaria treatment. Here's the instruction sheet. I'm going outside to look for any sick ones.' I grabbed my water bottle and a handful of paracetamol from the windowsill, stuffing them into my pocket. The waiting mothers watched as I ran out the door.

With Musa at my side we ploughed into the crowd. Ahmed stood on the stairs giving the bad news to waiting patients and asked only the very sick to remain. Everyone surged towards him. We felt foreheads, examined their tongues and put our hands on chests to feel for pneumonia. We had less than an hour to find the really sick people and to scribble a prescription on a piece of paper.

'Fever,' called Musa. 'Pneumonia. Suspected malaria.' He felt his way through the crowd and slowly we pulled out the sick ones. It was so basic, so unfair when we knew we could do better. These people deserved a lot more than our one second glance. But it was all we could do.

Back on the stairs Ahmed called to the crowd. 'You must all go home. The commander will return in one hour and we must be gone. Please go home. We will return when we can.' All around us women bent down, gathering their bags and water bottles, and they started to leave. No one was going to wait for the commander without us beside them.

We worked like fury. Some women called to us, hands reaching out, pulling, pleading, begging. Those with sick children needed to be seen, they were desperate.

'Ten minutes to go,' called Steve from the vehicle. 'Go, go, go.'

It felt like some mad race. We saw the sickest patients, handing paracetamol out to those who I didn't have time to examine properly. Just to be able to give them something that would help until we could return. Then the compound was empty, the tin trunks packed and sitting in the back of both vehicles. I ran to my table and gathered up the pens and stethoscope. 'Oh shit!' I shouted. 'What about Asha?' Lying quietly in the storeroom was Asha, waiting for us to take her to Nyala.

'Ahmed, take those boxes out the back of that vehicle. We have one patient to lie down and one family member coming with her. Musa, will you prepare two bags of intravenous fluid and a line. Adam Ali, come and translate for me!' I shouted as I ran, not remembering to say please or thank you. We had five minutes left and my mind was spinning.

We ran into the storeroom. I fumbled and dropped the bag and tubing as Adam Ali translated. The women stood quickly and packed their bags, stuffing scarves and basins into their wicker baskets. They had known nothing of Commander Ali's visit. We lifted Asha on her mat and half dragged, half carried her to the door. Her daughter followed us, dragging a mountain of bags. Our hurried departure left a tangled mess in the room. Rolls of tape, a pile of plastic tubing and an empty bag of fluid lay on the ground.

'Tell her she can take two bags only,' I said to Adam Ali. 'There isn't enough space for all those.' I nodded towards Asha's daughter.

We ran and pushed, carried and reorganised the vehicle as quickly as we could. In the front vehicle Steve sat with Musa.

'Come on, Lisa. We're over time. We have to leave *now!*' he shouted.

'I'm doing my best,' I shouted back. 'Just two more minutes. Please.'

By the time we drove out of the clinic we were late and Asha and her daughter were frightened. Steve had paid the clinic staff and told them we may not be back for a while. Commander Ali was angry with us and there was no sign of when we could return. I turned to look out the window as we left and watched as the midwives and guards stood silently on the steps of the verandah. The old guard raised his arm to wave. No problem, I had said. In my naïvete I thought things were getting better. We had a routine and a relationship with the commander. We followed his rules and he knew our rules and disobeyed them. Despite the tracer lights the night before I thought things would be all right for us. No problem. I was wrong again.

****

It was the day before my departure and the afternoon heat was unbearable. I sat under the rakuba and sprinkled water on my face. Steve sat with his back to me. We were both leaving the following day and I knew he was sad. I had watched as he said goodbye to the local staff that morning. I watched as they wept. But not Steve — his eyes were dry. Through gunfire and threats Steve had held the team together. He talked and negotiated, swearing and shouting as he worked to keep the project going. Despite the presence of the Janjaweed militia, despite the increasing displacement, despite our permits being refused and our activities blocked to the north and south he helped to keep things going. Despite all the obstacles we had managed to make our presence felt, to show the villagers and the displaced that we cared enough to stay and to care for them. In the evenings Steve lay on mats beside Adam Ali and the others and they talked of war and families and hope. At night Steve relaxed and I even heard him laugh. His mantle of responsibility and his veil of anger were laid aside at night and he became Steve their friend, their brother and their family.

But his year in Darfur was over. He sat on the ground beside the office, saying his last goodbyes. Musa crouched in the shade beside him, wiping tears from his eyes and drawing lines in the sand.

'We will miss you,' he said quietly. 'Who will keep us safe now, my friend?'

'You will have another team leader, someone who will look after you well,' Steve replied, his voice strong, his emotions hidden.

Musa shook his head. 'Things will get much worse. Already it has begun in the north. We felt safe with you, you kept us strong. Now we will be alone.' He hid his face and started to weep. They sat together for a while, Musa's silent tears and Steve's dry eyes each telling a story of grief and loss.

When Steve rose he saw another friend, waiting his turn. Adam Ali stood patiently. Waiting for his chance to say goodbye. His top button was tightly closed, two pens neatly tucked in his breast pocket. He held his hands behind his back. I didn't hear their words; I didn't want to intrude on Adam Ali's grief. My dignified friend with his immaculate clothes and broken heart wept like a child, his shoulders shaking as he farewelled his friend and leader. Steve stood tall, his eyes dry. They talked, nodded and embraced. I watched as Adam Ali clung to him, not ready to let him go.

'You are my brother,' I heard him say. 'I will always miss you, every day of my life.'

When you stand shoulder to shoulder with anyone, through pain and fear, your hearts draw closer. To live together, to survive together, is everything. For Adam Ali, to live apart was worse than death. It is hard to leave a brother, a friend, knowing your paths will never cross again.

'Goodbye, my friend,' said Adam Ali when at last he let go. 'I will never forget you.'

Steve nodded, and leaned almost imperceptibly in a bow.

'Goodbye my friend. And I will never forget you.' And he turned away. There is no right way to grieve in Darfur. We have many opportunities to perfect our own unique grieving. Every day.

****

I didn't know it as I was leaving, but I was never to return to El Wadi. Never to see Asha or her daughter after they left for Nyala. Asha died from ovarian cancer the following week. Her dehydration and weight loss were the result of her advanced tumour. I never saw the two children with gunshot wounds or heard of them again. I never saw Hanan with her healing abscesses or her tiny baby who filled me with hope.

The team from Saleem returned six weeks later to a very different El Wadi clinic and scaled down activities due to low patient numbers. Many of the people had fled the town. I never again stood under the rakuba on the edge of town, feeling the warm wind or listening to Craig David as he sang through the old, plastic speakers. Our end to El Wadi was unfair and unwarranted. But Commander Ali wished to make a point. And he did just that. He won. And we lost. Patients, villagers and MSF. We all lost. And I never saw any of them again.

CHAPTER SEVEN

At the start of a new journey every step is a mystery. Where am I going? Who will walk with me? How will I get there? These questions are all part of the excitement and the mystery. The challenge is to just keep going. In spite of the uncertainty. In spite of the unknown. In spite of the fear.

I sat on the floor of my thatched grass tuckul in Muhajariya and looked out. Amna, our compound lady, was sweeping, her little grass brush leaving smooth arcs in the sand. This way and that, she swept until she was hidden in a cloud of dust. Early-morning footsteps had trampled the pattern as sleepy feet ventured to the latrine and on to the shower. My eyes followed the steps. And in the calm of the morning my heart broke.

I had just returned from my three-week holiday, ready for the next part of my Darfur journey. Three weeks of bliss in Scotland; the call of seabirds on the wind as they wheeled above the cliffs, long, slow strolls along sandy beaches, stopping here and there to search for coloured beads of glass, rolled smooth in the east coast surf. I still woke suddenly at night. Lying there in the dark my ears strained for the sound of gunfire. But all I heard was peace, wind and the occasional mournful cry of a seabird somewhere out in the pitch-black night.

I was ready for the challenge of El Wadi's crowded clinics, Commander Ali's smiling face and lying eyes, ready for the African Union and all its shame. I sat in the office in Nyala, my bag waiting on the floor and looked at Helen, my supervisor.

'You won't be returning to Saleem, Lisa,' she said. 'The situation is uncertain and the team feels they can manage well without you. So we have made a decision, you are not going back.'

I looked at her.

'Not going back? But ...'

'Sam and Toby have things under control. The new doctor is energetic and the three of them can manage the programme adequately.'

Adequately? My mind screamed. Sam was exhausted, despite his smiling eyes. Toby could think and plan and procrastinate but achieved little on a good day. And the new doctor's enthusiasm sprung from his fresh start; this was his first mission, his first venture into war. Neil was alive with the thrill of it all.

We didn't get off to a good start, Neil and I. He arrived in the project just before I left for my holiday. I felt exhausted, my body weary and my soul bruised after three months of war. He sat quietly after our first conversation and looked at me.

'I would like you to treat me with respect,' he said, his feelings apparently hurt by my rapid-fire explanations and expectations of the project in my absence. 'You can't expect me to do anything if you don't respect me.'

I stopped writing and looked up at him. Respect him? My head was throbbing with all that needed to be done; the clinics, the witness statements and the reports that sat unwritten. My heart was broken in a dozen different ways with the wickedness and lies that lay all around us. I knew I wasn't as organised or as diplomatic as I should be but I was tired. So tired I felt raw, every breath just a moment away from tears. In his new Velcro sandals and just-out-of-the-packet white MSF T-shirt he looked comical. What I needed was someone strong to stand with me, to face the workload and share the strain. He had to hit the ground running. What I had was a petulant new boy with his bottom lip pouting. And he wanted my respect.

'Well?' he asked, his arms folded across his chest.

'I'm sorry,' I said, putting down my pen. 'I'm just tired. Let's start from the beginning. Tell me how you became interested in humanitarian work.' And I pushed the paperwork away from me, trying to forget the work that screamed out to be done. I reached for Toby's coffee sock and filled the kettle.

'Coffee?'

I tried to remember how I had felt in those first Darfur days three months before. The closed doors and closed faces that left me feeling outside and unwanted. All my dreams and patience and good intentions meant nothing to my team as I stood in my new boots and clean white T-shirt. Perhaps their hearts were breaking too, their souls bruised after months of watching children die, families running from war and the machinery of humanitarian aid woefully inadequate as the war rumbled on.

As I listened to Neil talk I tried to smile, to nod and listen as he talked of his dreams, his past and his plans. We all need to be heard. But my mind kept wandering, worrying about those people we were missing and those we met but couldn't help. I pictured the line of small, dusty feet waiting in the sand as we gave water to the children outside the African Union. And Neil talked on.

****

And now the team didn't need me. Adam Ali, Musa and Ahmed. My partners through the months of war; sharing, encouraging and supporting each other as we struggled to make sense of the world around us. Abdullah and Matthew, with their stethoscopes and a pile of textbooks at their side. We had talked and compared notes as we examined our patients, learning from each other in crowded, dim clinics each week. Memories of the last months flooded my mind, and failure roared in my ears. I had failed them all — I had not worked hard enough. I had left them waiting in the sun while I holidayed and forgot about their suffering. And they didn't need me any more.

'But what will I do if I don't go back?' I asked, swallowing back my tears. 'Are you sending me home?'

She looked at me carefully and tapped her pen on the desk.

'Do you want to go home?' she asked at last.

Home. To leave Darfur and all its misery. To forget the African Union and its lies. Forget the families living in the river bed, still waiting for our return. To forget my failures and instead bask in the false glow of my brief wartime experience back home.

'I want to stay,' I said. 'I'm not ready to leave Darfur. You can send me home, but I'm not volunteering to go.'

Despite my words and my inner resolve, my heart was breaking. I would never see Adam Ali again, never turn to him for advice in the crush of a clinic. Never feel Musa's hand on my arm, his touch reminding me I was safe. Never again to lie on a mat, under the endless starry skies and listen in the dark as Adam Ali spun a tale of love and hope as he lulled us all to sleep.

Friendships are precious. To me their beauty lies in their honesty. In true friendship we can reveal our hearts, our fears and our failures knowing that we are safe from shame and judgement. Perhaps in war and times of trial we let our masks slip in the rush to survive. I had let mine slip. I had revealed my anger and frustration, my foot-stamping impatience and my aching fear of failure. They had seen it all — Adam Ali, Musa, Ahmed, Sam and Steve. And still they welcomed me, wiped away my ears, laughed at my impatience and reminded me with a smile or a touch that I was okay.

In my mind I was standing by the dry river bed full of the displaced families. I saw Adam Ali's smile as he waved, 'I knew you would be busy so I have prepared everything for you.'

I remembered standing beside weapons in the marketplace in El Wadi, the rocket-propelled grenade launcher so close to Steve's head and the Janjaweed militia and soldiers at our backs. I felt Musa's touch. Come with me, it said. I will take care of you. And standing in the sun outside the African Union, the old woman touching her hand to her heart, saying thank you with her eyes.

They were all gone. And I would never go back. My tears fell and there seemed no end to my sorrow. I lay in my room and wept until my soul touched the stones, the small hard stones in the echoing shame of my heart.

And then the tears stopped. If I couldn't go back, what could I do? If I had failed and been turned away. Where could I turn now? Muhajariya. Many families had fled south, looking for safety with the SLA. The attacks still hit Saleem, people still fled at night from El Wadi and Saleem. Many headed to Muhajariya. Perhaps I could climb out of my grief and my shame in the south. And just maybe I could get it right this time.

****

My resolve was teetering as I contemplated the early-morning sand in Muhajariya. My new team was a mystery and the problems here were different to those in Saleem. My new boss was Dave, the Englishman I'd met on my first clinic in Darfur. Ten years in the British Army had shaped him into an efficient, insular man.

His chain smoking and unbrushed hair and unshaven whiskers made him look restless, as though he was always just about to go somewhere. He spent his days in the office, negotiating, writing and cursing.

Gertrude would be my anchor. My Khartoum pal as we traipsed to the German Club. She was a survivor and a rock in the busy hospital in Muhajariya. That much I could count on. And then there was Karen, my new team-mate and nursing partner. After weeks and months of running clinics on my own in Saleem I now had a colleague. Someone to share the load and the frustrations of life with.

Dave and Karen both left the day I arrived in Muhajariya. My early-morning helicopter carried them back to Nyala for a much-needed rest. Without a handover I didn't know what to expect of my new life. My heart sank as I watched the helicopter rise and turn to the west. I would have to start all over again, a new beginning. But then again, perhaps that is a very good place to begin.

****

'So, where do you guys want to go?' I asked the mobile clinic team.

They sat looking at me, at each other and at the floor. No one spoke.

'Should we look for the new arrivals or stay in the clinic?' I asked again. The five men sat in front of me in silence.

Peter coughed. 'Where do you want us to go, Lisa?' he asked. 'You have to decide.'

Tell the local staff what to do? I sat back. In Saleem the outreach workers worked independently, returning at the end of each day to tell me what they had accomplished. More often than not Adam Ali told *me* what to do. I always turned to him for guidance.

We had received reports in Muhajariya of a large influx of displaced people. A whole community had sprung up on the edge of town. They claimed to have fled Saleem following a new wave of violence two weeks before. Dave and Karen had seen them, but I could find no reports or plan of action. Should we go and talk to them and see if they needed help? Or should we stay and work in the hospital? The sixty-bed hospital in town belonged to the Ministry of Health. MSF now ran many of the services; the male and female wards, children and obstetrics. They always needed help. Stay or go?

I looked at the group. The five young men looked back and shifted on their plastic chairs.

'Well, I say we go and talk to the new arrivals. I feel like a challenge today!' I said, clapping my hands as I stood. 'Who's coming with me?' They all stood and smiled at me shyly.

'We are,' they all replied. And they followed me out into the sun.

Two hours later we stood beside the land cruiser and surveyed the crowds around us. Over 1500 people had arrived ten days before. They camped on the edge of town, waiting for permission from village leaders to enter and start searching for food. My mind flashed back to the African Union, to the ramshackle shelters and endless queues of empty jerry cans. All around us families huddled under trees and clung to the shade as it shifted and shrank in the morning sunlight. There were women and children, the elderly and the sick. Many watched us from their shelters but no one approached. They expected nothing.

'Where do they get their water from?' I asked, turning to look for a hand pump.

'There are thirty water taps in our new MSF water station just over there,' Peter pointed to a grove of trees. 'There is a lot of water and it is free.'

Peter was my translator, my new Adam Ali. He was from the Dinka tribe, from South Sudan. His smooth dark skin and upturned nose were quite different from those of the tribes around us. Three long, straight scars dragged across each temple and disappeared into his hair. Scarification is common in the south, as young men and women are initiated. They grow in beauty with scars, some with a delicate pattern of dots and dashes across their face and chest, others with rough lines cut into young skin. He fled the south during the endless civil war between North and South. He brought his family to Darfur in 2000 to escape the attacks and repeated displacement that were common.

'We lost our homes and crops many times,' he told me when we met. 'I am a father and I was afraid for my children.'

Darfur was to be their safe haven, a place to start again. But the war followed him. In 2003, the year before peace was found in the South, a new civil war started in Darfur. And now he was the humanitarian worker, our translator as we followed in the aftermath of attacks and displacement and listened to new tales of woe.

Behind the water station the African Union compound in Muhajariya sparkled. Sunlight reflected off the rows of corrugated iron sheds.

'What's that noise?' I asked, listening to the steady rumble in the distance. 'Trucks? A helicopter?'

'It's the air conditioning in the African Union compound,' replied Peter. 'Their generator runs twenty-four hours a day, every day. I think it must be very cold inside.' He laughed while I shook my head.

We broke into pairs and each set off in a different direction. I wanted to talk to as many people as possible, to listen to them and to find out what their needs were. My stomach felt tight and my skin cold as we started walking. These families were from Saleem, my patients, my colleagues, my community. What horrors would they have to tell us?

Stories of the displaced blend seamlessly into each other when you have heard hundreds in the burning heat of the day. But each still has its moment of clarity, a sparkle of humanity that secures it in my mind. As we walked towards the first group I was about to hear one I will never forget. We walked towards them, all sitting by the tree. My shoulder bag felt heavy, filled with references books, sunscreen and my warm water bottle. I was better prepared for the hours of walking and talking and the infinite number of people waiting to be seen. The African Union in Saleem had taught me well.

The oldest woman stood as we approached. She instructed a child to shake out an empty sack and then lay it on the ground for us. I kicked off my boots, leaving them on the sand. Peter and I sat cross-legged on the mat. We shook hands with each of the women, gently winding our way through the gracious stream of greetings.

We sat and listened to them as they spoke of repeated attacks and intimidation. They tried to stay in Saleem, tried to adapt to the restrictions on their movements and the night-time raids. The new rules were designed to trip them up, if not today then always tomorrow. The local militia and soldiers wanted them gone and their means were clever and relentless. But in the end these families had to run. They stole out of Saleem town by night, carrying the children and a few belongings. Their men hid in the hills, too afraid to follow them. They were hungry, tired, afraid and without hope.

I listened as the old woman talked, looking to see what they carried. One sack, one blanket, two pots and one cup for twelve people. She talked with her hands, pointing and gesturing and wringing them as she spoke. What had happened to her family was unfair, it was persecution and injustice. And all I could do was nod and listen and try to find a way to help her. As we stood to leave the old woman stood with us. She didn't ask for anything, but thanked us for our visit, her right hand on her heart. Then she took Peter's hand and spoke softly. She reached out and took my hand and we stood together in the sun. She was about the same age as my grandmother, standing in her rags. Her feet were bare and her skin felt rough in my hand.

'What did she say, Peter?' I asked when she had finished talking.

'She wants us to write this down,' he said. 'She says that Bashir (the President of Sudan) has thrown us into this fire and we are all dying. She is begging us to pull them out of the flames.'

She stood looking at me, her thumb stroking the back of my hand. 'Please,' she said and she started to cry. My heart broke at the sight of her, at the feel of her skin and the sound of her tears. But what could I do to help?

We walked in the sun for the rest of the day, stopping to talk to dozens of families. They all sat in despair, surrounded by the hopelessness of their lives. They asked for nothing and watched us with sad, tired eyes. Each time I thought of the old woman, my hand resting in hers. How can I ignore someone when I have felt their skin against mine? Separated by time and culture it may be easy for some to close their eyes to her tears, to close their ears to her pleading. But I can't. With her rough skin and her small bare feet she was with me, beside me, part of me. Burning in the flames fanned by a man I didn't know, a man who didn't care. I had to do something to help her.

That night I sat at the table and leaned back to gaze at the stars. The mobile team were gentle people, easy to talk to but hesitant to step forward. The youngest, Ali, was twenty-two years old. The oldest, Issa, was thirty-three. Having lived their entire lives in Darfur they knew all about the people, patterns of life and war. But when I asked them to explain, they just smiled and looked at their feet. This is how the life goes, they would say. I sighed. With over a thousand people sitting on our doorstep we would need more than reticence and acceptance to help them and to pull them from the fire.

****

The following day I waited outside the office while Ali went to fetch the car. We drove the five-minute journey to the other humanitarian organisation in town. In this quiet, SLA-held town we were allowed to walk freely, and needed no guard or escort as we did in Saleem. But for my first meeting with the others, I wanted to make a good first impression. Arriving hot and sweaty from the fifteen-minute walk would do nothing for my appearance.

I stood at the front gate and waited while their guard went in search of an expat. The French organisation distributed food to the residents and displaced, covering a huge area of south Darfur where others didn't go. People couldn't farm the land when they were forced to move so often and their seeds and tools were stolen with each raid.

'Shukran,' I said, touching my heart with thanks when the guard returned to his shady rakuba. He looked at me, bored, and shrugged. Then returned to his game of cards.

'Ah, welcome, welcome, welcome.' I turned to see Patrice, their beautiful coordinator as she crossed the compound, her arms open wide. Two kisses, one on each cheek, and I was invited into the shade. I looked at Patrice as we walked and then down at my own dusty clothes. Her earrings sparkled in the light and she chatted as she cleared the table for our drinks. I even caught a breath of her perfume. In the heart of Darfur, surrounded by war, French women still managed to look beautiful.

'Take a seat,' she said as she handed me a soda.

I sat and pulled out my papers. They were full of names and the number of those we had spoken to the day before.

'I would like to talk to you about the new arrivals and their food needs,' I said, ready to talk business straight away. The overwhelming needs of those we talked to were for food and shelter and we had no time to waste.

'Ah yes,' she said. She looked at my papers but didn't take them from my hands. 'We have food in our warehouses, but not very much. The World Food Programme supplies us with far less than we need and there is simply not enough for our current population. Already the arrivals of last month are on half and quarter rations, just to stretch what we have. An extra fifteen hundred is impossible to feed.'

She looked at me. 'What can we do?'

I thought this would be easy. World Food Programme (WFP) food rations operate on the principle of registration. One family: one ration card. Extra children: extra ration cards. On distribution day each month everyone queued patiently in front of their community leader and collected their rations: grain, oil, sugar, flour and salt. It wasn't enough to thrive on but it was enough to survive. But with WFP cutting their rations there simply wasn't enough food. Nearly three million people in Darfur were totally dependent on food rations. They had no other food. The UN politics of food distribution had now become my problem.

'So there is no food for these people?' I asked, not ready to believe what I heard.

'No, not at this stage.' Patrice shook her head. 'We will juggle our warehouse stocks, take food from other groups. There will be some food soon. But for now, there is none.'

When I returned to our compound I sat in the office with my

head in my hands. We were going to fail these people, I just knew it. First the displaced in the river bed, then the displaced outside the African Union in Saleem. When I came to Darfur it was with high ideals and I was ready to make a difference. But constraints of time and resources, as well as the bloody war, tied our hands every time. All I was really doing was standing closer to the front line, close enough to hear them cry, and I could do nothing.

I sat there for hours, lost in my thoughts. When the fly-screen door crashed open I looked up. Thelma stormed in, slammed the door shut and sat heavily on Dave's chair.

'Fucking engines. Why does nothing work around here?' she said taking off her glasses and rubbing her eyes. Thelma was Danish, a water expert who travelled around Darfur advising MSF on the water situation and trying to develop water programmes. She was tired, disillusioned and she struggled with the ridiculous constraints around us. She was in Muhajariya to cover for Dave while he was away. She did not want to be there.

'You look as bad as I feel,' I said after a while. 'Why do we stay?'

'We're sitting here on our arses, our equipment broken and not enough staff. There is a war on, people are starving and there isn't enough water. But life could be worse, yes?' She peered at me myopically. 'Look on the bright side, we could be in Khartoum.'

I nodded. That would be worse.

'So, what is your problem? Apart from this fucking war?' she said.

I told her about the newly displaced, their fear and their hunger. I told her of the old woman, asking us to rescue her from the fire.

'And there's no food,' I finished. 'WFP has cut all rations and there is no more food coming for them. So they just sit and wait. Some of the people in Muhajariya walk out of the town at sunset and give their leftovers to whoever they find. If they find some family members they can bring them into town. But the others just wait. And there's nothing we can do.'

'Like hell there is,' she said, slapping the table and standing up. 'We have got a warehouse half full of food and oil and plastic sheeting. If we are not allowed to give it away then those Frenchies can have the lot.' She yanked the door open and stormed out. I followed her as she muttered and kicked sand, and we made our way to the warehouse.

Over the following two days we donated truckloads of grain and non-food items to Patrice. With smooth efficiency it was distributed to the waiting crowds within days. I couldn't stop smiling. Each time we drove out of town the number of blue plastic shelters had grown. People were coming out of the bush and they had shelter from the sun, wind and howling dust storms. And they had food. We had won. It was a small success but we had done it. And so I learned my first lesson in the power of determination: push, request, demand and fight until you get what you want and what the people need. And never give up.

****

Muhajariya was a town of about 35,000 people. The displaced population sat in camps on the outskirts that often exceeded 20,000 people. Like in Saleem the roads were wide. Long sandy tracks ran alongside neatly fenced compounds. At dawn each day women emerged from their homes and stood sweeping the roads in the still cool air. They would sweep as they walked, legs straight and backs bent. Sweep and talk and laugh with their neighbours as they worked.

In the early-morning light they swept patterns in the sand, pushing rubbish and straw and leaves into a pile at each intersection.

Each pile was lit with a match before they returned to their homes, leaving it smouldering and smoking. The day would begin and trucks, donkey carts, school children and others would travel each road. But the smouldering pile was left untouched, except by curious donkeys. By nightfall it would be almost gone, an ashy mound just waiting for dawn and new sweepings to start again. So tidy and organised in the chaos of war.

The marketplace in Muhajariya was thriving, far busier than Saleem. A discerning shopper could find almost anything. David Beckham calendars, mascara and silk petticoats lay hidden in the dark recesses of the market's labyrinth. Chickens wandered through the alleyways and donkeys hung their heads in the sun while their owners talked and gossiped in the coffee shops.

The SLA presence was strong and there was no mistaking who held the town. Fresh splashes of paint announced SLA on buildings and signs. We often passed one of their vehicles, beaten and battered to accommodate their weapons of war. The young soldiers sat in T-shirts wearing heavy necklaces of leather and string. Each little leather pouch afforded 'protection' with its blessing and thin paper prayer inside. Protection from bullets and protection from disease were common. In a land consumed by war, where most people died without hospital care, their leather protection was all they had to save them.

In spite of their weapons and their numbers around town I didn't feel afraid. They watched us as we wandered through the market at the end of each day. And they sat in the shade and talked while we drank coffee at the end of a busy day with the team. It was so different from El Wadi and Saleem. The people wanted the soldiers in Muhajariya. They smiled and waved at brothers, uncles and friends sitting high on their armoured vehicles. The SLA grew out of Darfur, a rebel movement that claimed to be standing up for the people of Darfur. In a land with a myriad of tribes and changing allegiances the SLA seemed to be the people's army. Other armed groups held various areas of Darfur, splinter groups and ideologically different groups with their own weapons, uniforms and leaders.

But Muhajariya belonged to the SLA. Our working relationship was respectful, so we went about our work in peace. After the intimidating soldiers in Saleem and El Wadi, the roaring vehicles, shouting soldiers and weapons pointed at us, the quiet distance between us and the SLA in Muhajariya was so welcome. My stomach stopped turning, my headache stopped grasping at the sight of these soldiers when I realised they would leave us alone. My body relaxed with relief, my breaths came a little easier in the apparent safety of my new home.

****

On Wednesday evening I joined Ellie as she drove to the hospital for her ward round. The expat medical and nursing staff took it in turns at the hospital. One of us was on call each evening from dusk until dawn; a bridge of frenetic activity between the end of a busy day and the start of a new one. Being on call was tiring. If any local staff needed help in the hospital during the night they would call the expat. At night I heard sleepy voices through my thin tuckul wall as someone was called to the hospital.

I climbed in beside Ellie and we drove slowly to the hospital that evening.

'Why are we driving so slowly?' I asked Ellie. 'I could walk faster than this!'

She laughed. 'Because if we speed to the hospital in the dark the SLA are likely to fucking shoot us,' she said. 'We go slowly, always along the same roads, with our flashing orange lights. That way they know we are coming and they keep their big guns away. Otherwise we're target practice.' She roared with laughter.

Ellie was a treasure — an Australian outback midwife with a loud laugh and a raw sense of humour. Life had trampled on her many times, but still she laughed and fought to make a difference for the women around her.

'Life's a bitch,' she told me one evening. 'And I love her!'

We drove along in silence. Here and there I saw the twinkling eyes of donkeys and cows in the headlights. They lay on the sand or stood tethered to a pole in the pitch dark. After the 40-degree heat of the day, the night was a blessing with its cooler, calm air.

Ali reversed the land cruiser in through the hospital gates and I stood blinking in the orange flashing lights. I had forgotten to bring a torch. When Ali turned off the engine and lights we stood in complete darkness.

'Ellie, where are you?' I called, feeling my way along the side of the vehicle. 'I can't see a thing.'

'I'm in here,' a muffled voice called. 'After a while you don't need a light, you just know where to go.'

I felt my way into the nurses' office, my arms stretched out in front of me as I stumbled towards the door. Inside four local hospital staff sat quietly on long wooden benches while the nurse spoke to Ellie. The room was lit by a single kerosene lantern. The two of them peered at patient charts in the dim light. Without many qualified staff it was hard to run a hospital as busy as this. We relied on health assistants to do much of the work, locals with only basic schooling, and expats filled in the gaps. But these health assistants were good, they were trained to carry out tasks with precision and relative speed.

'Here, you carry that. Let's get this ward round started.' Ellie handed me the kerosene lantern as she passed, and disappeared into the darkness. I stood blinking in the sudden pool of light. Crickets, beetles and moths converged on the light and beat against my shirt.

'Hey, wait for me,' I called, swiping the insects from my skin. And I stumbled after her.

I followed Ellie as she stopped by every bed. She touched each patient, her soft hands touching and examining as she went. She listened and nodded while the nurse translated, then scribbled notes in patient files. Behind her stood the health assistants, their arms laden with files as they waited for instructions for each patient. They were good at their tasks but they often missed vital clues in sick patients, only calling at 3 a.m. when a patient was dead. So Ellie explained carefully her plan for each one. I knew I had to learn quickly. By Saturday it would be my turn and the health assistants would lean in to listen to me at each bed.

The glare of the sunlight kept patients inside each day. The long, narrow wards housed a single row of beds stretching left and right; one ward for males, one for females and a smaller one for children. The open wall of each ward faced into the compound. It caught the breeze and brought some relief from the daytime heat. At night, though, everyone moved out under the stars. Mats, sheets and beds with traction were dragged out of the ward and they lay at every angle on the bare ground. Without a blanket and just a soft breeze to cool them, everyone could breathe again. The icy cold nights of Saleem had passed as the rainy season approached. Even the nights were warmer now, and the dawn air had lost its shivering bite.

I stood behind Ellie as she worked. All around the compound families sat together on mats, talking, eating and laughing in the darkness. Little kerosene burners sat resting on the sand, tiny flickering pools of light dotting the compound. If anyone needed a light they could reach for a burner and carry it carefully as they

At the gate to the hospital a sign reminds visitors 'no guns inside'.

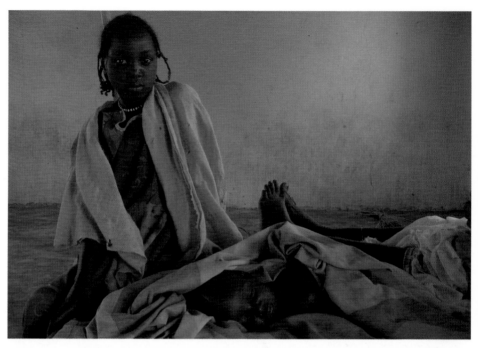

A young girl sits with her mother while her baby brother battles with pneumonia; a battle he lost.

The male ward of the hospital in the heat of the day; a hot wind tugs at the blanket while patients rest.

Beauty and hope in the face of a young girl.

Two midwives outside a war-damaged clinic; smiles in the midst of hardship.

A young boy from a wealthy family rides the family horse to the market.

A community focuses on the future as a teacher holds the first class of the day. Education gives hope.

An old woman shells peanuts at the side of the road; her work a labour of love that will feed the family tomorrow.

Beauty is in the eye of the beholder, but her strength is undeniable;
this old woman was over 80.

Outside my tuckul, or hut. Its woven grass walls and thatched roof provided little protection from the wind and rain.

A beautiful smile from our neighbour's daughter; without a shirt for her back but a wealth of laughter and hope.

A local leader sits quietly with his great-grandchildren.

Asha gently sweeping our courtyard; an early morning chore of beauty and patience.

walked. Patients blinked in our lamplight, shielding their eyes as they answered Ellie's questions. Soon we passed, leaving them to lie in the dark and return to their conversations.

It was 11 p.m. by the time we returned to our compound. The sickest patients had strict instructions from Ellie. She stood checking her radio battery in the office.

'If this thing dies in the night, I'm fucked,' she said, shaking her radio. 'It's happened before.'

She worried mostly about her women — those labouring in the dark of the delivery room with a local midwife. Women were her passion and the source of her exhaustion. In Darfur a huge number of women die because of complications in their circumcised labour. But those stories still lay in the future as I climbed into bed. I just worried about Saturday and how I would manage my first ward round in the dark. That night I dreamed about it, of tripping headfirst onto the nurses' office floor. 'Hello,' said the nurse in my dream. 'You must be the new expat. They always arrive on their knees.'

****

I made it through the first week, waiting for Karen's return. Thelma and I still glowed from our success with donating our stores to the displaced. But in Darfur there is never time to rest on past success. There is always another tragedy waiting in the wings.

Having survived my first ward round and not arriving on my knees, it was time to introduce me to mobile clinics, Muhajariya style. We drove out of town early, past the smouldering piles in the road. Villagers waved as we drove by, some whistled and sang when we waved back. Children chased us and laughed as they ran, three boys turned cartwheels in the dust. I sat back in my seat and took a deep breath. I had been there such a short time, but I had seen only smiles. As an SLA stronghold there seemed to be stability, the guns faced outwards, not at the townsfolk. There was no oppressive force controlling or intimidating the residents. There was no gunfire in the night, no screams or plumes of smoke. The queues at the hand pumps were long, but the women waited their turn as they gossiped in the shade. Everywhere I turned life looked normal and hands waved in greeting.

'Kawadja, kawadja,' called children. White person. They rushed to my side, taking my hand in theirs and stroking my skin with confidence. White people were a novelty and they just wanted to be near. After the brutality and fear of Saleem I felt tears well up as we drove out that morning. Muhajariya was going to be a very different experience, that much I could tell.

****

When we arrived in Labado it was nearly 10 a.m. Thelma had come with the mobile team, the second expat needed in Karen's absence. With a mountain of paperwork and an office full of broken pumps waiting for her in Muhajariya she was *not* happy. She was the 'donkey' for our clinic, our underappreciated workhorse.

'Why is it always me that has to go?' she asked that morning as we packed. 'Why does everyone assume I've got nothing better to do than be the mobile clinic donkey? I've got work to do, you know.' On and on she muttered as she smoked and frowned into the distance.

We needed a second expat to accompany us, or our clinic would be abandoned. Security rules demanded it. An expat had to sit in the front of each vehicle as we travelled potentially unsafe roads. There had been armed hold-ups and shots fired at vehicles in many project sites.

I stood with my arms folded outside the office and looked at her.

'So, are you coming or not?' I asked, feeling impatient. 'If you aren't then there are two hundred women in Labado who will be very disappointed.'

Thelma closed her eyes and dragged on her cigarette. 'I've got no choice, have I?' she said in a cloud of smoke. 'I'm coming.'

The first day in Labado proved to be easy after my trial-by-fire in El Wadi. Crowds of patients sat waiting as we drew up outside the clinic. The guards arranged them in rows, and lines of rope separated the men from the women. The latrine door was unlocked and hand-washing posts stood filled and ready for the day.

'A latrine!' I said as Peter showed me around. 'We even have a latrine!' I couldn't stop smiling.

He looked at me strangely. After months of clinics in El Wadi and outside the African Union this was my first clinic with a toilet. It was an exciting start.

We worked well together, the mobile team and I, triaging, treating and talking to patients. Two of the team, Issa and Ibrahim, worked as consultants in the other room. After their one year of training they were able to work as medics in this place where few people are trained at all. Both wore their stethoscopes proudly as they walked around the clinic and looked for sick patients among the crowds.

With the sole burden of care removed from my shoulders I felt relaxed as we worked through the day. Patients came and patients went. We heard no gunfire and the soldiers left us in peace. I saw SLA soldiers strolling past the clinic, hand in hand as they talked. Each with a gun slung over one shoulder.

I sat smiling to myself at the ease of it all. Thelma refused to leave the vehicle. She slept away her frustration of the wasted day.

'Why are you smiling?' asked Peter as we stopped working to drink tea in the sun. 'Are you happy?'

'I am so happy I could cry, my friend,' I told him. 'This clinic is so easy and no one is afraid. I think I will stay here forever.'

He shook his head and laughed. 'After six months in this place you will stop smiling. And no one lives in Darfur forever. They either run or die. But I am glad you are happy now.'

****

Buoyed with our success in Labado I was ready for another challenge. The weekly clinic in Angabo was suspended while Karen was away. As her R&R stretched into its second week, news came that she was sick. After two months of running the mobile team and outreach workers alone she was exhausted. She needed a rest. I could sympathise.

'I think I am ready to take on Angabo,' I said that night as we all sat down for dinner. 'Who wants to come with me?' I looked around. Thelma avoided my eyes and the others poked at their food. No one wanted to be the mobile clinic donkey. Gertrude and Harold, the surgeon, shrugged their shoulders.

'We have a hospital to run,' said Gertrude. 'We cannot leave.'

That left Jack.

'How about it?' I turned to him and smiled. 'Pleeease?'

Jack was our logistician, Toby's counterpart in Muhajariya. Where Toby procrastinated and prevaricated Jack just got on with things. He organised, built, planned and achieved every day. With his open, smiling face and his lilting northern English accent he was the favourite with the team, both locals and expats.

'I'll go,' he said as he ate. 'But I've got to bring my iPod. It breaks the monotony of the clinics for those of us who come as a donkey.' He smiled and raised one eyebrow. 'A guy's got to have some fun.'

And so we made plans. Angabo wasn't far as the crow flies, 50 km or less. But with security checkpoints, dry river beds and long potholed tracks the journey could take days. We packed our bags to stay for three days, a long time to be away from Muhajariya in a time of change and growing displacement from Saleem. We couldn't help everyone, so we had to choose a few. Muhajariya or Angabo, the displaced north of Muhajariya or the homeless south of the town. The needs around us still crushed in, but I had learned to close my eyes and ears to much of it. To focus instead on what we could do — the clinics we could run.

Everything was prepared in plenty of time — drugs and equipment, barrels to store water and mats for our evenings under the stars. I stood back and looked at the vehicles on the morning of our departure. Both vehicles were already loaded, their roofs piled high with boxes and the back of each filled with metal trunks of equipment. I loved this place already. Jack had packed the night before and all we had to do was leave. He could teach Toby a thing or two.

There won't be any nights spent sleeping on the cold, metal floor, I thought as I watched the team pile into the vehicles. Soft pillows and iPods were more Jack's style.

We set off at 9 a.m., amid clouds of dust and shrieking chickens.

'Are you guys okay back there?' called Jack on the radio.

'Yep, the team are singing in the back seat and we're ready to go,' I called back. Gone were my fears of the radio, my nervous shrinking at Steve's sharp tone as he called. Instead there was Jack.

'Right, let's get this show on the road,' he called back. 'And let's have some fun!'

So we lumbered out of town, past the hand pumps and the dry river bed behind the hospital. Past the displaced families with their new plastic shelters and stores of food neatly stacked in the shade. I can do this, I thought with a smile. And I turned to join in the singing.

****

By lunch time the following day I stood amongst the crowd and my skin burned in the sun. My confidence was wavering again. We had arrived the day before and set up our belongings in a rented compound in Angabo. Our new compound was still being built on the far side of the marketplace. We bought ice-cold sodas in the market and retired to our mats in the shade to drink them.

Our clinic in Angabo was a new venture as we spread our project to the east. The resident population was around 6000 with another 10,000 displaced living in areas around the town in makeshift camps. Some walked for hours to visit the MSF clinic. They sat in the sun in scattered groups and pulled at my clothes and clicked their tongues for attention as I passed.

Haroun, our local triage man, stood beside me with a smile.

'Very good,' he said in English. 'Yes, very good.'

I looked at him. He couldn't read mercury thermometers — our three digital thermometers had mysteriously disappeared — and he had forgotten how to measure children for malnutrition. The plastic band for measuring their upper arms dangled from his pocket. When Jack had seen him measuring children's wrists and ankles instead of their upper arms he called me over. I stopped Haroun from using the band, but he insisted on carrying it in his pocket.

'I couldn't understand why so many children were appearing with severe malnutrition written on their card,' said Jack. 'They looked thin but not at death's door.' Then he spotted Haroun kneeling on the ground measuring little ankles.

Without a competent triage worker I was left to sort and identify the sick as they spread across the vast compound. My Arabic was improving in leaps and bounds as I worked without a translator. Peter worked with Jack, organising local staff and translating for a meeting with local leaders. The other five members of the team worked inside the small tuckuls, seeing patients and dispensing treatment at a furious pace. With over three hundred people waiting to be seen everyone worked at top speed.

Haroun followed me as I worked. 'No problem,' he said over and over. 'All is good.' And he patted my arm. Somehow I didn't feel reassured.

The women kept changing groups as they gossiped in the sun. I had given up trying to keep them together. I watched as mothers stood up to leave, holding my red cards in their hands. Red cards were reserved for seriously ill patients, severely malnourished children, those with pneumonia or malaria — receiving one meant they could go to the front of the queue. But my Arabic was obviously far from perfect. These women gathered up their belongings, a smile on their faces, and started to walk home. They were just happy with their red card! So I ran after them, trying to explain that their children were too sick to leave, and shepherding them towards the consultation room where Issa and Ibrahim worked.

By sunset the sickest patients had been seen. Those who had walked for hours to complain of 'gas in abdomen' had received their advice and a few antacids for their time. I walked over to Jack.

'I'm knackered,' I said, kicking off my boots and falling onto the mat. 'Three hundred people in an area the size of a football stadium is too much. I can't keep track of them all.'

'You should use Haroun more,' he said, handing me a soda. 'I've heard he's very good.'

I took the soda and rolled my eyes. 'Yes, so he tells me,' I said. My nose was burned and my shoulders ached from the day in the sun. Haroun had followed me every step of the way, smiling and nodding but not actually working.

'Don't worry, Lisa. We'll get this place sorted,' he said, holding up his soda bottle. 'To team work!' And we clunked bottles in a toast.

Later that evening I stood brushing my teeth in the far corner of the compound. I loved those still evenings at the end of a long, hectic day. I watched the evening star as it hovered in the west, above the horizon. I thought of El Wadi and the evening star watching over us as we lay on our mats at the end of a bruising day. I closed my eyes to the star and spat on the sand.

The mobile team sat washing their feet under the great spreading tree. They were preparing to pray. They knelt or stood in silence, each lost in their prayers as they gave thanks for the day. The constant devotion of their faith was soothing in the face of such hardship. No matter what evils they met, or pain and suffering they encountered, come dusk they would give thanks. I watched as they stood side by side, and bent in unison, murmuring in the dark. And I thought of Musa. Calm, quiet, patient Musa as he prayed in the dusk light of each day.

I wandered over to Jack and sat down.

'I'm going to bed early,' I said. 'It's been a long day.'

'But the music is about to start,' he protested, holding up his iPod. 'What about the dancing?'

I laughed and put down my toothbrush.

'OK, I'll stay for one dance. But I'm ready for bed, so I'll just watch. I can't dance in my pyjamas!'

Moby's voice crooned softly as Jack knelt to adjust the speakers. Ali and Ibrahim walked over, their prayers finished, and bent down to watch him.

'What do you want, guys?' he asked. 'Moby, Seal, a spot of R&B?'

They shrugged. I lay back on the mat and watched the stars through the leaves above me. How could it be that we laugh and dance and have fun when all around us people are being crushed by the most brutal violence imaginable, I wondered. My sanity had nearly been destroyed by Saleem's violence. I listened to Jack laugh as the others started to dance, and felt tears well in my eyes. I remembered Adam Ali and his smiling eyes. 'If we don't laugh then our heart dies,' he had said. To give in to the misery around us would destroy us. Finding friendship and laughter would give us strength and through it, hope. God only knew we needed hope.

The last I saw as I climbed into the back of the vehicle to sleep was Jack and Issa swaying to the music of Seal. The others lay on their mats and clapped in time. Darfur really is a place of extremes, I thought as I tucked my blanket under the mattress. Fear and evil, laughter and dancing. And all just a breath apart.

****

Our last morning in Angabo ran much more smoothly as Jack organised people and stood guard at the gate. Those women with their red cards were not escaping! I worked with Haroun and by lunch time he was able to read the mercury thermometer. I was almost ready to trust him with the upper arm band for the malnourished children. Not perfect, but it's okay, I thought as I watched him work. He smiled and nodded constantly as he worked. And maybe okay is enough for now.

We parked the vehicles in the marketplace before leaving Angabo at lunch time. The Oomda, the most senior district leader, wanted to talk to us. As we crossed the hot sand Jack pointed ahead to an armchair in the shade.

'That's him over there,' he said. 'A very nice man and well respected.'

We approached the tree and the Oomda rose. His chair was made of wood and rope, its seat covered with old sack cloths. His white jelabiya gown tugged in the breeze as he walked towards us, his arms open.

'Welcome, my friends. Come and sit with me,' he said smiling.

We sat in the shade and talked while a young boy sliced open two watermelons and handed them to us on plates.

'Eat, eat,' urged the Oomda. 'The tea will come shortly.'

'Oomda I am afraid we have to leave soon,' said Jack. 'We must be in Muhajariya by 5 p.m. and already it is late. I'm sure you understand.'

The Oomda nodded. 'But everyone must finish the watermelon.' He pushed the plates nearer.

We all bent forward and pulled great chunks of sweet, pink flesh from the melons. I dripped and slurped while Jack talked to the Oomda. It was too delicious to miss.

The hospitality of the Sudanese is astonishing. Whether they were homeless and living on the run, or an Oomda on a throne of old sack cloths, they shared what they had. We were welcomed with offers of tea or food and when people had neither they offered us water in old, battered bowls. They weren't asking for sympathy or trying to win favours. Their tradition and their pride required them to share, regardless of what they had. And they did so with grace.

We sat with the Oomda far longer than we should and shared his hospitality. He sat shelling peanuts as we talked. When we stood to leave he handed Jack a roll of newspaper, filled with his dry salty peanuts.

'For your journey,' he said, touching his heart. 'Shukran.' Thank you.

Jack touched his heart in return, and bowed his head in thanks.

We drove back to Muhajariya an hour behind schedule.

'What will happen if we're late?' I asked Hamid as he drove. I thought of Commander Ali and the security officers in Saleem.

'Nothing,' he said shrugging. 'Thelma will be upset, I think.'

So we drove on unhurried and I relaxed, my arm resting on

the open window. The late-afternoon sunlight flooded the fields with golden light as we neared Muhajariya. We passed an SLA checkpoint, the only one that day. The soldiers barely looked up from their game of cards and waved us through absent-mindedly. Their AK47s lay in a jumbled heap on the ground beside them.

We arrived in Muhajariya, tired and dusty, but still singing Peter's hymns. Thelma was upset, as Hamid had predicted. But all was well. I stood at the gate and waved as the team left, walking to their various homes around town. Two children crossed the track, leading a donkey. They shouted to me.

'Kawadja, kawadja, what is your name?' Jack had been teaching them English.

'My name is Lisa,' I called back, and they burst out laughing. 'Lisa' in Arabic means 'Not yet'. Who would be called that, they wondered, and laughed at the ridiculous name.

I didn't care who laughed. I was happy and the day had been good. We had seen sick patients, treated everyone who needed help and made a difference in Angabo. When the days are good in Darfur you relish every one. You never know — it may be your last.

CHAPTER EIGHT

Karen's return to Muhajariya marked the beginning of a time of purpose, laughter and achievement. I was already halfway through my mission and the months were about to get even busier. Karen sat quietly for the first few days, still recovering from her weeks in Khartoum's hospitals and clinics. She looked pale, both hands resting on her abdomen.

'Bloody doctors in Khartoum poked and prodded me until I was ready to scream,' she told us on the first evening. 'And then they told me what I already knew and sent me back to Darfur.' She leaned forward to stub out her cigarette and winced with pain. Giardia and ulcers in her bowel left her feeling exhausted and weak. 'It's nothing that a pack of cigarettes and a cup of strong coffee won't fix.'

Dutch people are hard to keep down.

Karen was another veteran of MSF missions. Like Sarah in Saleem she was blonde and beautiful, almost out of place in the chaotic swell of our mobile clinics. But where Sarah was elegant and trailed a breath of perfume, Karen was down to earth and the word 'elegant' didn't spring immediately to mind. She wasn't a morning person, preferring to sleep until lunch time on her Fridays off. With tousled hair, a sleep-wrinkled face and short temper she was to be avoided before her morning fix of coffee and cigarettes. While I stood with the mobile team outside, packing and organising the vehicles after breakfast, Karen sat scowling in the early-morning light while her coffee cooled.

By mid-morning, though, Karen was on fire. She worked tirelessly. She triaged, organised, shouted and consulted her way through the crowds. I started to call her the Mobile Princess, the darling of the clinic. Seeing her at work in Labado, I was in awe. Surely I hadn't been like that in El Wadi, I thought. The tiny room in Labado was packed with patients; they stood, sat and crouched on every inch of the floor. The old Ministry of Health clinic had been bombed directly during an attack in 2004. The corrugated iron roof lay twisted and broken, barely held to the blackened rafters by rusting nails. The walls were pockmarked and crumbling, bullet holes and shrapnel had weakened every surface. But there on her knees, in the midst of the crush, Karen worked.

We all worked hard in mobile clinics. Facing crowds with only our metal trunks of equipment, we were alone with our team. We worked without doctors or specialists, pharmacists or laboratories. We were all the villagers had. Will I ever be like that, I wondered? As I watched Karen work I worried that we wouldn't be enough.

I had forgotten El Wadi and stood in my anxiety alone. I forgot our achievements, the constant battle to treat and care for our patients under Commander Ali's threat and the small successes we created. I forgot my sense of purpose, my inner reserves and the strong team that surrounded me. All I remembered was failure — the team in Saleem didn't want me any more, I couldn't even say goodbye. I hadn't worked hard enough. I was afraid I would make the same mistake in Muhajariya.

'We'd better get going,' Karen said at 3 o'clock as our first clinic drew to a close. 'Janjaweed militia usually hit this town in the late afternoon. If there's a raid they come before sunset, then head home, knowing that no one will follow them in the dark.'

I looked around at the smiling faces around us. Behind their smiles there was fear — it was the same story with every Darfuri. Nothing is as simple as it seems.

The crowd parted as we walked to the vehicles. Some laughed as they helped to carry our heavy trunks. It was all so different from El Wadi. These people knew we would return each week, Sunday was their clinic day. Come rain or shine we arrived on time and ready to work. Instead of the desperate faces and aching wounds of El Wadi they brought their families. Children with coughs and babies with diarrhoea sat waiting in the shade. The time of malaria had passed as the dry season advanced. To the 25,000 people of Labado we brought a service, a community clinic in the absence of any local care. In El Wadi we brought a lifeline.

I sat in the front seat as we drove away and rolled down the window. It had been a good day. The shutters in my mind hid Saleem from view. They didn't want me and the suffering in the north was theirs now. I didn't know what I had done wrong, why my failure was worse than any other and why my colleagues had turned away from me. Behind my smile I still ached. But in Darfur there is little time to dwell on the past. When the dead are buried and the children are safe, people carry on with the business of living. The past was behind me and Muhajariya was my present.

****

I walked past Ellie as she sat on the low wall of the clinic just after sunset. I gave her shoulder a squeeze. She looked flushed and tired, her damp hair clinging to her neck. She was in her late 50s, but her energy and enthusiasm outpaced the rest of us. She worked tirelessly for the women.

In the delivery room two women were labouring and Ellie

always worried about her women. In Darfur almost every woman is circumcised by puberty. Their genitals are mutilated as the traditional midwives cut away the clitoris and labia with a razor blade, suturing the gaping wound closed with old catgut. The rights and wrongs of female genital mutilation filled our evening conversations. The problem is complex and beliefs are firmly entrenched. The reality is that women inflict mutilation on women and Ellie had to deal with the consequences. The war and its business of starving, displacing and dying filled our days and many nights. There was no time or resources to take on the practice of mutilation — stopping it would save lives, but to change it was almost impossible. One problem too many in a land burdened by wrongs and destruction.

'How's it going in there?' I asked, almost afraid to hear her answer in my early-evening tiredness.

'Fuckin' awful,' she replied, leaning forward and hanging her head with tiredness. 'I've got a 14-year-old in there and a woman with twins labouring in the dark. It's hot, I'm tired and the fuckin' solar lamp has just died. That's how it's going.' She looked at me. 'You want to join the party?'

My heart sank and my shoulders ached. I felt exhausted by the day in Labado and all I wanted was sleep. But every moment was a chance to learn. I'd rather learn with Ellie at my side.

I nodded. 'Let's get in there.'

We ducked into the heat and darkness of the delivery room. The entrance was low and every woman ducked and scraped their clothes as they bent to enter.

I followed Ellie to the furthest bed, and knelt beside her in the dim light. On the floor a kerosene lantern flickered, casting shadows as we moved. Ellie reached over and gently held a cup of water to the young girl's mouth. She drank noisily. In the shadows stood two women, mother and grandmother perhaps, their arms folded.

'She's only 14, not married and twenty-four weeks' pregnant,' whispered Ellie. 'I reckon they've given her something so she'll abort the baby. Here, you give her some water and catch the baby when it comes. I'll be behind the curtain with the other woman. Call if you need me.' She handed me the cup and disappeared into the shadows.

I knelt in the dark, holding the cup. My stomach growled with hunger and I was desperate to go to the toilet. Oh shit, I thought. I knew very little about babies and even less about circumcised birth. The young girl started to groan quietly. Oh shit, oh shit, oh shit.

On the mat beside me was a pair of sterile gloves, tape to tie the umbilical cord and a razor blade. A green bucket of clean gauze swabs stood at the foot of the bed. The young girl was sweating and started breathing quickly. Her contractions were minutes apart and when she bore down to push she made a strangled groan in the dark. Sudanese women deliver their babies in near silence, their mutilated bodies straining against the scar tissue with barely a sound. It made me shiver each time I watched a birth.

I put the cup on the mat and pulled on the gloves. And then I sat in the dark and waited. The baby was going to come out, no matter what I did. The young girl cried, a thin stifled sound and fell back on the pillow.

'Oh shit. Ellie. I think she's had the baby. What do I do?' I whispered loudly. I crawled towards the bed and lifted up the sheet, holding the kerosene lantern in one hand. Lying on the bloodstained bed was a tiny baby.

'Ellie, help! What do I do with the baby?' I whispered. This was no 'normal' circumcised delivery, with a healthy baby waiting for my care. This was an unwanted baby lying in the shadows.

'Is it alive?' she called back.

'Yes, it's breathing and moving,' I said, peering more closely. 'I can almost see its heart beating, the skin is so thin.'

'Oh fuck,' came the reply. And I heard her footsteps next door.

The two older women still stood in the shadows behind me. They talked quietly to each other, but neither came forward.

'There's nothing we can do. Not for such a small premmie, it's at least four months early. We've got no oxygen, no incubator or drugs that this little thing needs,' said Ellie, kneeling beside me. 'It's a perfect baby but she can't have it. Not at 14. They'll wait for it to die,' she said, gesturing towards the women. 'Then they'll take her home and leave the baby. She'll be punished but only the family will know.' She moved to massage the young girl's abdomen, helping her to expel the little placenta.

I couldn't take my eyes off the baby; this breathing, beating, moving thing. I reached down and lifted its little body with my yellow-gloved hands. Beside me Ellie wrapped the white tape around the umbilical cord and cut the soft rubbery tube in half. I wrapped the baby gently in a sheet of white cotton gauze. Its left hand reached out through the covers, fingers stretching. Its skin looked soft and downy in the half light. I lifted the covers and wrapped the little arm inside.

I stood stiffly and walked over to the two women.

'Here, look at her baby,' I said. 'It's alive.' I held out the baby.

They both turned their shoulders. No, said their body language. Take it away. For the young girl's future and for their pride and dignity it was better that the baby didn't exist.

I carried the baby back and laid it at the foot of the bed. I sat back on my knees and watched while Ellie disposed of the placenta. She wiped up the blood, the unfortunate mess of the unwanted baby. Beside me, the white cotton still moved, though less often.

I sat close to the bed while the baby died, my hand on its head and with shame in my heart. It was unwanted and unloved but I would not let it die alone. I whispered the Lord's Prayer and prayed for forgiveness. I had stopped praying months ago. Why bother when my prayers felt weak and the suffering continued. This was the reality of unprotected sex. This was the reality of a culture of abstinence before marriage. A slowly dying baby, wrapped in a white cloth, lying in the dark.

I pulled back the cloth after an age of waiting. My feet were numb from kneeling. Inside, the tiny body was still, its chest still, its life gone. In the shadows of the lantern the baby looked like a doll, tiny but perfect. I placed the lantern on the floor, hiding its face from the light. And I wrapped it again, enveloped in the soft, white cloth, protected from the world.

When we finished washing the young girl we helped her to stand. She was tiny, her adolescent head barely coming up to my chest. Ellie guided her to the spare bed in the corner and she lay down on the clean sheets. She turned her face to the wall and hid in the darkness.

'You can leave the rest to me,' said Ellie gently. 'I'll clean up when I'm finished next door. She'll sleep here tonight and they will take her home tomorrow. I'll get one of the guards to bury the baby tonight. You can go back to the compound.'

I nodded and walked quietly across to the table. I picked up my water bottle and carried it outside. I stood on the rough, stony ground and looked up at the stars. My shirt was wet with perspiration and beads of sweat ran down my neck. I thought of the baby, lying alone inside. I don't think I can ever forgive myself for what I did. I walked away in the darkness, my hands guiding me along the brick wall. When I came to the end I dropped to my knees, my whole body shaking in the dark. I felt so ashamed.

In the rush to care for the people broken and damaged by the war there was little time to help and console those with ordinary needs. The young girl deserved counselling, time to heal and to process the pregnancy, birth and death. This pregnancy wasn't the result of war, it was the result of life, of abstinence that doesn't work and of a culture of silence. Circumcised in silence, conceived in silence and delivered in silence. The young girl deserved to be heard. But we couldn't offer her that. This war kills and consumes. Not just on the battlefield, but in homes and villages caught up in the damn chaos. Women's rights, the freedom to speak and be heard, support and encouragement for those who survive the war are undeniable rights for all. We expect them for ourselves, for our children and our societies in the West. And we fight for them when our rights are ignored. But living in a broken, damaged society far from our own, the young girl lives on, forgotten, overlooked, silenced.

****

The following week we returned from the Angabo clinic, arriving in Muhajariya late again. Dave's anger was explosive. We stood in front of the whiteboard in the office and listened while he raged.

'We have rules for a reason,' he said, looking at Karen and me. 'The security level is orange, see that? O-R-A-N-G-E.' He tapped out the word with his finger. 'That means you are back before 5 o'clock and in my sight before dark. This place is not safe, got it?'

We nodded and murmured our apologies. Tribal clashes in the south and Janjaweed raids were becoming more frequent. They were still far away, but never far enough. Trying to get all the work done and follow security guidelines seemed an impossible task some days. If only the bloody war would go away and leave us to get on with our work!

The clinic in Angabo had been busy, the crowds more insistent than before. Dehydration, malnutrition and chronic problems pushed steadily towards the front gate. Over fifty school children arrived just before lunch. While Karen and the rest of the mobile team laboured inside the compound I triaged in the sun with the ever-smiling Haroun at my side. The school prefect stood waiting beside Haroun, his uniform neatly pressed. When I turned, he handed me a notebook. Inside, carefully written in English, were the names of each child and a summary of their complaints. The Sudanese love of bureaucracy was incredible. It must have taken the headmaster *hours* to write, I thought.

1. Musa Ibrahim. 12 years old. Headache.
2. Hawa Adam. 13 years old. Sore tongue and feeling like wind in the legs.
3. Adam Hussein. 11 years old. Burning feet and not eating vegetables.

'Hang on,' I said, grabbing at the prefect's shirt as he turned to bring the group of children inside. They sat and lay on the sand around us, laughing and talking while they waited for their consultation.

'These kids don't look sick to me,' I said looking around at the group. 'You're lucky you can go to school, do you know that? You just want a day off school!'

'No,' replied the prefect in English, his face looking serious. 'They are very sick and their families are worried.'

Beside me Haroun was smiling. 'Very sick,' he said. 'Come, come, come,' as he ushered the school children into the compound.

So I gave them the benefit of the doubt. I slowly worked my way through the group, asking questions and palpating them one by one. Not all illnesses are obvious and it can take time to tease out the real problem. Post-traumatic stress, sexually transmitted infections and a myriad of medical problems were always possible diagnoses.

Inside, Karen was working with the more serious patients. I wanted to do my share to help. But when I finished at 3 p.m. I realised my instincts had been right — not one child had a genuine problem. By doubting my abilities I had fallen for their joke. I turned to the prefect and shook my head.

'Sick, huh? Very funny,' and I stood up from the sand.

'Thank you for your time,' he replied cheerfully. The children cheered. I watched as they left, walking slowly out the gate and down the dusty track. Their laughter and hoots filled the air.

'See you next week,' called the prefect with a wave.

'No you bloody won't,' I muttered, kicking the sand. I was not going to fall for that again. Children are children, wherever you go.

Standing in front of Dave as he lectured and growled, I sighed.

'I understand, Dave. We won't be late again. I promise.' And I'll break their ankles if they come back, I thought angrily, as we walked out of the office.

****

I went to bed early. I needed to so I could cope with the sweltering days and the endless crowds. Daytime temperatures touched 45°C and the sweat ran freely while we worked. I imagined Adam Ali sitting at our desk in El Wadi and wondered whether he still looked so cool and relaxed in the staggering heat. I think he did.

My 9 p.m. bed time was a source of mirth to Dave and Karen.

'Children's bed time, Lisa,' called Dave as I crossed the compound with my towel and toothbrush. He and Karen often sat up until midnight and beyond, their cigarette ends glowing in the darkness. But by 9 p.m. I was finished.

I lay in the dark and listened to the voices around me. My new tuckul was made of woven grass mats, so unlike my mud-brick tuckul in Saleem. The mats were stitched together and pulled around a circle of posts driven deep into the sand. Through the grass walls I heard the night sounds: crickets and bats squeaking, donkeys braying, a nearby corral of camels snorting and grunting in the darkness. I listened to the sound of a hedgehog eating a beetle under my bed, crunching and wheezing quietly in the dark.

My favourite sounds were the voices, sleepy and low, just behind our fence. A family compound lay on the other side of the sandy track. In the still night air they sounded close. I rolled over and listened as the children giggled and whispered in the dark. An adult voice shouted out now and then, warning them to go to sleep or else. When the children's voices softened and they slept, it was the turn of the adults. The women sang and whispered, telling stories and murmuring consolation over some wrongdoing that my ears strained to hear. A group of men always lay outside the compound, their mats on the still-warm sand. They talked and debated, laughed and told stories long into the night. I thought again of Adam Ali and Steve. I imagined them lying on a mat in the dark, talking and laughing as I drifted off to sleep.

There in the dark I forgot I was in Muhajariya, forgot the hurt and the ache that filled my quiet moments every day. I listened to Adam Ali's voice and fell asleep.

****

The MSF hospital was the centre of our life in Muhajariya. Morning ward rounds, surgery and the rumble of the generator filled our days, and night-time call-outs with sleepy voices over the radio filled our nights. For Karen and me the mobile clinics were a blessing, a welcome escape from the routine and complaints the others faced in the hospital. When we were in Muhajariya we sat around the table and listened while the others complained about their frustrating day.

'Isaac didn't restock the pharmacy today,' someone would sigh.

'Idriss forgot to prepare the patient files for the ward round last night,' complained another.

'Who used the last roll of toilet paper and didn't fetch more from the storeroom?' called a voice from around the corner.

'And I'm tired of tomato stew,' was Craig's frequent cry. He was from London and this was his first, and I suspect only, venture to Africa. He worked hard and managed his patients diligently, but he often seemed to forget he was in Darfur. He never left Muhajariya and didn't see the hungry faces in the bush.

Lost in their familiar pattern each week the same complaints arose often. Small annoyances were common. Karen and I looked at each other — we were just glad to escape to Angabo and Labado, for all their frustrations. To lie under the stars at night and paint pictures in the sky, or sit shoulder to shoulder as we ate lunch in the small, crowded consultation room in Labado. The crowds and the chaos were worth it for our quiet times with the team. It was our world and we liked it. We also had our own rules about when to restock the toilet paper.

'No. No. No! Not that tomato mush again. I refuse to eat it!' said Craig, his arms folded across his chest. His round glasses were dirty and he squinted through the lenses.

We were a million miles from home, living in a war zone and he was having another tantrum about the food, I thought. We'd all heard it before, but that evening I closed my ears. If I listened I'd only get angry.

Hanan was our cook and she tried her best each day. She arrived every afternoon at 1 o'clock to prepare our evening meal, her routine always the same. She walked through the front gate looking like a desert beauty, covered from head to toe in the softest, silkiest fabric that shimmered and floated in the hot wind. She crossed the compound and stepped into the kitchen. She took off her wrap, blew her nose loudly onto the sand and started to prepare the food. Six hours later she would walk home, dressed again in her exotic colours and two-inch heels. She left us an astonishing array of small pots on the table, the largest of which always contained tomato mush. Six days a week, come what may, she placed it in the middle of the table before she went home, patted the lid and smiled.

'Table stew,' she said each time. Vegetable stew, I think she meant. A Western specialty taught to her by one of the previous expats. It was her pleasure and delight to present it to us each evening. She had been told the expats loved it. It was her labour of love in the small, hot kitchen. And every night Craig complained.

True, it contained more tinned tomatoes than any other ingredient. The tiny mouldy potatoes were peeled with infinite care and added to the pot. There were tinned mushrooms on a good day, or a dozen emaciated carrots from the Jebel Mara mountains on a bad day. And a handful of 'secret herbs'. But by the time it had been boiled on the gas cooker for two hours it always looked the same. Tomato mush.

Tiny cubes of tough, boiled beef usually filled one small pot, devoid of colour or flavour. A cup of soggy rice stuck to another. Local beans were a rarity and eating them was often fraught with danger, with little bean-coloured stones just waiting to crack a tooth or dislodge a filling.

The food was lousy, that much was true. I had tried to teach Hanan a new dish, with limited success — a creamy curried vegetable dish that made even the worst vegetables taste good. It was relegated to small pot number four when I stood beside her on Thursdays. We peeled and chopped in the kitchen together, my poor Arabic and her poor English standing aside while we made friends. But obviously my dish didn't pique her interest the way the 'table stew' had.

I wished that Craig could see Hanan as she worked; slicing and concentrating, stirring and mixing. She sang and danced and hummed her way through every afternoon in that hot brick kitchen, the office generator thundering in the logistical compound next door. And every evening I tried to see her before she left at 7 o'clock.

'Shukran, Hanan! I love your table stew,' I said. Thank you.

And every evening she beamed. 'Alawajip,' she said, touching her heart. My pleasure and my gift, said her smile.

If only Craig could see that beauty. But instead he clanged the lid down, and skulked off to the storeroom to search in vain for something better to eat.

****

The first drops of rain started to fall on a Thursday. It had been seven months without a smell of rain, but that day the air was heavy.

'Do you think it'll rain?' I asked Jack as I stood in the office.

'I don't know,' he replied, his attention still on the computer screen. 'If it rains, it rains. If it doesn't, it doesn't.' He had a very Sudanese perspective on life by this stage of his mission.

I walked outside and breathed deeply. I could smell rain.

I slept outside every night by April. I had been in Darfur for six months. The months of icy cold dawns had given way to hot, airless nights as the rainy season approached. The oppressive heat of the tuckuls and the windless nights suffocated me. Just before nightfall I dragged my bed, mattress and all, and set it firmly in the sand outside my tuckul.

There in the dark I found an escape from the heat and fell in love with the stars. With the lightest sheet to cover me I lay watching the night sky, thinking and dreaming about life away from the heat. We sweated and burned though each day, our wet clothes forgotten as we ran through clinics and ward rounds, barely keeping up with life's demands. I'd stopped wiping the sweat as it tickled and dripped from my chin. Stopped complaining about tiredness as the others yawned around me. Stopped thinking of failure and sadness. There was more to life than complaints. And so I started to smile and enjoy what small achievements there were in each day.

That afternoon we were sitting in the shade, making plans for the week. Where to go, who to visit, what clinics to open in new areas of need. The first drops fell. We stopped talking.

'Did you just see that?' I asked Karen, not wanting to turn my head in case the rain heard me.

'I didn't see anything,' she replied, not wanting to curse the pregnant air.

We resumed our discussion, perspiring hands writing on damp paper as we worked.

Drop. Drop. Drop.

The first fat raindrops started to fall and the sand was soon pockmarked with heaven-sent splashes. The sky quickly became dark as a thunder cloud loomed overhead. If you have experienced the dry season, the aching months of waiting as the land cracks and dies in the heat, you will know the real smell of rain. We put down our pens and walked out into the open. The rain fell, the warm drops running down our arms. As the rain fell harder our shirts clung to our backs and my hair dripped puddles down my neck. How we danced! We spun in the cooling air, racing to catch drops in our mouths. Jack walked out into the rain, his arms out wide.

'It's bloody marvellous,' he shouted. 'Just like I told you, if it rains, it rains.'

And so the rainy season started; late, short but so desperately needed. The displaced living in the bush would have puddles and wells to collect their water from instead of walking for days to hand pumps. Without money they often couldn't afford enough water. At most hand pumps the owners charged a fee. If people were living on the run it was hard to make the money they needed. Farmers could stop standing in queues every month, their hands out for food. Instead they could plant and grow and harvest the way they used to do. If only the war would give them a respite, just long enough to plant. All over the village women sang, children whooped with delight and men prayed as they all gave thanks for the rain.

By nightfall after the first rain, it had passed and the air was cool and still. I dragged my bed outside, leaving deep gouges in the wet, sticky sand. Above me the stars shone for Africa and a single satellite spun slowly across the sky. I sat on the edge of my bed and kicked the sand from my feet. I can't stand a sandy bed. I pulled up my blanket and whispered thanks for the rain and the singing and new beginnings. I still couldn't bring myself to pray like I used to, giving thanks and asking for strength and help. So many prayers went unanswered, and the suffering only grew. But surrounded by the beauty of the night, I couldn't help but give thanks for the rain. And I fell asleep to the sound of voices, talking softly in the dark next door, as they too gave thanks.

****

We left later than usual on Monday morning. The vehicles were packed with staff, patients and babies on our way south. We planned to assess an old village, knowing of its past insecurity and the growing numbers of displaced now moving to the area. We planned to drop off the three patients and their babies along the way, saving them hours of exhausting travel by foot.

My impatience exploded as the team stood watching me work: carrying, lifting and organising the vehicles while they reclined in the shade. Sometimes those men drove me crazy as they reverted to the Sudanese way — the women worked while the men relaxed. When we finally drove out of the compound at 8 o'clock in a cloud of dust and flies, my head ached. Karen sat in the vehicle behind, her eyes closed and cigarette in her hand. It was still too early for her.

Two hours later my impatience had eased. We drove past green grassy fields and watched children playing in mud puddles. The team softened me with their singing and their eternal optimism that everything would be all right.

We arrived in the village a little after 10 a.m. Breakfast was replaced by fatuur in Darfur — a mid-morning meal that could stretch on for hours. With people, bags, babies and water finally unloaded in the marketplace we were ready for fatuur. I just hoped it would be a short one. The MSF circus had come to town! The growing crowd certainly seemed amused by our presence as we all sat squeezed into the back of one vehicle to eat.

When the plates were empty, hands wiped clean on our trousers and the vehicle floor swept free of salad, bread and bean stew we started to work. After a short meeting to discuss our plan of action, most of the team dispersed. They were off to talk to women in each household, with clipboards in hand. What was life like, were things getting better, did they feel safe? Women hold the key to every community. They may not be invited to meetings or hold positions of importance on village boards, but they know the inner workings of their community.

But I'm sure our team learned more about village gossip that day than they did about security and health in the village. Eight young Sudanese men with big smiles and smart new T-shirts marched into their homes and the young girls fluttered. It certainly got tongues wagging — by midday the old women had organised a group of pretty young women as prospective wives. They stood smiling and blushing by our vehicles in the marketplace. We left them to work and went in search of the Oomda.

Karen, Peter and I were shown into one of the small tuckuls to meet the community leaders. Women may hold the key but men still have the power. Peter walked in first. Being male and a Dinka he was a step outside of local tribal politics. And we used every advantage to get to know communities.

We sat together, squeezed onto a hard bag of grain in the cool, dim hut. Men ducked in periodically, taking a seat on the ground, their jelabiya gowns pulled tightly around their knees. No one was in a hurry. Not all were leaders but if there was a meeting happening, the men wanted to be involved.

The Oomda arrived when the room was full. As the most senior man in the district he commanded respect. Karen and I were instructed to give our names; birth name, mother's name, father's name, married name, which we both duly did. Karen and I made up married names to avoid the usual follow-on conversations: 'The Importance of Marriage' and 'Why a Sudanese Husband is Good for a White Woman'. We then waited while the designated scribe was sent off to look for a pen and paper so the Oomda could record the information.

Our unmarried status was a constant source of interest. I was offered a husband regularly, any size or shape, I only had to ask. Or I could have a brother to keep me safe, someone to be my protector. Surrounded by village leaders in other meetings, we were asked how and why we were not married. MSF seemed to have too many unmarried women, they said. And this was a worry for them. Women need a husband, a man who will provide for us and protect us.

'The world is not a safe place for an unmarried woman,' we were told. 'A man will keep you safe.' Which was curious, given that men seemed to fuel the war around us. No one was safe in Darfur.

Despite our reassurances that women in the West were different, and that an unmarried woman was acceptable, men in Darfur would shake their heads. It was an unassailable fact — women must marry. So we gave up trying to convince them otherwise.

In the long, quiet wait while the scribe was away, I explained that I was from New Zealand.

'It will take you twenty-three hours to fly to my country,' I said to give them an idea of the distance. 'And it is three hours to fly to Khartoum.' The conversation around us stopped as Peter translated.

The Oomda put his hand to his mouth. 'Really?' he said.

'Yep, right now it's night in New Zealand,' I replied.

Peter translated and I waited to see their reaction. The Oomda sucked air in through his teeth. All around the room heads were shaking, foreheads frowning.

'Thank you for coming to Darfur,' said the Oomda at last. 'And thank you to your parents for allowing you to come so far on your own.' He put his right hand over his heart and bent his head in thanks. I blinked quickly to keep back my tears.

Three tea cups arrived on a silver-coloured tray. The scribe had still not returned. We sipped the tea slowly while the men watched us, sitting in the shadowy cool. They couldn't afford tea and sugar for themselves. As I sat drinking I looked back at our hosts. They were hungry, war-weary men with holes in their shoes. We hadn't yet started our questions or stated the purpose of our visit. But their hospitality flowed over us. Even now the memory of those dignified men nourishes and sustains me. They gave their gratitude to my parents and their thanks for my visit, asking nothing in return.

I closed my eyes for a moment, overwhelmed yet again by their kindness and gratitude and ashamed by how little we ever offer them in their time of need. The war, our inadequate supply of resources and endless bureaucracy stifled our every attempt. And at home these men meant nothing to my friends, neighbours and colleagues as people closed their ears to the war.

We drank our tea and learned about their lives. More displaced people were arriving in the village as the fighting in the north pushed them on. They had no seeds or tools for planting and the rains had already come. The Oomda worried for their children and the long rainy days ahead. We sat and listened but there was little we could do. Our own warehouse was empty and the number of people who needed supplies grew every day. Anticipating their needs and ordering the resources to match them was difficult. It could take months to get more blankets and sheets of plastic. And it wasn't our responsibility to supply them with tools. Others were trying but it was never enough. But we told them we'd try. We have to keep trying, I thought. Because they deserved more, those dignified men with their sad, sad eyes.

****

Later that week we explored closer to home. We visited the camp for the displaced south of Muhajariya. I had become used to the crowded, noisy bustle of the north camp with their plastic-covered shelters and long queues at every water point. We drove through the camp two or three days a week as we went about our work. The south camp was different. It was more barren than the north, with fewer shelters scattered over the plain. More desolate, more battered by the daily sand storms that sucked the life from the land as the rainy season started.

We wanted to talk to new arrivals and to learn of their lives. The heat of the wind was exhausting. It was like standing in front of a fire, eyes squeezed shut to the flames. My skin prickled and stung as eddies of scorching heat came and went. There was no escape.

The air was brown with sand. Children stood together with their eyes narrowed, trying to watch us as they were battered by the wind. Peter and I stood shaking hands with the men but I couldn't concentrate. Their words were lost in the roaring wind around us. We ducked into an abandoned shelter. The entrance was low, with sticks and thatching creating barbs to catch my clothes as I crawled and stumbled in. The others folded themselves gracefully, drawing their jelabiya gowns in close before they bent low to enter the hut.

Inside the air was gritty, a light rain of sand fell through every hole and break in the plastic-covered roof. One of the women scratched patterns in the sand as she talked, one hand protecting her eyes from the falling sand and hiding her tears as she told us her story. Another story of loss and fear.

Some men came to join us, their heads bound with lengths of white cloth to protect them from the fury outside. Their eyes were all I could see as they talked and nodded. It looked so exotic, that godforsaken place with those beautiful people and their sorrowful eyes. I wished for a camera, a way to capture the moment so that others could see. But all I could do was listen, wipe the sand from my face and watch them as they talked. They had given up asking for help in their camp. Our small water point saved them walking far in the heat but their food supplies had dwindled and their days were unbearable. We struggled to provide enough water to the new arrivals on the north side of town. These people sat at our back door and waited, hoping that more could be found for them.

'We will try,' I told them as we bent down to leave.

'Inshallah you will help us,' replied one of the men. 'We can do nothing for ourselves.'

****

After a week of stifling heat the rains started again. Tall columns of cloud built in the west and the air was heavy with the smell of rain. I couldn't sleep as the first drops started to fall that night. It should have been peaceful; we had been longing for rainy evenings after a week of building heat. But instead I kept picturing all the new arrivals on the edge of town and those still hiding in the bush as they huddled under trees or in makeshift shelters. They looked hopeless and tired and now they would be wet. My feelings of purpose and achievement in Muhajariya faded as I thought of the displaced. For all our clinics, our donations of plastic sheeting and attempts to talk and listen to them, how much were we really achieving? I fell into bed exhausted at the end of each day, at least knowing I had tried my best for the people around me. But we missed so many, families hidden from us as they ran, children dying in the sun as they waited for peace. What was the point in even trying when we failed so many?

What would people say at home if they were driven from their own homes and had to live as people do here, I wondered. Would they refuse to leave? Would they phone the police? Just imagine the unhappiness and the outrage as they left, their children crying in the dark. Then imagine the scene in the rain. It would never happen at home.

Dave reminded me often that I couldn't fix every problem. That I needed to prioritise the problems that we found. We walked from group to group each day, looking into shelters to learn about their lives and to find out how they were. Families just sat together and watched us. They didn't expect much any more.

We collected a list of what they needed. Each item was priority number one — shelter, water, food and jerry cans. None would buy them happiness and none would meet all their needs. I'd empty my bank account at home to buy the little that would keep them alive if I could. But each time we heard the same answers and we'd shake our heads at the unfairness; not enough resources, not enough time, it simply isn't possible.

'There's a war on, Lisa. You have to prioritise.'

'You try looking them in the eye and telling them no,' I wanted to shout. 'You sit and listen to them cry or scratch circles in the sand when they tell you the story of their lives. Please don't make me do it again.' But it was no use — there weren't enough resources to help everyone. It was that simple. That night my eyes were wide open as I listened to the rain, picturing families hiding in the bush.

I was listening to the rain drip through my roof when I heard Harold's radio crackling in the tuckul next door. It was past 11 p.m.

'I can't hear you,' I heard him shout as the rain pelted down.

'They need the surgeon in the hospital, there's a woman in labour,' shouted Peter over the radio, translating for the exasperated nurse. I gave up trying to sleep, so I struggled out of my wet sheets and called out to Harold.

'Do you want an extra pair of hands?' I shouted into the rain. He was our surgeon and the most senior in our team.

'Ja, ja,' he called back. 'Let's go together.' I loved Harold's soft German accent and his calm gentle ways. In the midst of any storm he was always unflustered, ever the gentleman. He reached for my hand as he stood in the dark, and together we slipped and skidded our way to the office.

I stood in the lamplight watching streams of water pour off the iron roof while we waited for Dave. The rest of the team was already in the hospital and we couldn't leave one expat behind alone in the compound. If most of the team were in the hospital then we all had to go. So the three of us drove through the rain together, peering through the windscreen into the night.

We arrived at the clinic and jumped out onto the muddy track. Harold and Dave joined the others in the operating theatre. I left them to struggle with the generator and to dry the light fittings that dripped from the theatre's ceiling. Karen had been in the hospital for hours and she was searching through the muddled tangle of keys to open all the cupboards.

I went to look for Ellie. If there was a woman in labour then I knew where Ellie would be. I put the torch inside my sleeve to keep it dry and walked slowly through the rain to the delivery room. I turned down the narrow pathway and found myself walking through a river that was soon up to my knees. Builders' bricks, pieces of wood and lost shoes were stuck in the mud along the path. I tripped over every one as I waded slowly in the dark.

Inside, Ellie had her labouring woman warm and dry. She was covered with a blanket and surrounded by her family. She was 18 years old and had been in labour for four days.

'Circumcised women go through this hell every week,' Ellie muttered. 'I fuckin' hate it!'

I stood at the door, dripping in my raincoat, leaving puddles on the dry concrete floor. Ellie crossed the room and handed me a kerosene lantern.

'Take her to the theatre,' she said, turning and walking back to the bed. 'I've got more work to do.'

'Are you crazy?' I asked. 'It's pouring out there, the lantern won't last a second and she can't walk through that river.'

'Well, I don't bloody care how you do it,' she said in her Australian drawl. 'Just get her there. I've got another one now, just arrived. Three days' labour. It fuckin' chokes me!' She turned and disappeared behind a curtain.

With her sister to help me, we guided the young girl towards the door. The rain thundered down around us, lightning flashed as we hesitated on the top step. The six-inch drop down into the river sent us all tumbling. I fell against the wall, tripping on an underwater stone. I caught her as I fell.

Her sister stood behind us, carrying the bag of intravenous fluids and her catheter. 'Malesh, malesh,' she said, clicking her tongue. Sorry, sorry. 'This is not good.' Even with her hands full, she managed to reach out, rubbing her arm with encouragement. 'Don't worry. No problem, soon we will be there.'

What a sight we must have been, inching our way along the path in the dark. I lit the way with the torch in my sleeve, my other arm holding the young girl around the waist to steady her exhausted body. We stopped every few seconds as she leaned against me, too tired to go on. Without raincoats or umbrellas the two of them were soaked in seconds, their dresses clinging to their bodies, and their feet cold in the water.

We arrived at the entrance to the operating theatre after what seemed an eternity. We stood dripping and shivering on the verandah. Dave pushed the fly screen open and we stepped into the light, dry room.

'Get inside,' he said as we stumbled past. 'You guys are wet.'

'No kidding, Sherlock,' I muttered.

She climbed up the small wooden steps slowly and turned at the top to sit on the edge of the operating table. She looked so frail sitting there. Tired, wet and just too young to be suffering the trauma of a circumcised birth. Her shoulders shook with exhaustion.

Harold performed the caesarian section, while Karen gave the anaesthetic. The baby was dead. Four days of contractions had crushed and exhausted him. But the young woman survived. By the time Harold closed the wound an hour had passed. We were all yawning and aching for sleep. The two theatre staff carried her out into the rain on a stretcher and back to her family. I covered her with my raincoat as they lifted her from the table. It was precious little protection from the driving rain. But as she lay in her post-anaesthetic sleep I couldn't let her shiver in the rain.

It was 1 a.m. by the time we shuffled back into the office. Karen and Ellie stayed in the clinic, watching over the new woman in labour. Watching and waiting, hoping that this baby would survive. I sat in the office, my torch lighting the page, and started to read my book; *Shantaram*. A tale of life and suffering and love. In those pages I ran away to India to forget the misery of Darfur. The rain hammered down on the iron roof above me. My bed would be soaked after a night of hard rain. So I sat with the hedgehogs and read until dawn, pausing just once to change my batteries when the torch light started to fade. Escaping the rain and dreams of people hiding in the bush. And hoping and praying that the next baby would live.

****

Team life was challenging. Some days we laughed and pulled together and some days we wanted to pull each other apart. We woke up each day and stood waiting at the water barrel to brush our teeth. Karen appeared much later. Craig showered each morning when the water was still icy cold. We listened as he oohed and ahhed in the cool morning air, as the water hit his warm, sleepy skin. The rest of us waited until dusk. The water barrel was warmed by the heat of the day, giving a heavenly bathe in the evening light. Behind the fence young children herded cattle towards the wells and we heard them whisper and giggle as they peeped through the fence into our compound, trying to see the kawadjas (white people) in their home.

Every morning Craig, Harold and Gertrude drove to the hospital at 8 a.m. Some days I envied their routine, their safe days surrounded by the sick and healing.

'Come, come, come,' Harold would call as he sat on the back seat, the vehicle ready to go. And Craig would hop and stumble out of the gate, a piece of toast still in his mouth.

When we stayed in Muhajariya, Karen and I took some time to just sit in the quiet of the morning after the others had left. Amna swept the sand around us, leaving us coughing in the clouds of dust and leaves.

'Can you wait one hour?' I asked every day. 'The coughing is not good!'

And every day she smiled. 'No problem,' and she moved two feet to the left. The storm of sand and coughing followed her each time. I gave up asking after a month, and we sat in the office instead.

Life in the office had its routine, as the staff went about their work. Radio calls to Nyala and staff complaints about pay seemed to fill their days. When any MSF vehicle was on the move in South Darfur, the office staff relayed its position, the numbers of people on board and their destination. Abraham radioed the information to Nyala every thirty minutes until each journey was over. Every vehicle movement and every staff member could be traced by Nyala in a land where the situation could change in an instant. An armed hold-up, robbery or intimidation could happen at any time. Yet again, nothing was as simple as it seemed.

When the team returned for lunch, we sat together and shared stories from the day. Mona's spaghetti stew and baked bean salad were usual on weekdays. I sat and stirred the food, hoping that mixed together it would taste better. We never discovered where and how the ladies learned to cook. The food was unappetising, but painstakingly prepared. Each lunch time was the same. Craig complained. Harold sat quietly and nodded to himself. Gertrude gave us feedback on patients we had brought to the hospital from our faraway clinics. Jack ate quickly so he could return to the warehouse. And Dave and Karen hid in clouds of smoke as they relaxed in the midst of the talking. Ellie usually stayed behind in the clinic, guiding another young mother through the trauma of birth.

Other expats came and went: visitors, specialists from HQ in Amsterdam and coordinators from Nyala. The tide of the hospital swept them all along and we soon forgot they were there. There were always new faces, those coming to examine the project, to write reports or to create more work for us as they introduced new spreadsheets or data collection forms. We left them to it, lost in our own work until a meeting was called.

For Karen and me, our office days were precious as we wrote reports on our clinics and our findings from the bush. Each time we hoped it would be different, that we'd get permission and the resources to head back to those groups with all that they needed to make it through the week. So we made plans to look for new groups that we heard about each week. Surely we could help some of them, I kept thinking. We have to keep trying.

Each evening we came together, showered and refreshed, to share stories from the day. Our bathroom was quite simple, with its smooth concrete floor and high sorghum fence. The water barrel, a jug and a small black bucket. Jack introduced a luxury — two garish flower-shaped mirrors hung from the sorghum wall, one red and one blue. I tried to avoid looking at them, my sad, tired eyes reflected my soul more than I wanted to see. I had saved a pile of toiletries, some luxury to lighten my sunset hours. Pears soap, sweet-smelling lotions and a stack of face masks to soothe away the day. We suspected that Amna had developed a taste for our toiletries, Ellie, Karen and I. Each week we found something missing in our tiny, muddled tuckuls. So we shared what little we had, not having the energy to deny her the few treats she found.

And so the days passed, in routine and with purpose. The others off to the hospital and us to the mobile clinics. I had already been in Darfur for seven months. With only two months left I felt a screaming sense of urgency in our work. So much to do and so little time!

I couldn't help but feel the others were lucky in their ignorance, safe in their quiet familiar days. They listened as we told them stories of loss and fear and need. But they didn't feel the sun burn or hear the tug of plastic in the trees as they stood watching the frightened families, hiding from the war. Craig nodded and Harold shook his head, but they didn't really know. I wished with every breath that the displaced would go away. If we couldn't help them and the war kept pushing them on, why did I have to keep seeing them and listening to their stories? Nightmares played with my fears, leaving me panting and afraid to go to sleep some nights. I saw their eyes and heard their screams and watched as they burned in the flames. I envied the ignorance of others.

****

The clinic in Labado became busier as the weeks passed. We saw an increase in the number of malnourished children belonging to displaced families, and in diarrhoea and dehydration as families started to drink from waterholes and open wells as they filled with the rain. The workload was still bearable but I faltered when Karen left again for Khartoum. This time she left on holiday, an overdue break for her weary body and tiring spirit. We lay in the dark and talked of Egypt and the luxuries that awaited her there. I worried how I'd manage with my right hand so far away. I didn't have to worry — Jack stepped forward, smiling.

'How can I help, Lisa?' he asked when she left. That was all I needed, a helping hand and we were off.

We arrived in Labado the next day, the mobile team with Jack in one vehicle and me trailing behind with Ali in the other. The night had been long and my dreams left me tired, so I was grateful for the quiet on the hour-long journey.

'Music?' asked Ali when we passed the edge of town. 'I have Bob Marley.' So we listened to Bob for the rest of the journey, Ali tapping gently on the wheel as he drove.

When we got to Labado my first thought was 'chaos'. The normally wide empty verandah was crowded, sick children lay everywhere while their parents sat fanning them frantically. I negotiated my way through the gate and past all the animals. Donkeys, carts and camels blocked the entrance. Donkey carts always meant trouble — they were used to carry the unconscious and dying.

'Please come quickly,' called the guard. 'These children are sick.'

I left Jack to unpack the vehicles while Issa, Ibrahim and I moved from mat to mat, examining the children.

'Diarrhoea and fever over here,' I called. 'What about you guys?'

'Same here,' said Issa. 'We just start working early. See you for lunch!' And he disappeared into his consultation room with the first patient carried in behind him.

I pulled pieces of paper from my pocket. Moving from child to child I felt, listened and looked at each little body, trying to identify the sickest ones first. I handed the paper to the parents of the sickest children only. They were numbered from one to twelve with hasty scrawling strokes.

'Bring in these ones,' I asked Abdulla, our local drug dispenser. 'Number one first.' And I turned to go inside.

I walked into a consultation room and tried to pull open the metal shutters. They creaked as the old, rusty hinges twisted. With the shutters closed the room was quite dark and I could barely see my hands. I climbed up on the windowsill and dragged open the bolt at the top. A big black spider ran over the bolt and down my arm.

'Bloody spiders,' I muttered, shaking my arm and trying to not fall off the sill. With the window open and the cobwebs pulled from my knees I was ready to start work.

I heard the sound of an aeroplane and looked out through the metal grill. I held my breath. In the courtyard behind the clinic the patients and caregivers stood or sat in silence, all looking up.

'Antonov,' said a man standing outside the window. 'Ma tamam.' Not good. He shook his head. Antonov planes were used for aerial bombing. Their sound was distinctive. No one moved for several minutes as they listened and waited. The plane passed overhead, too high for a bombing raid. I moved away from the window when the crowds started to relax. If they relaxed then the threat had passed. There was too much work to do for me to worry unnecessarily.

'Okay, bring in the first one,' I called to Ibrahim.

Peter came in behind them. 'How can I help you?' he asked, his face serious.

'Let's start at the beginning and just keep going.' With twelve seriously ill children lying just outside my door we had to work quickly. Darfur had taught me to stop, take a breath and do as much work as I could without panic or fear. Sometimes I remembered the lesson and sometimes I forgot. That day I remembered and we got on with our work.

By mid-morning the crowd was thinning as the less serious cases were sent home and the day-care cases lay outside. But there was still so much to do. Outside in the shade some children lay stretched out on mats. Each parent trickled rehydration solution gently into their child's mouth, whispering and praying in a world of their own. They'd received antibiotics and paracetamol and the rest was up to the children. We were winning outside. The sickest ones lay inside, each with an intravenous line in a thin arm as we fought to beat the dehydration caused by giardia. All the children had been drinking contaminated water.

Jack had volunteered to help. He worked in the pharmacy, urging his little baby to live. The baby boy was seriously ill with pneumonia and dehydration. His three-month-old body was too hot and exhausted after four days of battling the infection. I showed him what to do and had left him to work earlier that morning. Jack knelt beside the mother and wrapped the baby in a wet towel. His big hands looked awkward as he worked, the towel a tangle of wet clothes, nappy and sand. Every time he dripped water into the infant's mouth his lips pursed with concentration, his forehead creased. He was a cricket-playing lad from Leeds, not a doctor, but he worked with such concentration.

He stood as I came to check on them an hour later. His trousers were wet where the cooling water had spilled as he fought to bring down the baby's temperature.

'I think we're doing okay, Lisa,' he said. 'I'm trying, anyway.'

The baby's mother still held him, her back against the wall, her long, thin legs stretched out in front of her. The wet towel had left her clothes damp and the flies sat drinking the moisture. She closed her eyes and took a deep breath, exhausted.

'Thank you for helping. I don't know how we'd manage without you today,' I said, trying to encourage him while somewhere a guard called my name.

He smiled and rubbed a sandy hand across his forehead.

I knelt down to check the baby, pulling open the wet towel. He was so thin, his breathing ragged and shallow. And as I watched his fevered body, now cool from the towel, he took his last breath. Like a candle blown out he died. I looked up at Jack.

'He's gone,' I said.

Jack closed his eyes and his shoulders fell forward.

'He can't be. I've been watching him for a long time.' He opened the towel and looked over my shoulder. 'But I was trying,' he said quietly. 'I did what you said.'

'I know you did,' I replied. 'And now another baby needs you. All you can do is try. That's what all of us do, every day. Sometimes it works and sometimes it doesn't.'

We stood as the young mother started to cry, holding the wet bundle of towels on her lap as she rocked back and forth.

'I'm sorry,' I said as the rest of the family rushed in. 'I'm so sorry.' They sat around her and prayed while they stroked the mother's arms and legs, wailing for the lost life. Another child taken and there was nothing they could do.

I led Jack next door and found him another sick child to care for. The clinic buzzed with the sound of a hundred voices, all talking and complaining. Every now and then a guard shouted as he tried to organise the crowd, herding new arrivals into the waiting area. The women shouted back and babies started to cry.

When I had shown Jack what to do I left him. He was down on his knees, murmuring to another sick baby as he drizzled cold water into his mouth. I rested my forehead against the doorframe as I watched them together. If anything gave me hope in Darfur, it was seeing compassion in others. What else was there to hope for?

At the end of the day most of the children were awake and their parents were smiling with relief. The anxious buzz of conversation had calmed and women talked together in the shade. Mona, the tea lady, carried cups of tea as women called her over with a wave. Long-term solutions were almost impossible in a war and we were only barely keeping these children alive week by week. They needed water from a deep borehole, clean and free. Boiling water was impossible for them, there wasn't enough firewood for everyone to use. If they couldn't afford to buy clean water then they would continue to use water they found in puddles. The diarrhoea would never end. But for now they had rehydration solution and medication, and the children were alive. It was all we could do.

I sat down at the table beside Peter.

'I got some tea for you,' he said as he handed me a glass. Mona had left two cups to sustain us through the morning. He leaned back on his chair and called for the next patient. I sipped from the glass and took a deep breath. One by one, that's all we can do, I thought. Looking at the big picture is too frightening.

A middle-aged mother entered the room, leading her son by the hand. He was three years old, and his name is forever etched on my heart: Musa. They sat on the chairs opposite me and I waited for the woman to speak. I reached for a new health card and wrote the date in the margin. A little voice piped up beside her

'My name Musa. I am not sick and I want your pen.' He spoke in Arabic and he looked at me quite seriously, his head to one side.

I had to bite my cheeks to stop myself laughing at his seriousness. I put out my hand to shake his and introduce myself. He slapped my hand with a confident swing. Not aggressive, but *pow*! He raised his eyebrows. The challenge was there.

His mother said he was not eating so I leaned forward to examine him. I tickled his stomach, looking for a smile.

Not funny, said his eyes.

I asked him to poke out his tongue, as I did with every child.

Don't be ridiculous, said the eyes again, and he folded his arms and leaned back in his chair. He had confidence and presence with a cheeky twinkle in his eyes. Beside me Peter was choking himself with laughter. His message was clear: my name is Musa, don't forget it, and don't treat me like a child.

I examined him as best I could. His attitude came from a strong, well-fed body. His father was a local merchant and the family could afford what they needed. There was nothing wrong with him. I wrote down the important details while Musa watched me in silence. I wrote with my new pen, a present sent from New Zealand by my mother. She sent me care parcels every few months — skin cream, moisturiser, chocolate and more. We waited for the mail each week, when the pouch arrived from Khartoum. We had all taken it in turns to carry the green, plastic pouch, knowing that it contained untold gifts. DVDs, herbs and spices, chocolate and magazines that we could share and enjoy.

I reassured Musa's mother, telling her that everything was fine. Musa sat beside her and pursed his lips together. I stood up as they left. Musa gave me an over-the-shoulder wave as he sauntered off behind his mother.

'See you next time,' he called. 'And thank you for the pen.'

My special new pen sat tucked in the neck of his T-shirt. How could I resist his charms?

When we were ready to leave I wandered round to the back of the clinic, looking for Jack. He lay stretched out on the mat, with the baby snuggling beside him. They talked in smiles and whispers as the boy played with Jack's yellow wristband.

'Look at this,' he said as I knelt beside them. 'This one's alive and he likes me.'

All afternoon Jack had been nursing the baby to life with his green bottle of rehydration solution and the patience of a healer. He was not going to let this one die.

'Come on, little man,' he said as he stood up. 'Time to go home.' He lifted the baby from the mat, and watched as the mother tied him safely to her back.

'Shukran,' she said, smiling at Jack and touching her heart.

He waved as they walked away. Another small success in a hot and crowded day. And perhaps it was just enough to carry us through the unhappiness around us and into a new day. We lost three children that day, one more died in our hospital that night after we brought her back to Muhajariya for more treatment. Four needless deaths, four children who needed clean water and medicine to give them a chance. They had no chance. But we had to keep going, one by one for the sake of the others. What else could we do?

CHAPTER NINE

Everything changed for me the day the soldiers attacked Arto —
safety, trust and my belief that Darfur had hope. After weeks of calm
and small successes before the attack, I was happy. Walking through
the marketplace I recognised faces and had my favourite shops:
Omar's knickknack shop and Hawa's coffee shop. Children still ran
behind me as I walked the sandy tracks to the clinic. Now they called
me Lisa and giggled as they hid behind fences and trees. Life was
good. I had forgotten that in Darfur, nothing is as it seems.

Karen was still on holiday. With the mobile team I juggled the
workload and we still managed to get out of town to work. We knew
that Karen could be away much longer as giardia played havoc with
her gut. Her weight continued to fall and she winced with pain
when her bowel flared and twisted every day. She needed more than
hotels in Egypt to heal her wounds. I didn't realise when she left
how much I'd miss her in the weeks ahead.

It was Monday. We planned a gentle day to recover from the
rush and chaos of Labado the day before. The deaths of the four
children in Labado left us all feeling low, dispirited at the start of
a new week. But on Monday I had a day of paperwork and report
writing ahead of me, with a cup of strong coffee in one hand. For
once I wished I smoked. The day passed quietly, in contemplation,

as I typed reports, ordered stock for the week and sat listening to the hedgehog that slept in a hole beside my chair. He snored and grunted through the heat of the day, waking only to turn and rustle while he found a more comfortable spot to lie.

It was my turn to do the night round that evening. I loved the night-time world of the hospital, with lamplight and sleepy voices, just me and the nurses in the quiet of the night. Ali drove slowly as we bumped along empty tracks. The orange light flashed on the roof rack, throwing a blink of light on each compound as we passed. Cattle, goats and donkeys watched us from their roadside shelters.

'Let's make this a quick ward round, Ali,' I said, my arm hanging out the window in the warm night air. 'I think we're both tired tonight.'

But it was me who was tired, Ali always looked at peace. He smiled a soft, slow smile and nodded every time.

'Inshallah,' he replied. God willing.

As we approached the clinic I reached for my solar light and prepared to get out. The old guard stood at the gate and put his hand out to stop us reversing inside.

'What's he saying?' I asked. I searched the darkness for a donkey cart that usually heralded trouble. Obstructed labour, a dying child or some such tragedy often waited in the night.

'There is a problem,' Ali translated and he turned off the engine. We sat in the dark and I waited while Ali listened to the guard.

'Come with me,' he finally said, opening the door. 'A man wants to meet you.'

That didn't bode well.

I followed as he crossed the open ground in front of the clinic. In the daylight the area was full of animals: donkeys and camels waited in the sun while their owners sat in the clinic. But now it was deserted.

'Wait for me,' I whispered, stumbling in the dark. I had left my lantern in the car.

When my eyes grew accustomed to the dark I saw a group of men approach us. SLA soldiers. I stood next to Ali and waited while one spoke. I couldn't see his face and his voice was quiet in the dark.

'There's been an attack,' Ali said. 'And they are asking for our help.'

I held my breath and waited for the blow. Would the attack spread, would it hit Muhajariya next? Would we have time to warn the others? Behind me more than fifty civilian patients lay sleeping in the hospital. Another hundred or so family members slept beside them, on mats and blankets on the sand. Where could we hide all of them if an attack came out of the darkness? My mind was racing.

'There has been an attack on Arto and the wounded are coming tonight,' he said quietly. 'The first truck will arrive in two hours, the second one after that. We must be ready.'

Arto was a village 60 km north of Muhajariya. It sat close to the front line, that nebulous scratch in the sand that men fought over every week. It had been a safe haven for the displaced who fled Saleem. I'd heard its name often from those who sat outside the African Union's compound. And they had been hit in an attack that morning. I felt sick.

When the soldier finished talking he stepped back and the group disappeared into the darkness.

'You go and tell the clinic staff,' I said at last. 'I'll call Jack and organise the rest.'

Ali and I walked back to the vehicle in silence. I watched as he walked through the front gate of the hospital and soon he was surrounded by the staff. I reached in through the window and picked up the radio. Dave had left on holiday so our team was smaller than ever.

'Jack, this is Lisa. We've got a problem.'

The drive back to the compound was achingly slow. My mind raced with thoughts of what we needed. Harold would operate on the wounded and Bridgette, the new nurse, would run the second operating table on her own. Craig and I would work outside, stabilising patients while they waited their turn in theatre. Gertrude would supervise the post-operative patients while Ellie watched the rest of the hospital. At home in New Zealand there had been order and other teams to call on when we needed help. We performed assessments, blood tests, X-rays and referrals as team members worked together in a 'real' hospital. But here in the dark the wounded would arrive on trucks. They would be dropped at our feet on the sand as the soldiers unloaded, and our work would begin. Without a laboratory, oxygen, X-rays or blood transfusions to help us. We would have to be a strong team if we were to make it through the night.

I leapt from the vehicle and ran down the hill to the office.

'We've got two hours to get organised. Ali's waiting in the car, let's go.' I stood in the doorway of the office and blinked in the bright light.

Craig pushed past me, pulling on an old MSF T-shirt.

'You can leave it to us now, Lisa. You go back to bed.'

I turned to look at him as he walked up to the vehicle.

'Excuse me?' I said, not believing my ears.

'Thank you for the message. We will take it from here.' He waited in the shadows while Harold and Gertrude pulled on baggy T-shirts and followed him out the door. All staff had to be clearly identifiable at all times of the day and night so everyone wore an MSF T-shirt. If trouble hit town at least they would know who we were. I watched as the three of them disappeared. Jack came running from his tuckul.

'Wait for me,' he called.

And then they were gone.

'But, but …' I started to run after them.

'Don't bother, I've already tried,' said Bridgette. 'Craig said the "real" medics will manage fine without us and that the girls can stay at home.' She sounded bitter.

'Why that …' My anger suddenly flared. Two commercial trucks were lumbering through the night towards Muhajariya and Craig could manage them without us?

'But we're a team,' I protested.

'Sit down, honey.' Bridgette dragged a chair over to where she had been sitting. 'And let's change the subject.'

Bridgette had arrived two months before and led a rather frustrated life in Muhajariya. The outreach worker programme I ran in Saleem had been informal, with my ladies cheerful and proactive as they worked in a difficult environment. Bridgette had over sixty outreach workers here and the needs and demands in Muhajariya's huge community were huge and complicated. She had teams of men and women who represented nearly every tribe in Darfur. Managing a group of people always takes skill. Add tribal tension, jealousy and pride to that group and it can be like walking on egg shells while you work amongst them. At the end of each day she slumped in her chair and sighed.

'Another day over,' she'd say loudly. 'And still we got nowhere. Don't you love Darfur?'

Tribal squabbling and grievances were a very real and potentially volatile part of life in every community. And each situation had to be dealt with, while treating everyone fairly. Perceived favouritism could actually be dangerous. One sector of town needed health education, another needed roving health workers to look for sick children who weren't coming to the hospital in time. But if one sector received some input from our team then all the others wanted the same. And there wasn't enough time or resources to go around So Bridgette met with community leaders, discussed and explained and compromised day after day while her team struggled to get their work done. And so again, nothing was as simple as it seemed.

'This is not about our ego, so just let it be. If he says he can manage then leave him it to it,' she sighed in the darkness. 'We should go to bed and do as we're told.'

'But I've been in Darfur for seven months and I'm part of the team,' I started again. 'And you're a surgical nurse practitioner...' My ego was bruised but what about the patients as they were unloaded from the trucks, I worried. There was more at stake than ego.

'Just look at those hedgehogs,' she stopped me and pointed to one snuffling at the office door. 'There are doctors and there are hedgehogs in Craig's medical hierarchy. He is a doctor and you and I are hedgehogs. That's just the way it is.' She sniggered.

We sat in the dark for a while and listened to the night. The hedgehog chased beetles as they flew into the screen door, trapped. He crunched their shells and slurped water from the tap stand. I sighed. I suppose I could cope with being a hedgehog, snuffling in the dark. Let Craig's ego carry him through the night and see how he felt by daybreak, I thought to myself.

'Love it or hate it this place is still home,' said Bridgette, as she stood and stretched. 'Goodnight, little hedgehog,' she called as she disappeared round the corner.

I sat a while longer and tried to imagine the trucks driving through the night. What must it be like to be wounded as you're thrown around in the back, I wondered. Hard, cold and painful if they survived the journey at all. I didn't envy Craig's workload. But if I was being sent to bed then that's where I would go. I stepped round the hedgehog and walked to my tuckul. In the compound behind me a woman started to sing softly as her children went to sleep.

****

The following morning we sat together at breakfast. I avoided Craig's eye. I was still angry.

'How was the night?' asked Ellie, her face still lined with sleep. 'Did something happen? I slept like a bomb.'

'There was an attack yesterday and truckloads of patients arrived last night,' I said as I reached for a banana. 'But don't worry, Craig saved the day.'

'And we took care of the hedgehogs,' laughed Bridgette.

Ellie sat looking at us. She rubbed her eyes. 'You guys are fucking weird.'

The trucks had arrived and unloaded the wounded just after midnight. Men and women now filled the wards. Most families with children had fled into the bush around Arto, their wounds unseen. No one knew how many were dead. Craig, Harold and Gertrude had worked through the night. The hospital staff worked alongside them, not even stopping for a break. The following day they continued, stopping only to eat and drink when Jack brought them supplies. Gunshot wounds filled each bed and the generator rumbled non-stop while the operating theatre greeted each patient in turn.

All the while Bridgette and I watched. We went about our work and met during the day to compare notes. My clinic in Angabo was cancelled — no vehicle movements were allowed in the wake of an attack. Who knew what or where would be hit next. I thought of our regular patients, those who had walked hours to see us in Angabo. They would arrive early and stand waiting at the gate this morning. With no means of communicating with the village we couldn't tell them of our change of plans. They would hear of the attack in Arto, but still they would wait and hope. As Tuesday turned into

Wednesday they would still wait, thinking 'maybe they will come today'. And finally they would go home, as Wednesday faded and the sun started to set. Two days of waiting with their children, hoping our vehicles would arrive. The people of Darfur wait and hope and pray every day. But they are used to being let down.

****

By Wednesday my frustration had boiled over. With no Angabo clinic and my services not required in the hospital, I was restless and angry. I had fiddled and procrastinated, played with hedgehogs and watched Amna sweep the compound. I'd even tried sweeping myself. When there was so much need and desperation around us it was unbearable to just stand by and watch. Living in Darfur is an exercise in frustration. My head throbbed after another night of exhausting dreams. I turned the mirrors to the wall when I had a shower, too afraid to see the crying eyes they reflected. And I'd given up asking why; why does this war go on, why doesn't someone stop them? As much as I loved my way of life in Darfur, I would give anything to make the war stop so they didn't need us any more. I'd give up my friends, the nights under the stars, the flush of achievement at the end of a good day in a clinic. Just take away the crying, bleeding, pointless pain.

I marched into Jack's office after breakfast.

'I'm sick of doing nothing,' I announced. 'And I am worth more than a bloody hedgehog.'

Jack looked at me and frowned. 'A hedgehog?' he asked.

'Forget the hedgehog. The others are working flat out in the hospital. Bridgette's pushing shit uphill with her outreach workers and getting nowhere. And I'm here doing nothing. I've had enough!' I stamped my foot.

'Just relax,' said Jack. 'If you're not needed, then put your feet up. Enjoy the break.'

'Break? Relax?' I spluttered. 'This is Darfur. When is there *ever* nothing to do?'

'Okay, so what do you want me to do about it?' he asked, leaning back in his chair.

'I want to talk to each patient and listen to their stories. I want to find out how they're coping and see what they need. I want to do something to help these people and make a difference in this fucking war. That is what I want.' I felt calmer now he was listening.

'Okay, take Abraham from the office and get down to the hospital and start,' he said. 'And whatever you do, relax!'

****

An hour later I stood with Abraham in the shade of a tree outside the hospital.

'I want to hear their stories,' I explained as I pulled a pen from my bag. 'Just listen.' There were no ulterior motives. I just wanted to show people we could listen and if they needed us we could help. If it was the last thing I did in Darfur I would help these people if they asked.

'All right,' said Abraham. 'But you will listen with tears. Are you ready?'

I nodded.

Abraham was the rock of Muhajariya. He was the one member of the team around which all things revolved. Without him Muhajariya simply wouldn't be. He was a local man, but had spent years working abroad. His polished English, subtle humour and passion for European football lifted him out of Muhajariya at a glance. Barcelona, Real Madrid and Manchester United peppered every conversation. When I first mentioned David Beckham, the only footballer I knew, his eyes sparkled.

'And what about Ronaldo and his game last month? Barcelona versus Chelsea, did you see it? What did you think?' he asked as he leaned forward.

I shook my head. 'Only David Beckham,' I said and hung my head with mock shame. Abraham was very disappointed.

But standing outside the clinic that day football was forgotten. With patience we were going to listen to whoever wanted to talk. It was a day I will never forget.

I followed Abraham as he crossed the compound. My skin burned in the sun and the glare of the light hurt my eyes. In the male ward blankets were hung across the doors to keep out the light. Above us the corrugated iron roof clicked and popped in the heat. We approached the first bed slowly. I waited while Abraham explained to the family why we were there. The patient lay on the bed, a colourful sheet covering his legs. He had been shot in the legs as he ran away from his attackers. Family members stood around him, worried uncles and cousins who had come to hear the news.

'They came from every direction and I tried to run,' Abraham translated as the patient started to speak. 'I shouted to my wife to run and I watched her take the children to the trees. But my camels, my camels,' he covered his eyes and took a deep breath. 'I have no money, no home and no land. But I had my camels. And they stole them all away.' You don't often see a grown man cry, it's not what men do, especially in Darfur. But his shoulders shook and he covered his face. He had lost everything he owned, and I could not imagine how that felt.

When he had finished talking he wiped the tears from his face with the back of his hand.

'You can write it if you want,' he said. 'But no one will listen.

They never do. You will leave this place and you will forget us. Everyone forgets us.' He turned his head away and our meeting came to an abrupt end.

I felt sick inside as Abraham translated his words. I knew they were true. What else could I do, but hope and pray that this time someone else would listen. I murmured an apology and we moved to the next bed.

'Hello, my name is Lisa. Could we talk to you?' I asked. When the family nodded I knelt down beside the bed. Abraham sat beside me, his knees drawn up under his chin, and we started again.

'We saw the soldiers first,' said the man. His chest was covered with bandages and flies sat in clusters on his blood-stained arms. With every sway of his wife's paper fan the flies rose, only to come to rest again with each pause.

'The soldiers came in vehicles and they ran around the village. When I ran from my house I heard one man shouting "Shoot him, shoot him". I saw him pointing a gun at me. Someone shot me in my arm and also in my chest. After that I went to sleep on the ground. My son watched from the trees while the Janjaweed stole everything from the village. Our mats and cooking pots and our clothes and our shoes. They tied them onto the donkey carts and took them all away. Now I have nothing and my youngest child is missing.' He closed his eyes and was quiet. 'That is all I can say,' he whispered.

We stood in the silence and I thanked them for their time. His wife resumed her fanning and the flies rose and fell with her strokes. My back was beginning to ache and my ankles scraped on the sandy floor where I sat. It was going to be a long morning.

We made our way from bed to bed, and listened while they talked. We didn't listen to gather information, rather to show them that we cared. They didn't ask for food or blankets, they just worried for their families and all were afraid to go back. I couldn't heal their wounds or take away their grief. Some just wanted to talk and their stories seemed without end. They talked of the sound of the helicopter as it circled the village before the attack, the screaming as the shooting began, with soldiers on every side. They talked of their fear as they ran with their children and the pain as they lay on the sand and waited for the end. I brushed the flies from my face and shifted my raw, aching ankles as I looked up from the floor and listened. And each time I nodded and thanked them for their time.

All around the hospital families gathered in grief and love. Cousins, in-laws and children from Muhajariya brought food and blankets and clothes to share in the quiet of the first days of grief. Even in Muhajariya possessions were scarce as people struggled to survive. But in their own poverty they shared what little they had. The hospital compound usually hummed with voices as people talked and laughed as they whiled away the time. But on that glaring Wednesday morning the hospital was quiet, despite the crowds. Groups whispered as they shared stories, women touched and healed each other in the shade. No one would shout their grief out loud, they buried it in the quiet, the way they always do.

The only noise to break the quiet came from bed four. Wailing, sobbing cries filled the air. He was twenty-five years old and he had just lost his fight for life. He and his brother had been shot from behind as they ran from the soldiers. His brother watched from the trees as the soldiers walked to where the young man had fallen. One stood with his foot on the body, another raised an axe. Again and again the axe rose and fell, his brother stopped counting the blows. As we passed his bed the young man died, his head wounds too severe to survive. Soldiers. With an axe. Shot from behind. The words throbbed in my head as I reached for Abraham. I followed him onwards, my hand on his back and my eyes blind in the roaring darkness that consumed me. I thought I would faint. Will anyone believe me when I tell them this tale? I thought. It took all my strength to keep walking.

And so the morning passed. Wave after wave of suffering until my heart felt empty and cold. We still hadn't seen the women and the midday sun was burning. Abraham and I walked to the nurses' office and sat in the shade while we drank water. Inside the nurses sat quietly, they too were aching from the attack. We closed our eyes for a while. Abraham sat beside me, his head hidden in his arms.

'Are you okay?' I asked.

'I am just praying that next time it is not my family,' his muffled voice replied. 'And I pray for their souls.'

I hadn't thought to pray. Instead I concentrated on my ankles, now red from the scuffing sand. That a man could chop at another, his axe deliberately destroying another, was beyond me. People don't do that any more, I thought. Rwanda and Sierra Leone happened long ago, and people are different now. But I saw the young man's body in front of me, saw him shiver and twitch with seizures while he lived. I had proof that people don't change. And the thought made me sick.

After a while Abraham touched my arm gently.

'Do you want to continue?' he asked. 'We can stop if you want.'

I shook my head and stood slowly. Not listening wouldn't make their stories go away. I wanted to go on.

We walked to the female ward and ducked low at the entrance. Sitting propped up in the corner was a young woman on a metal frame bed. Abraham led me there first. All around her women sat, whispering and singing in the dim light of the ward. A gauzy veil of mosquito netting hung around her, a vain attempt to keep the flies at bay.

Her breathing was shallow and her head was turned to the wall. Beside her sat an older woman, fanning her with a small piece of cardboard as she cooled her perspiring skin. The air was stifling.

'Hello, my name is Lisa,' I said, crouching beside the bed.

The women moved, some stood and stretched in the corner. They had been sitting with her for hours.

'How are you?' I asked, reaching in to touch her cheek. She was hot, fevered and in pain.

'Better,' she whispered. 'I have tablets and the pain will go.'

She was breathless after those few words. I waited.

'I can come back tomorrow,' I said after a long pause. She looked like she was falling asleep.

'No, talk now,' she said lifting her head. 'For my baby, we talk now.'

Oh no, I thought. Not a baby.

What she said took an hour, as she panted and sweated in the hot, airless dark. The flies buzzed all around us, clinging to her bandages until someone pushed them away. When she stopped talking she lay quietly, her breathing shallow with the pain. Abraham translated each time, his words quiet beside me on the bed.

'I was travelling on my camel, to see my sister for the day. My daughter was only eight days old, so I travelled slowly to be gentle for her sleep. I heard shooting sounds around me. The camel was afraid. I fell from the camel when it started to run. My baby was on my back so I made myself land on my hands. The soldiers came running to my place and I threw my baby to the bushes. I did not want them to hurt her. He started to kick me with his shoes, my head, my arms, my stomach. It hurt very much and I was telling him to stop. I heard one man say, "Shoot her in the head." Another man was laughing. He said, "No, she is a pretty girl, we will take her." They shot me here.' She pointed to her left breast. 'And they kicked me here and here.' She pulled down the sheet, and lay in her naked, swollen bruising without shame.

I pulled the sheet up, not wanting to see more of her wounds.

'When I was lying bleeding a woman came to me. She found my baby and lifted her up. She said, "If there is a brave man here, he can have this baby. Who is brave?" And she shouted to the men. She was Janjaweed. A soldier said, "Don't take the baby, this is not good." The Janjaweed laughed and then she threw my baby on the ground. The other Janjaweed stood all around me, shouting and talking about what they would do to me. I shut my eyes and I waited. I was bleeding and my baby was crying.'

I closed my eyes as she talked. Abraham had stopped translating as her breathless words took longer to form sentences. I listened as the fan swung back and forth — click, cluck, click, cluck. At the foot of the bed the baby girl lay wrapped in a red scarf. She was sleeping. I thought of another baby, alone and unwanted at the foot of a bed as it slowly died. I opened my eyes and shook my head.

The old woman with the fan had tired and she dropped it on the bed as she stood to stretch. Abraham reached for the fan. The sheet had slipped down, exposing her wounded breast. The bandage smelled of blood. In any other moment it would be unheard of for a man to be with a woman who was not his wife. Her nakedness and pain were not his to see, he didn't even know her. But Abraham was no ordinary man and this was no ordinary day. He lifted the sheet to cover her shoulders, then started to gently fan her as he murmured and nodded in the dark. Click, cluck, click, cluck. He was a gentleman and a healer, with his sad eyes and patient hand. He cooled her as he listened and his eyes were filled with tears.

When she fell silent he turned to me and he sighed.

'Do you want to hear the rest?' he asked. 'Or do you want to go home?'

I knew her story would hurt to hear, but what was my pain next to hers?

Then he relived her story for me, repeating her words as she fell asleep behind the net.

She was twenty-five years old, young and beautiful. She survived her injuries, but lost much of her breast over the following weeks. Her newborn daughter survived, her bruises and fractures healing with time. But this young woman's fear will never leave her. When will they return and what will they do? she asked herself over and over. Lying on the ground as he started to kick her, what could she do? Listening as the Janjaweed woman offered her baby as a trophy, what could she do?

She did all that a Darfuri woman can ever do in this war — she waited. Patiently, prayerfully and with hope that soon it would be over. She waited for the kicking to stop, the woman to go away and for the pain to make her go to sleep. She didn't expect help, because Darfuri people know it will never come. I sat beside her as Abraham talked and I couldn't hold back the tears any longer.

For the love of God, I wondered. When is someone going to stop this war? The beatings, kicking and murder happened every day. And this day it was me who had to listen. If others were listening would they care more? For the love of God, I prayed, please make this all go away.

****

The others continued to work on the wounded in the days that followed. The nurses and assistants walked through the hospital quietly, their laughing eyes and gentle smiles gone. They went about their work without a break, treating, dressing wounds and washing away the blood.

After the stories were recorded I left the others to work in the hospital. They didn't need extra pairs of hands, the local staff were used to dealing with these attacks. They worked round the clock to care for their patients.

We drove north towards Arto to assess the area on Thursday. Dave had returned to Muhajariya following the attack, his meeting over in Nyala. We knew there were many more displaced families now. But before we could look for them in the bush, we had to assess security out in the open. The team in Saleem would meet us on the ridge near Arto and we could talk face to face. It had been months since our last meeting.

Dave and I left after breakfast, with Peter sitting behind me on the back seat. In a land of tribal warfare we had to be careful who we worked with when tensions built up again. Being a Dinka, Peter was seen as neutral, not Darfuri at a time when neutrality really mattered. He sat tucking in his MSF T-shirt, his face serious and eyes unsmiling.

'This is not good,' he said as we left. 'They attack anyone. Maybe they will attack us. Does the T-shirt stop them?' 'They' were the government soldiers and Janjaweed.

'I don't know my friend,' I said, turning to look at him. 'But they know we are coming, we have permission to travel. They won't hurt us. They know us.'

'But what if they make a mistake?' he asked. And he sighed.

We drove slowly and close to one another, our two vehicles plain to see in the early morning light. Our T-shirts were clean and bright. No one would mistake us. Ali approached the first SLA checkpoint, his hazard lights flashing and all windows down. The soldiers walked towards us. Their heads were wrapped in layers of green cloth, with only their eyes revealed. There were no card games or smiles that day.

Peter spoke to them through the window as Dave explained our journey.

'Be careful,' said the first soldier. 'The front is on the ridge now, the fighting will happen at any time.' He slapped the side of the vehicle and gestured for us to drive on.

'If the front is on the ridge I don't like our chances of crossing it today,' said Dave when we stopped further from the checkpoint. We spoke through the open windows as the two vehicles idled. 'We'll stop below the ridge and see how we go.'

Ali drove on again and we all strained our ears for the sound of gunfire or helicopters on the wind. There was no one to talk to, no official report to tell us where to go. We would write that report when we got back. But first we had to experience it.

The landscape around us was lush after the rain and great baobab trees dotted the plains. Their thick grey branches spread in the sun and stood far taller than anything else around. Despite the desert sand and heat, grasses and shrubs still grew. Underground springs provided water and the vegetation grew thickly in dips and shallows in the ground. After the rains in the last week, a blanket of small white flowers now covered the sandy ground.

We slowed at one of the water points when Dave's vehicle stopped ahead of us. Ali pulled in front of him and parked in a small patch of shade. I climbed out of the vehicle and walked to Dave.

'So, what do we do now?' I asked, putting on my sunglasses.

'Wait and listen,' he replied. 'The team from Saleem will leave their compound soon and tell us what they see. If all goes well we'll drive up to the ridge and wait for them there. Just relax and see what happens.'

I groaned at the very idea. I was not good at relaxing. I wandered over to the hand pumps to talk to the small group of women as they filled their jerry cans. Usually the hand pumps were crowded at this hour as women queued for water from miles around. But because of the recent fighting, people stayed away. Many collected water at night, feeling safer as they stood in the open and waited. I said hello and smiled at the women but no one wanted to talk. They smiled back, but they didn't want to linger at the pumps. So I turned to walk back to Dave.

An old man had walked up to our vehicles. His clothes were threadbare, his white jelabiya gown was torn and dirty. Men value their jelabiya gowns, they treasure them and wear them with pride. But this old one pulled and tugged against his legs as the hot wind blew, dried blood covered both arms. His feet were bare, the skin dry and covered with sand. A man his age should have been resting while his family took care of him.

He stood looking in through the back window, asking Peter if he had seen his missing donkey. He had lost everything in the attack on Monday. His house, his belongings, his food and his animals. Everything.

'Please, I've lost my donkey. Have you seen her? She's brown with a white nose. She's my last donkey,' he asked.

'No sir, sorry. We haven't seen it,' said Peter through the back window.

'I need to find my donkey,' the old man repeated. 'I haven't eaten for two days. I need to sell my donkey so I have money to buy food.'

'Sorry, my friend, I can't help you,' Peter replied. We had instructions from Nyala not to linger at the water point. There was no time to search for a donkey.

I stood watching and my heart broke a little further. We were in the middle of nowhere, and it was hot. The radio call could come at any time to give us the go-ahead to drive further up the ridge. We were all feeling tense, sitting so close to the front line. And this old man was asking for our help.

Dave sat in the front seat, his face red from the heat, his cigarette hanging out the window. He pulled a chocolate biscuit from the packet beside him and offered me one.

'Dave, how can you eat in front of this man?!' I was nearly in tears listening to the old man talk. 'He hasn't eaten for two days and you're eating chocolate biscuits in front of him!'

'I was eating them before he arrived,' Dave replied. 'I didn't ask him to come over, so why should I stop? Besides, if you help one then you have to help them all. And I don't have enough biscuits for the whole of Darfur.' He held the packet out to me and waited.

I took the last biscuits and offered them to the old man. Peter reached out through the back seat window and held out his biscuits as well. He looked at me with sad eyes. I pulled a few dinar notes from my pocket and gave them to the old man quietly. He put the money and biscuits in his pocket.

'Shukran,' he said as he touched his heart. He walked away slowly, his eyes focused somewhere in the distance. And he talked quietly to himself. 'Where's my donkey? I need my donkey. Please, where is my donkey?' But there was no one to listen.

I walked behind the vehicle and sat down on the sand. Surely everyone would have done the same if they had seen his eyes. His sad, lost, hungry eyes. Oh God, why is this still happening? I said to the sand at my feet. I sat crying until I heard Dave call my name.

'Come on, Lisa, we've just had the call to move.'

Ali and Hamid started their vehicles and revved the engines, ready to go. I stood up and wiped the sand from my trousers and the tears from my eyes. It's easy when you can turn off the sound and walk out of the room, but what was I supposed to do when that man stood beside me? Eat another chocolate biscuit? My heart despaired for Darfur and the poor, hopeless souls around us.

We made it to the ridge and stood on the sandy track and waited for the others to approach from Saleem. This would be the first time

I had seen the team in four months. There were new expats now, new faces in my old, familiar compound. But the core team stayed on — Adam Ali, Musa and Ahmed, Matthew and Abdullah. As I stood in the sun I felt nervous about meeting my old friends again.

All around us SLA stood on rocky outcrops or sat watching from shady ledges. This was a major advancement in the recent weeks; taking the ridge meant the SLA had come within spitting distance of Saleem. This was serious for the government troops in Saleem. To our right a vehicle sat half hidden in the bushes. A machine gun stood on the back, rising above the branches piled around its base. Spent cartridges lay on the ground beside me.

This is real, I thought. And I felt a brief thrill of anticipation. But as we waited I pictured the old man we had met earlier. What thrill is there in his pain, what excitement in his lost eyes. I sat down on the ground and drew patterns around the cartridges with a stick. The thrill had gone.

After a few minutes I heard Dave call. 'There they are,' and he pointed to the road below us. Moving slowly along the track were two MSF vehicles. I wanted to see them all again, but my head throbbed in the glaring sunlight and my heart ached with memories.

'I just want to go home,' I said to Ali as I stood up. 'I want Bob Marley and a shower.'

'Inshallah you will have both,' he smiled. He reached up and tapped the sun visor above his seat. 'I have Mr Marley waiting for you here.'

As the vehicles drew up the ridge I felt myself getting nervous. I had heard rumours about why I was not allowed to return to Saleem. It came down to team dynamics and grudges. Toby and I had never gotten on. With his ponderous ways and his apathy even in the face of chaos, I found him exasperating. Neil and I had got off on the wrong foot, his ignorance of the project and focus on himself angered me. I tried to like him, tried to calm my fears as I listened to him talk of his home and dreams. But he wasn't the strong, dynamic person the team needed. Perhaps I pushed myself out of Saleem. I should have smiled more and been more tolerant. But my tolerance for less than the best was at an all-time low when I left Saleem.

I knew that Toby and Neil had requested I didn't return, but what about the local staff in Saleem? In my months of grieving for my old team-mates had they forgotten me and found they didn't want me either? My heart and my ego struggled as I shielded my eyes from the sun. I was about to find out as both vehicles crested the ridge.

The local commander stepped forward and he and Dave exchanged a few words. Then the soldiers pulled back into the shadows as the new arrivals climbed out of their vehicles. There was no threat to them from us. I watched as Dave shook hands with Tom, the new coordinator in Saleem. They smiled and talked as they clapped each other on the back. Today's meeting was a big step in our freedom of movement. Weekly trips between Saleem and Muhajariya had been normal when I first arrived in Saleem, seven months before. Patients were transferred to the hospital, supplies from Nyala were routed through Saleem and on to Muhajariya. But permission had been denied for any crossing of the ridge for months, while the land became increasingly contested. But now that it was confidently in SLA hands we had permission to pass.

I stood behind our open passenger door and waited shyly. I wasn't sure who had accompanied the team. I saw Rebecca step out of the second vehicle, the nurse who replaced me after my unexpected departure. The team found they needed help in my absence. But it wasn't to be me.

I started to walk towards Rebecca, to greet my colleague with the respect she deserved. And then I saw the others, standing behind her: Adam Ali, Musa and Ahmed. Adam Ali walked towards me, his arms outstretched as he smiled.

'My sister,' he said softly. 'We have missed you.' I ran towards him and held him tightly while I cried. My brother, my guardian angel and my friend. The man who protected and guided me in those frightening days of Saleem and El Wadi. It is not usual to show such emotion or to touch Sudanese men, beyond the usual greetings and gently touching each others' hearts. But I didn't care that day. I couldn't let go of Adam Ali and my tears fell, I couldn't have stopped them if I tried. Behind me Musa touched my shoulder.

'Where have you been, my sister? We have been waiting,' he said quietly. 'Everything is different now that you are gone.'

Ahmed touched my cheek. 'Don't cry,' he said. 'We are together now. Be happy for this time.'

But my tears only fell faster. My friends had missed me. Their kindness washed over me as I stood in their arms. We were surrounded by the soldiers, our feet scuffing cartridges in the sand and looking down on Saleem from the front line of war. And I wouldn't have been anywhere else in the world.

'How are you, my friends?' I asked when at last I let Adam Ali go. 'I have missed you too.'

Adam Ali led us away from the others and he stood with his back to the vehicles as he talked. 'Things are much worse,' he said quietly. 'Every day we go to the African Union and the families suffer there. We fight for water and we count the shelters and then we go home. We sit in the bomb shelter when the fighting gets very bad. And every day in the market the Janjaweed are coming to make trouble. I am a forgiving man but I cannot forgive Saleem. We all want to leave.'

'If Steve were here things would be different,' said Ahmed. 'Steve would talk to the commanders and make things better. But now we just listen and say thank you when the meetings finish. And every day the life gets worse.'

'But are you all safe?' I asked, worried for their lives.

'When the Janjaweed are in town then no one is safe,' said Adam Ali. 'After the attack on Arto, Saleem was full of Janjaweed. There were hundreds of cattle at the hand pumps in town before they took them back to their farms. All the cattle were stolen and we knew they came from Arto. Cows and goats and sheep all together. Donkeys and camels also. We saw them leaving in crowds when we drove to Tala yesterday.'

The Janjaweed had joined the government troops in their attack on Arto. They followed with their carts and wagons and picked the village clean. They worked together, approaching Arto in a tight circle. The villagers had nowhere to run. When the fallen were dead and the shooting had stopped the soldiers sat back while the Janjaweed moved in. At each bedside while the wounded spoke and the sand rubbed my ankles raw, I heard it over again. That old man by the hand pump was still searching for his donkey while his stomach ached with hunger. He would never find his white-nosed donkey, no matter how hard he searched. His donkey belonged to Janjaweed now, a greedy vulture on a blood-stained leash.

I listened while my friends talked and I reached out while I could. This might be the only time we met and I wanted to remember the touch of their hands and their kind words. Adam Ali's shirt was still smooth, without a crease. His MSF waistcoat carried two pens in the top pocket and his shoes shone in the bright sunlight, the tips scuffed with sand. Musa's gentle smile soothed me, but he still shook his head as we talked.

'Why did you leave us, Lisa?' he repeated. 'We needed you every day.'

Ahmed just stood quietly, his hands behind his back, and he nodded while he listened.

'We need Steve back,' he said at last. 'If this place will get better we need Steve to fight for us. With him we had hope. Now everything is wrong.' Gentle, patient Ahmed who would do anything to help us, stood with his eyes brimming with tears. 'We need Steve back.'

Steve was gone, who knew if any of us would meet him again. He was good in Darfur, he could talk and negotiate and shout his way to any resolution. He knew when to fight and when to stand back. But he wasn't coming back. I wasn't going back to Saleem either. My work was in Muhajariya now. We had thirty precious minutes up there on the ridge, while Dave and Tom discussed the security situation. Such a short time to talk and listen and grieve for the past.

'Perhaps Steve will come back one day,' I said, reluctant to deny them the hope. 'He loved Darfur and he loved you.'

'If he returns then we will all find him,' said Musa. 'We will stand with him forever.'

We all stood in the sun, shoulders together as we talked of the present and Adam Ali despaired of the future. His wife wanted him to return to Nyala, news of the dangers of Saleem worried her. Their baby daughter was growing fast and he saw her too little.

'She is frightened I will die here,' he said. 'I tell her I am safe, but she worries. Now I worry too.'

All too soon we heard Dave calling. It was time to leave, our time on the front line was over. Adam Ali, Musa, Ahmed and I hugged each other, and they bowed as we touched our hearts in farewell. I would never see my friends again. And my heart grieves for them still.

****

Karen returned from her holiday at the beginning of May. I hugged her tightly when we met. Weight loss and pain had plagued her time away. She had been gone for three weeks and we both had just five weeks left of our contract in Darfur. Arto and all its tragedies had filled my waking hours and the long hours of darkness. We held our mugs of coffee and sat in silence.

'So, what are we going to do?' she asked after a while.

'Nothing,' I replied. 'It's all fucked, so there's no point. Our clinics are all cancelled, the number of displaced out there grows every week and all we can do is watch. We don't have enough supplies to help them and we can't get out to them because of insecurity. The people are fucked and the place is fucked.' I sat back and stared at her, my heart empty.

'So are we just going to sit and watch them?' she asked.

'Yes. That seems to be the plan.'

So Karen and I sat in silence, contemplating the future.

'We could go and look for them in the bush,' she said in the quiet.

'Why? So we can see their misery and write a report again?' I asked. I remembered the families who had waited an eternity for us to return to the river bed, south of Saleem.

'We don't have the food or shelter to help them, so why torture ourselves?' I asked.

'Maybe we could find them and actually do something to help. Isn't it worth trying?' she asked.

I shrugged.

'I suppose we could try,' I said when my coffee was finished. If we didn't try then there was no point in being there. 'But if we let them down this time then I will scream blue murder.'

After the attack on Arto more families had appeared on the edge of Muhajariya. They spent their days and nights under trees and waited for food and shelter. I had visited the other NGO in town again, with a small splash of my perfume and a clean T-shirt. I didn't want to be scruffy around the elegant French.

'What can we do?' said Patrice with a shrug. 'We fight for the supplies we have. We know it is not even enough for the people we have registered already. And we know there will be more fighting and more people looking to us for food. But what can we do? We can't get more food. WFP has no more to give us.' She looked tired and despondent. 'Every month it is the same and every month we say, "Please, we need more food." But nothing happens.'

I tried to imagine her job, standing in amongst the crowds while they begged for food. And every month there was less food to give. I was glad I was not there to see it.

But Karen and I were willing to try one more time with the displaced outside town. If we didn't try then we had given up on the people. The following week, on a hot, still Wednesday morning we headed out of town with the mobile team. We drove towards the front line, meandering through the bush as we searched for the missing families.

We brought Hassan with us, one of the local staff who worked in the office. His family was from Arto and he knew the area intimately. With him to guide us we drove east and north, through stony river beds and past rocky outcrops. At one point he called 'slow down' from the back seat.

'Do you see those rocks in front of us?' He pointed through the open window. 'Every man in this place owns a gun. If we drive quickly here we will be shot from a hundred places. Drive slowly, please.'

We drove on at a snail's pace. We found many groups that day. Our rough estimate was two thousand people, scattered on the plains. Some sheltered under trees, some made shelters from blankets. I recognised some from the market in Muhajariya, on the days when we sat and drank coffee and watched life go by. They were merchants and cattle farmers who came into town to sell their goods. And I recognised some from Saleem. They belonged to those singing, laughing voices that passed our compound each night as they carried their last load of water home. One woman called out to me and kissed my hand as we talked. Her clothes were torn and her family sat hiding from the sun under a shrub. I had treated her daughter in Saleem all those months ago, and she remembered me still. I had forgotten her face. There had been too many crying, desperate faces since then. But I touched my heart as she talked.

'Alawajip,' I said. My pleasure for your daughter.

With each group that we met, Hassan drew a breath before stepping out of the vehicle.

'Do you know them?' I asked each time.

'They are my cousins,' he replied. Or his in-laws or his aunts or his friends from long ago. He knew them all by name.

We drove into Alhadi village on our way back to Muhajariya after a long, weary day. We had marked and plotted each group, recorded their numbers and identified what they needed as they waited in the bush. Some had food for days and some had blankets for the nights. And some had nothing at all. All were afraid to come to Muhajariya — their feeling of safety shattered with the shooting and the threats in Arto. They felt safer hiding where they were, where they could move at any time.

In the Alhadi village they heard us approach. The men stood in a line, their faces unsmiling. The hot wind pulled at their jelabiya gowns and they held their hands behind their backs. Hassan moved to open the back door.

'Do you know them?' I asked again.

He nodded. 'Two are my cousins and one is my father's brother.' He opened the door and jumped out.

I watched as Hassan approached them, his arms at his side. He walked towards the eldest man and bowed slightly. The men started praying as one, their voices rising and falling in the stillness of the afternoon. There had been no greetings, the endless salutations that accompany every Sudanese handshake. Instead they murmured blessings to each other, over and over again. The power of their prayers and the sorrow in their eyes were profound. These men had grieved before. All of them had lost family and friends and belongings, not only this time but many times before. Seeing Hassan they drew together in prayer, not knowing whether they would ever meet again. The rest of the team sat silently as we watched. Peter wiped his eyes in the quiet.

'Inshallah,' he whispered to himself. God willing their grief will end.

When the prayers were over Hassan approached them one by one. They shook hands briefly, reaching forward to touch each other's heart and nodding as they spoke. By the time Hassan turned to face us, his eyes were full of tears.

'We must go,' he said. And he walked away from his family without looking back.

We found out later that all those men were armed. They had taken lodging in the deserted village following Monday's attack. It was close to the front line and gave them a base while they prepared their weapons. Their women and children fled south in the days that followed. This exhausted group of hungry men stood ready to fight. They were protecting their families, giving them time to run. They looked more like priests, I thought as I looked out the window as we left. A gathering of priests whispering blessings in the sun. One was a teacher, another an elder in the local village mosque. The rest were farmers without land or tools. None were soldiers.

It was nearly four weeks before we were able to return to the sites we marked on that day. Four weeks of rain, sun and waiting. Four weeks without shelter or clean water, where they had to beg others for food. And they waited. Security constraints, our own lack of supplies, poor road conditions and another attack kept us away. And still they waited. When we finally made it back it was days before I was to leave

Darfur. We piled supplies in both vehicles and drove for hours in the sun. And we didn't find one family in the places we had marked. We found only fallen grass shelters and small clearings around the trees, the occasional blackened stone where a fire had burned before. They knew we weren't coming back so they moved away. The rains had pushed them further, as they moved away from the low ground and boggy plains. And we never saw any of them again.

****

The week after our exploration with Hassan, life was settling down as people recovered from the effects of the attack on Arto. The hospital was less busy as patients slowly healed and were taken home by relatives. Not home to Arto; there was nothing to go home to. But home to family around Muhajariya. The male ward was still busy, though. Many of the men had been shot in the legs as they ran from the attack. Fractured femurs took a long time to heal as the patients lay in traction for weeks. Harold didn't have the equipment to fix metal pins and plates to their fractures as he would at home in Germany. So the men lay for endless weeks and played cards while their bones slowly healed.

I woke with a smile. Only four days until my next break in Khartoum! And only four-and-a-half weeks left in Darfur. This time I was ready for the swimming and the food, the long days of dozing and for the nights lying under the ceiling fan. I would sleep with my light on to chase away the dreams. If I could do nothing to help in Darfur I would rather help myself in Khartoum. What a change from the tearful journey I made from Saleem when Steve had sent me out in November. This time I would run to the waiting helicopter on Wednesday morning. Darfur could suffer without me for five days.

CHAPTER TEN

On Sunday night I dragged my bed outside, ready for sleep. It had been a long day in Labado and my break in Khartoum was still three days away. Noise, chaos and not enough time left my head aching and frustration exhausted me. Why was there never enough time to help people? But all that was behind me, and the long night ahead. I sat on the edge of my bed and looked up at the clear night sky. There were no storm clouds on the horizon — my night outside was assured.

The sagging rope bed held me in its cradle of warmth. Some nights I was woken by raindrops on my face as a storm blew in from the east. I'd slip on my sandals and drag my bed back inside, eyes only half open. Pulling on my raincoat I could get back to sleep before my sheets were too wet from the leaking roof. Some mornings I surprised myself — I hadn't remembered moving. But then I looked down at my raincoat, hurriedly pulled over my pyjamas in the night. It was all worth it to be able to fall asleep under the star-filled sky. Please let tomorrow be better, I sighed. Please.

Karen and I met after breakfast to plan the Tuesday clinic in Angabo. After three weeks of waiting in Muhajariya it was finally time to head back to the people of Angabo. I would be away in Khartoum but Jack was going with the team, giving them a chance to get back to work. Dave was out of the project again, this time in management meetings in Nyala. It was 10 o'clock when Jack crossed the compound and ducked under the rakuba.

'Sorry to interrupt,' he spoke quickly. 'There's been another attack. It's all hands on deck in the clinic. The first truck will arrive in an hour.' He turned to leave.

'Are you sure Craig needs us this time?' I asked, not forgetting my anger and frustration at his last snub.

'I said all hands on deck. We work as a team.' He ran back to the office.

Ten minutes later the three of us stood at the hospital gates. I watched as the staff prepared for the influx of patients. Bags of intravenous fluid hung from trees, the plastic tubing primed and swinging in the breeze. Mats covered the ground, ready for new arrivals. The midwives stood in the shade, with Ellie leading the preparations. They were making thick padded dressings because we didn't have enough in the storeroom. One midwife cut large gauze pads, one wrapped cotton wool inside and one rolled the dressing and tied it with a bow. Soon a mountain of dressings stood piled on the table.

Karen and I pulled gloves from a box and stuffed them in our pockets in anticipation. All around us staff were talking, shouting and running. Once everything was prepared we all stood in the compound and waited. It was already hot, the early-morning cool had burned off leaving the air still and oppressive.

'What happens now?' I asked Karen. 'I feel like we should be doing something.'

'The old patients have been discharged or moved outside to make way for the new. Gertrude is taking care of that,' she said, pulling a stethoscope from her bag. 'Every patient gets the same treatment out here while they wait for the surgeon. The health assistants know the routine — antibiotics, fluids, pain relief and a wrist band. Just keep your eyes open and you'll find a job that needs doing.' She smiled. 'And remember, keep breathing.'

I thought at the time it was an odd thing to remind me — to breathe?

We stood together as the first truck reversed up to the gates. Two soldiers jumped down from the front seats and walked round to the back. They pulled at the bolts that held the iron doors shut. As they opened the doors the canvas roof was sucked in, then it billowed in the draught. Jack and I stood peering into the dark recess in the truck. Inside, a dozen or more patients lay tangled and groaning in the darkness.

'What the ...' I started to say.

'Watch out, here come the first ones,' Jack pushed me back and the soldiers lifted the first patient out.

Within minutes most of the mats were occupied. The staff were on their knees in the sand beside each one. Our normally reticent health assistants were in action as Karen called out instructions. She had seen an influx previously and knew some tricks to get the staff moving.

'Musa, over here,' she called to one. 'Hawa, you take this one.'

There was only one task not yet covered — documenting patients' wounds and preparing them for theatre. I grabbed my bag and knelt in the corner.

'Hello, what is your name?' I asked as I lifted his bandage. Underneath, his chest wound sucked and bubbled from a huge, gaping hole. 'Karen, this one needs theatre *now*!' I screamed. She pushed her way through the crowd, leading the theatre staff who carried a makeshift stretcher.

'Right, we've got him,' she said and we lifted and dragged him across to the theatre door.

Inside Craig and Harold were preparing their tools for the morning ahead — a saw, some pliers and all the suture material they could find.

I rushed back to the rakuba and knelt beside the next patient. My knees were sticky with the blood of the first man, puddles lay congealing on the mat.

'Abu, can you do something about the blood and the flies?' I called to the guard. All around us the bleeding wounds were covered in flies as they hummed and drank from the wounds. The sight made me sick.

'Hello, what's your name?' I asked gently as the young man lifted his hand from his eyes.

'The pain is too bad,' he said between shallow breaths. I pulled more gloves from my pocket and lifted his shirt. He had been shot in the abdomen and a bullet had shattered his right arm. Bleeding tissue and shards of bone lay under his torn shirt sleeve. I fanned his abdomen with one hand while I examined it with the other. The flies were everywhere. They clung in a rainbow line from his intravenous tubing as it stretched above me.

'Abu, what about these flies?' I shouted.

'No problem,' he said behind me as he started to spray. Abu sprayed the mat, my shirt and into the patient's wound with his toxic shower of fly spray before I realised what he was doing.

'Stop, stop! You can't spray his wound.' I spluttered, pushing him away.

'But you want flies to stop,' he said, looking hurt. 'Spray stops flies.'

'Forget it,' I said, too busy to explain. 'Flies no problem.' They were better than poisoning every patient with his toxic spray.

I crawled from mat to mat, drawing sketches of each wound to help Harold and Craig in their work inside. Patient wounds were everywhere — head wounds, chest and abdominal wounds, fractured arms and legs. But I didn't find an axe wound — it was my biggest fear that day.

When the last patient was examined and the pain relief and fluids were running, I stopped working and sat down on a clean mat. Flies stuck to the blood streaks on my arms and my jeans were wet with blood.

If that was it, then we managed okay, I thought looking around. The dozen or so patients lay in a row against the operating theatre wall. They lay in order of priority, the sickest by the door. It was all so hopelessly inadequate, but it was the best we could do for now. Inside Harold, Bridgette and Craig operated on the most injured patients. Outside Karen, Ellie, Jack and I stood in the shade and looked at each other.

'Hate to tell you but there's another two trucks coming,' said Jack. 'That was just a sample.'

Karen and I groaned and leaned back against the wall.

Two minutes later we heard the rumble of an engine as the second truck lumbered into view. It stopped, reversed and again two soldiers jumped down from the front. I filled my pockets again with gloves and smiled at Ellie.

'Good luck!' I said. And we both walked forward to help carry patients.

The second truck was far more crowded than the first — forty patients lay crammed together in its hot, dark bowels. They lay bleeding and groaning in the crush, some dazed from the two-hour journey from Labado. One of the men screamed as the soldiers dragged him towards the door.

'I'll take that one,' I called, and guided the soldiers to the blood-stained mats in the shade.

Ellie and her midwives worked frantically as they passed out swabs and hung intravenous lines from the tree. They whispered and nodded to each other with encouragement. Soon the branches looked like a Christmas tree, the plastic tubing sparkling in the sun from dozens of swaying lines. The buckets of soiled dressings, filled with flies and muck and sand, sat beside every mat as we examined and treated patients as fast as we could. The health assistants worked without guidance by now, concentrating on one patient at a time. Every now and then one would shout, 'I need gauze', or 'bring me fluids'. The buzz of flies was worse than before and the groans and cries of patients filled the air. I remembered what Karen had told me and I stopped to take a breath. Flies stuck to my face and my arms, and the sweat poured down my back. The smell of blood made my stomach turn.

Our hard-working mobile team sat working in one corner. We were so used to working together, running a clinic in an open field or between blackened walls. They took to the chaos with enthusiasm and I had to smile when I saw their progress. Issa and Ibrahim stood sweating in the sun as they triaged and treated the patients at their feet. Team work; when the shit hits the fan, there's nothing like it.

I saw Abraham and Hassan arrive, our office staff, translators and guides in the last weeks. They walked between the mats, lifting sheets and looking at faces.

'My father is over there,' said Abraham when he walked past my mat. 'And my brother.'

After the initial chaos other family members started to arrive, looking for the dead and praying for the living. Abraham was always a gentle man, a calm smiling face when the rest of us were feeling overwhelmed. I thought of him as we talked to the patients from Arto. The way he fanned away the flies while he listened and soothed the patients' fears. Now he stood in front of me, his hands on his head and his eyes welled up with tears.

'These people are my family, my family,' he groaned as he started to cry. 'Inshallah, inshallah,' he said as he walked away. His shoulders were shaking. I could hear him crying as he grieved for his own family, after weeks of grieving for others. My heart broke a little further to hear his cries. He was always the proud one, the one to console others. And now it was his turn to weep.

At my feet a patient pulled on my trousers.

'Please, I have pain. Please help me,' he whispered. He was only about fifteen years old. I knelt down beside him and waved the flies from his broken, twisted legs. Pulling a vial of Tramadol from my pocket I injected the pain relief into his plastic tubing.

'No problem,' I said and I watched him relax. And I pulled the sheet over his head to keep the flies from the wounds on his face. 'I will come back. Sleep now.'

'Next truck coming shortly,' called Jack from the front gate. 'Hope you guys are ready.' All around the compound patients lay on mats. We had started organising them in the shade, but when the shade ran out we lay them in the sun. Women were mixed with men, the dying with the living. The line outside the operating theatre had grown and inside Harold and Bridgette worked steadily and carefully, well aware of the queue outside. They amputated and repaired wounds as best they could.

Bridgette excelled in her field of expertise, instead of crying with frustration with her outreach workers. When I peered in through the screen door I saw them working in silence, each lost in their world of damaged tissue and shattered bone.

I felt a cold shock on my arm and jumped away from the window. Jack stood holding two bottles of soda.

'Fanta or Stim?' he asked as he held them out.

I reached for the sweet, apple-flavoured Stim drink. The icy coolness was a blessing.

'Have I told you that you are the best logistician?' I asked, resting the bottle on my forehead.

'No problem,' he said smiling. 'I just want to help you guys do your job.' He turned and walked back into the crowd, distributing cold bottles of soda to all the staff.

By the time the third truck arrived an hour later, the late-afternoon shadows stretched across the compound. The burning sun had gone, but the flies remained. I crawled and sketched while I worked, my pockets now full of gloves and Tramadol. If there was one thing I could do it was to ease their screaming pain. There wasn't time to check names and ages or to enquire after allergies and such. A piece of paper lay under each mat, where staff could record their treatment. Many of them didn't read or write English. But they knew more about war than I did, and they could copy our 'T's' and 'I's' as we wrote Tramadol for pain and Intravenous line for fluids. I said thank you often, so grateful to be part of the team and proud to see them work. 'No thanks for duty' was always the reply. They considered their work a duty and an honour. And on they worked.

It was sunset by the time the compound had regained some order. The screaming cries had dulled to the occasional groan and the flies had tired of their feast of blood. It was the turn of mosquitoes, crickets and moths as we worked by lamplight. Jack had erected halogen lights. They stood on long poles and swayed gently in the breeze. The generator chugged noisily behind the operating theatre, bringing our lights and plugs to life. All over the compound empty soda bottles littered the ground. Karen had let some of the staff go home. A long walk home in the dark was never safe for a woman, even on a good day.

Abraham returned later that evening, his tears dry and his face composed. He sat cross-legged beside his family, ready to wait the whole night as they lay waiting for their turn in the theatre. His patience was without end.

I spent the rest of the evening moving from mat to mat outside the theatre, making sure those who waited were stable and without pain. When a patient deteriorated I called the guards and we carried them to the front of the queue. Ellie's tree of intravenous fluids was depleted and her midwives started to pack up their wares to go home. Ellie sat on the low, brick wall. Her hair looked wild, her face was flushed as she raised her arm to wave them goodbye. I lifted two bags from the branches and draped one over each shoulder.

'Shukran,' I called as the midwives left, and I touched my heart with my hand. Thank you.

'No thanks for duty,' they called in unison. They touched their hearts, just glad they had been able to help their friends. I turned back to the row of patients and pulled a handful of Tramadol vials from my pocket. The cries of pain had started again as the first dose wore off in the dusk.

****

In the days that followed, the hospital groaned with the huge number of patients. Our small, tidy wards were crowded and overflowing. Barely inches separated beds from each other and mats stretched across the compound. Each patient had at least one family member to take care of them. Changing sheets and fetching food from the hospital kitchen was not done by the staff. It was the duty of the family. The number of people living within the hospital walls was over two hundred. The compound was built for eighty.

Despite the crowds and the endless line of patients waiting at the theatre door, the hospital was strangely quiet. Few voices, no laughter and no murmuring while the women stood at the hand pump outside the gate. People stood together in their grief, they prayed and touched and wept. But in the heat of the day all we heard was the clang of steel instruments as they were dropped into the autoclave, and the creak of the theatre door as another patient was carried in or out.

On Tuesday evening before I left for Khartoum I stood in the nurses' office and prepared for the night round. The pile of patient files in front of me was huge. It would take hours to see them all. Our scrawling notes from the first moments of chaos on Monday were Sellotaped to each yellowing folder. I followed Ali out into the darkness. I had learned to see better in the darkness, not stumbling with my arms outstretched as in the early days.

We walked to the children's ward first. Dehydrated and malnourished children filled the beds. Many had walked from our distant clinic sites. With our mobile clinics cancelled for weeks on end, the children slowly weakened as their sicknesses went untreated. When their mothers eventually made the ten-hour journey on foot to Muhajariya it was often too late to save them.

I sat on the edge of the first bed. The young mother shielded her eyes from the light. Her tiny baby lay swaddled in damp towels beside her. She had carried him from Angabo, a journey that had taken her fourteen hours as she walked and rested. I didn't have the heart to tell her that there was little we could do. His fevered body and rattling chest were exhausted by severe pneumonia. He had stopped feeding three days before.

Why don't they bring their children earlier? I had railed when I first arrived in Darfur. But soon you recognise the choices that these mothers made, to stay or go when sickness struck. Stay and care for their five fatherless children at home? Or go, leaving the eight-year-old in charge while the mother walks eight, ten or fourteen hours to our nearest clinic. These choices face them every day. Who was I to judge them?

We moved from bed to bed and finally I stood waiting for Ali at the door. The airless room made me dizzy. Some past expat had hung mobiles in an effort to brighten up the ward. Colourful dolls and clowns hung limply from their strings in the shadows above me. The children's ward always made me sad. In this war of fear and hiding, it was the children who suffered most. Their little legs could hardly keep up, their small feet burning on the sand as they followed their families into the bush. Their stomachs rumbled with hunger and their heads ached for want of water. But the children have no choice.

We stepped out into the cool darkness of the compound. Tiny kerosene burners flickered and glowed all around us. A quiet murmuring had built as the sun had set and more friends and families came to visit. Small picnics were unpacked, home-cooked food was always better than the hospital fare. It's the same the world over.

'This one stopped talking two hours ago,' said Ali and I followed him to the first bed. Under the sheet the patient lay unconscious. And so the evening ward round began.

****

On Wednesday the helicopter came to take me away to Khartoum. My mind and body ached. Amna had washed the blood stains from my jeans but my head still echoed with the screams and cries of Monday. I was leaving the team to cope with chaos; overstretched and under-resourced. All our planning and forecasting for our future consumption of equipment and drugs lay in tatters. Our warehouse of supplies, newly stocked to last six months at least, would be empty in no time as the new patients consumed everything. Drugs, bandages and crates of intravenous fluids were signed out to the hospital pharmacy every day. The empty shelves would last for weeks or months while the new order slowly made its way from Amsterdam.

I couldn't wait to get on that helicopter. To leave behind the noise and the need, the long, rainy nights when my bed dripped and my raincoat barely kept me dry. To forget the sobbing cries as another child died in the small, hot ward. I had seen and touched and smelled Darfur's pain every single day for months. I had watched as our best efforts failed them, the government failed them and the war lumbered on. And still they waited for help.

I didn't say goodbye that morning. I walked quietly to the gate and hopped in beside Ali.

'Mr Marley is OK?' he asked and he reached for his old cassette.

I nodded.

We drove slowly to the landing strip while Ali gently tapped in time to the music. The last I saw as the helicopter rose was Ali. He turned slowly and drove back along the sandy track to the hospital. Ready for another day of work, Bob Marley at his side.

****

I spent the night in Nyala, then sat waiting five hours for the flight to Khartoum. A sand storm in the east kept us waiting as the pilots waited for it to move. I looked around the waiting room to pass the time. I didn't enjoy passing through the airport but, to leave Darfur, people had no choice. The colour, noise and disorganised nonsense of officials was overwhelming. The airport was nothing grand, but if you sat quietly there was a lot to see.

Arriving at the front entrance on time, with ticket and passport in hand, a novice might be excused for his unrealistic optimism. Airport, ticket, waiting plane — how hard could it be to leave?

Nyala is not that easy. The portable X-ray scanner sat a few doors down, hastily inserted in a narrow doorway some years ago. Once I found this first discrete entrance I dropped my rucksack on the three-foot-long conveyor belt. Each time I had to run to the other side before my luggage was ejected from the belt at speed. Invariably I found it buried under sixty-four pieces of UN-issued luggage that was also thrown at speed from the conveyor belt moments after mine. The two black-gloved ladies sat watching the X-ray monitor. They seemed to pay little attention to the monitor in front of them. In seven months I didn't see them stop a single piece of luggage while they talked and yawned.

Checking in was fraught with anxiety as boarding lists were misprinted or tickets bought yesterday were deemed invalid. With luck and persistence passengers would finally be given their little yellow tag. They were one step closer to leaving. With its low ceilings and tiled floors the waiting hall echoed with the voices of the hundred other passengers as they talked, shouted and laughed. I learned to always take paracetemol for my airport-induced headaches.

The seats were plastic, three or four bolted together in short rows. There were cherry-red seats and pale olive-green seats. I always chose a red one. The other passengers around me were mostly wealthy-looking locals with well-dressed children. The children often looked uncomfortable. The boys wore little starched green suits, the girls in candy floss tulle and satin dresses. They were off to Khartoum to show grandparents their affluence in Darfur. War is good to some. Their parents called out and waved to friends, some sat shouting into mobile phones.

There were no decorations on the walls, just one clock. It always stood at 8.45. The electrical sockets had been inserted just below ceiling level. I could never work out why. Who would want to climb the walls to plug in a laptop or mobile charger? All were incomplete, some with wires protruding, their little white boxes hanging loosely and unfinished. Above each socket the wall was smudged with soot, fanning out in a blackened blur, each one a testament to an electrical fault that flared and burned the wiring. I would never use one.

After hours of waiting, false flight calls and trips to the 'restiraunt' for sweet tea and malted biscuits, waiting passengers became anxious. Each time a flight was called, everyone assembled for the next round of travel permit checks, X-rays and baby frisking. Most were turned away, it wasn't their flight. The muffled voice that announced each flight seemed equally incomprehensible to the locals. They would look at each other, asking where and who and when. Those lucky passengers who made it through then shuffled to the next room where they waited all over again. When at last their flight was called they walked out into the sun. The icy coldness of the air conditioning inside had caught me more than once — I sat shivering in the waiting hall and watched the runway shimmer outside in the scorching heat. Once released, passengers walked across to the tarmac and waited again. All the checked-in luggage was lined up beside the plane and each passenger asked to stand beside their bags. If the UN team was flying, other passengers had to be prepared for a long wait. The team would weave and wander beneath the wing as they retrieved their mountain of scattered luggage.

The whole performance, from check-in to take-off, could take two or more hours on a good day. It was fraught with anxiety, frustration with mobile-phone-playing guards and a feeling of utter helplessness. At any moment one of the over-inflated uniform-wearing officials could block a passenger. They could find fault with a permit or lose a name on their list. When that happened there was no use protesting. All those unfortunates could do was return to their seat, tea and biscuits in hand, and hope that the next shift would be more lenient.

Welcome to Nyala International Airport, I thought with a sigh, where waiting is an art form and the passengers are patient sheep.

When at last I boarded my flight, five hours and twenty minutes late, I almost wished I hadn't. I was in a bad mood, tired and worried for the team in Muhajariya. Two bumpy landings along the way allowed more passengers to embark. At the second stop a young woman sat down beside me. I kept my sunglasses on, wanting to avoid conversation. But she wanted to talk.

'I work for the Red Cross,' she said with a smile. 'How about you?' She didn't pause so I could answer but continued with her chat. 'We're educating the military because education is the future.'

I looked at her.

'I run classes with local military leaders in the north, telling them of their responsibilities under international humanitarian law. I think they're really listening.' She nodded vigorously.

I watched her more carefully from behind my glasses. Her soft linen trousers were creased and hung loosely round her ankles. She wore thick, chunky bracelets, the 'ethnic' kind you buy in Accessorize in London. Her expensive glasses were dusty in the afternoon light and she touched them often while she talked.

'If we can just teach them the rules of engagement then this war will change dramatically. And civilians won't be at risk.'

Fuck off! I wanted to shout. Take your education and lessons on law and just fuck off. My jeans were still stiff with the soap Amna had used to clean away the blood. My ears rang with the sound of flies and crying. Men with guns don't go to class and follow international humanitarian law. They kill. They shoot and kill and they use axes while they work. I took off my glasses and looked her in the eye.

'I think you and I disagree on some fundamental points. You are dealing with the ideal situation, how people should behave. I deal with the reality, how soldiers and militia actually behave. We don't live in an ideal world and we never will. Your programme assumes that people want to be good, want to change and want to move towards the ideal. They don't. But I don't want to talk about it because I am hungry and tired.'

She looked back at me and adjusted her glasses.

'But I was just saying,' she started.

'I hope your classes go well and that every soldier attends.' I put my sunglasses back on and turned my head to the window. We didn't speak again.

****

As the plane approached Khartoum, seven hours behind schedule, the pilot's voice came over the intercom.

'There appears to be a sand storm over Khartoum so we may not be able to land,' he said slowly. 'We will fly on to Port Sudan instead and the lucky ones will find a bus to Khartoum tonight. Thank you.'

All around me people groaned. I pulled my scarf around my shoulders and pushed my sunglasses further up my nose. Great, I thought. This couldn't get any better.

We did eventually land in Khartoum, the sand storm had passed slowly but just in time. The MSF car had given up waiting. My flight was expected at 2 p.m. and it was now past 10 p.m., so I crossed the front courtyard and raised my hand to call a taxi. One roared up in front of me and a smiling man stepped out.

'The doors do not open, so you can use mine,' he said and stood back to welcome me in.

I handed him my rucksack and climbed over the driver's seat and into the back.

What else can go wrong? I thought, as the driver punched and shoved my rucksack through the broken back window.

'No problem,' he shouted over the roar of the traffic. 'In Khartoum everything is fine.' He smiled at me over his shoulder as we swerved into the stream of traffic.

I closed my eyes and pulled my sunglasses down. Outside it was dark. There was no use in worrying about safety. Either we would get there or we wouldn't, that was the Sudanese way. And I didn't much care which it was.

****

Those few days in Khartoum were bliss as I blocked Darfur from my thoughts every day. I swam and splashed, ordered ice cream and sat dripping in the shade. On the long walk back from the German Club to the expat house I crossed the road often to avoid the beggars and the cars. With my sunglasses on I slipped by unnoticed. That way I could cope with the heat and dust and noise.

One evening Rebecca and I escaped the house to go to a restaurant for dinner. She was also in Khartoum on a much-needed break. After four months in Saleem she was exhausted by the struggle and frustration as the violence increased and clinics were cut short. I didn't envy her. Life was worse than ever in Saleem and the team was blocked at every turn.

We walked to the restaurant together, through the warm early-evening light. We crossed deserted blocks of land, scattered with bricks and the detritus of a city with no effective drainage or rubbish collection. Along narrow streets of packed earth and potholes, jumping over ditches in the half-light, skirting around puddles lest we fell in. Past the Coptic Church, the sound of chanting rising through the spires. The church was lit inside with great round lanterns. Past apartments, most in darkness, some with bright lights beyond the balcony. One apartment was lit, showing a ceiling fan turning slowly in the hot and airless room. I saw the silhouette of a mother, standing with her baby, watching the world from her crowded, concrete platform. I wondered what she was thinking, surrounded by such luxury and stench.

We arrived outside the Lebanese restaurant and waited while a family pushed past, talking and laughing in their after-dinner bliss. We found a table by the air-conditioning unit and sat breathing in the cool, noisy air while we browsed the plastic menus. We drank water in brightly lit, noisy chaos, watching the comings and goings of workmen and customers. There were well-dressed locals eating in groups, overweight men from the north, pale skinned and with sullen faces. The two men who ran the restaurant were obese, their trousers barely containing the mass within. When the younger one sat at a table to rest his feet, the chair groaned and I was sure his belt would give way at any moment.

His young son was working behind the pizza counter. He shouted 'Papa' when he wanted advice and a blur of conversation, incomprehensible to me, flew between them. He looked about seventeen. He was preparing and cutting the most delicious-looking pizzas, thin, crisp, cheesy slices of heaven. His hair was greasy, combed tightly to his scalp. The longest locks escaped at the bottom into an oily wave. He wore a petulant look on his face as he worked and shouted at the Sudanese workers beside him.

The food was good and hot and fast. I ordered a guava drink with mango juice, made right there with fresh warm fruit and crushed ice. It was so thick and fruity that I couldn't draw it up the straw. In the end I resorted to a spoon, and sat dipping and slurping while I turned my head to catch the noisy breeze behind me. For a moment I was happy, just happy to be there. There was no fear, no gunshots and no hunger. Just life and noise and light. We sat long after dinner and just smiled and talked and relaxed. If heaven was a Turkish restaurant then we had found it in Khartoum.

We left after the meal, giving a tip to the bullied pizza men at the oily counter. I didn't thank the petulant boy, but eyed his pizzas longingly. And we walked back to the house along the same dusty streets. We stood at the gates of the Coptic Church again and listened to the singing. The yellow light on the sweeping spires, the bars of the gate warm under my hands. I felt at peace. When I rested my forehead against the iron gates I thought I would cry. Why should I know such beauty and such peace in a week, a month or a year when others were suffering such terror in the distance? But I rested in the dark, taking deep breaths and losing my fears in the beauty around us.

****

When my rest in Khartoum was over I sat in Nyala airport waiting for my helicopter. I contemplated the four weeks ahead of me, my last weeks in Darfur. What could we achieve in such a short time? Or would we simply see more of the same and stand by helplessly?

As the helicopter approached Muhajariya I pulled off my red earmuffs and rubbed my hot ears. Some people didn't mind the noise in the thundering machine, but it gave me a headache every time. When it landed the sand rose in a whipping fury. I peered out the window and saw the African Union soldiers guarding the landing strip. They stood spread out in a wide circle, their backs to us and their guns held low. They were there to protect and defend our precious selves. Their grey-green helmets looked hot and uncomfortable in the sun.

When the engines were cut we sat in the silence, ears still roaring from the noise. I climbed out slowly, the only passenger disembarking in Muhajariya. In the space of a week knee-high grass had sprung up in every direction. The heavy rains beat life back into the earth. New leaves sprouted, flowers quickly bloomed and all around us cattle sighed with pleasure as they ate fresh grass for the first time in months.

Karen and the mobile team stood waiting in the shade. I don't think I can face this, I thought to myself. The clinics and the failures stretched ahead of me. As the blades of the helicopter started to turn, the shaking, thundering noise resumed and I clutched at my ears to protect them. Take me back to Nyala, I wanted to shout at the pilot. Don't make me stay!

But I also knew that I couldn't give in so easily. I knew that the patients needed us. For them I knew I would stay. For the queue of worried mothers, for their children waiting in the sun. For the victims of last Monday's attack who I had helped in those first frightening hours. I knew many of their wives and families from our weekly clinics. I owed them my care and my respect. For them I went back to face failure, knowing we could never do enough to help. I walked slowly over to the vehicles and smiled at the team.

'We've missed you,' said Karen, jumping down from her seat. 'Come on, let's do some work.' The others sat smiling from the back seats.

'There is much to be done,' called Peter through his back-seat window. 'Inshallah we will do it now you are back.'

I threw my rucksack in the back of Ali's vehicle.

'Okay, I'm ready!' I called to them. I climbed in beside Ali and wound the window down.

'Hello, my friend,' I said, glad to be travelling with this quiet, gentle man.

'Hello, Lisa,' he smiled. 'Bob Marley is coming with us.' He reached forward and slipped in his cassette.

For the next four hours we hardly spoke a word and the quiet was a blessing. With the windows open and the warm wind blowing we drove slowly across mud-covered plains, through sticky bogs and fields of grass. In places where we had bumped and bounced along dry, rutted tracks the month before, we now drove at a snail's pace.

The wheels sank in the mud and spun when we became stuck. My worries disappeared as I concentrated on the road, drawn back to the present, instead of dwelling on the future.

****

We arrived in Angabo later than usual. The muddy tracks had only become worse as we neared the village. Our usual route took us past the Oomda's tree and through the marketplace. As we slowed to enter the town Karen called on the radio.

'Do you see those people?' she asked.

I peered ahead and looked through the trees and shelters. A crowd of colourful fabric stretched across the marketplace. As we got nearer we saw them more clearly. Hundreds of women and children sat waiting in the shade, their endless line of jerry cans sat empty across the marketplace.

We retraced our path and stopped under the Oomda's tree.

'What's going on?' Karen asked as she looked around.

'The borehole is broken and there is no water for the town,' said Ibrahim, walking back from the first group of women. 'They say they have been waiting for two days and they just receive a few cups of water to drink. There is no water for the animals. No one knows when it will be fixed.'

I walked across the sand and stood at the gates to the water compound. A thick, rusting chain held the gates tightly shut.

'Mafi moya,' called the old guard inside the compound. No water.

He stood with two other men and they were talking as they squatted beside the broken engine. Each borehole had a pump house with a diesel-powered engine to draw water from the depths. The borehole was lined with metal pipes, stretching 40, 50 or even 70 m underground. Engine failure or dislocated pipes often caused a disruption in the flow of water. Some engines had been running since 1945 and we saw the old brass plaques proudly displaying their English origins. This engine lay silent. Wet twine, rope and Elastoplast tape covered every leaking joint and pipe where they had tried to fix small problems in the past. But all to no avail. In an area of 16,000 people there was no clean water. That left puddles and muddy streams, and we all knew what that would mean for us — a stream of patients in the clinic with diarrhoea and dehydration, poor feeding and death for children.

'Oh no,' said Karen, standing beside me at the gate. This also meant *we* had no water. And we planned to be there for two days. 'Let's call Jack,' she said, kicking the sand with her boot. We turned back to the vehicles. This was not an auspicious start.

Our new compound had been completed and I smiled as we approached the gate. After the scattered, stressful clinics when I first started in Angabo, this new clinic was a dream. The Oomda and local leaders had chosen the spot for us. Karen and Jack had sat drawing plans in the sand as the men gathered for their meeting months before. Together with teams of local men and women, the compound had been built in a week. We had separate tuckuls for consulting, for midwives and for our lunch. No longer working back to back in tiny, stifled rooms. We had light and space and a proudly constructed latrine. Jack and Ali had supervised and laboured over it for weeks. It stood on a rise, its concrete base set to last a lifetime. It was the crowning glory of our new clinic.

The waiting area was empty. After weeks of our cancelled clinics and the newly broken pump people stayed away. So we unpacked and swept and settled in while we waited for work to arrive. I radioed Jack about the water pump. The beauty of modern communication brought us an answer within minutes. Oxfam was already on the case. A new pump had been ordered from Khartoum and was coming sometime soon. But what good is 'soon' when it has already been two days and the sun is burning while you wait?

The damaged pump could run a little, enough for cups of water only. The Oomda agreed to give us some so we could stay and run the clinic. How precious those few cups were. We drank and shared every cup. I will never forget the pleasure or the guilt.

By late afternoon some patients had arrived and our work began at last. Our regular malnourished children came first, wearing the red bracelets around their ankles that showed their priority. I sat with one while Peter measured the baby's height and weight. His name was Idriss. He was only eighteen months old. His mother had taken him to a traditional healer who inflicted pain in an effort to heal his diarrhoea. He had burns to his anus to 'dry' the diarrhoea and razor-blade scars on his belly to 'treat' the fever. Idriss lay limply in his mother's arms and I just knew we were too late. But you try telling a mother that there is no hope for her baby. I couldn't. So I watched while Peter hung him from a soft, black fabric harness and we admitted him to our clinic. The scales registered his barely living body weight. Most children cried and kicked as they fought the frightening scale. But Idriss just hung there, his harness slowly turning on the hook. He was too tired to care.

He wouldn't drink or eat, so we decided to feed him through a tube. Peter held his head while I passed the tube into his tiny nose and down into his stomach. When it was done, Haroun my smiling helper sat for hours in the shade as he trickled water down Idriss's tube. He brushed the flies away with one hand as he drew more water into a syringe. Concentrating, frowning and trying his best.

Later that afternoon I stood paralysed as the sound of gunfire shattered the air. Vollies of shots echoed in the market and my heart was in my throat. I pictured all the women and the children with their jerry cans. I pictured the thirsty donkeys as they leant against the gate.

Oh, please no, I prayed. Don't let anything happen out there.

'It's okay, Lisa,' called Peter. He stood at the front gate and pointed towards the market. 'The peace agreement team is here to celebrate Abuja.'

The Darfur Peace Agreement had been signed in Abuja, Nigeria on 5 May 2006. After lengthy negotiations, mediated by the African Union, the Government of Sudan, SLA leadership and various fractured rebel groups had reached an agreement. It promised peace, sharing and development for the people of Darfur. It was all the people had ever wanted. SLA vehicles filled the marketplace. They had weapons, trucks, speakers and a hastily erected stage. Flags fluttered in the hot breeze. When the wind blew towards us their voices were loud and clear. This team was moving through Darfur to explain the peace agreement to the people, confirming their support. With noise and colour and whoops of joy the crowd danced and cheered. They were still thirsty and tired and life was far from easy. But if you could have seen them dance you would have seen hope for the first time in years. Hope for the future, hope for their children and hope that the wicked war was over.

I stood watching them from the gate and I even allowed myself to hope.

Let this work, I prayed. Let them keep their promises and let this damned war end now.

None of us realised how catastrophic the Darfur Peace Agreement would be. It marked a change in the war, as fighting worsened and tribes split and sold their loyalties. Not everyone signed the agreement and those that didn't became targets in horrific attacks. The non-signatories didn't believe in the agreement, didn't trust that its promises were true. But standing in the late-afternoon sun as the guns fired in the marketplace, we all had hope and our hearts were soaring.

****

More patients started to arrive as the afternoon wore on. They heard that we had water. Many came to see us, but not all needed our care. We had bought two barrels full when the last blast of the engine sounded for the day. The Oomda always looked after us well, knowing how important we were to the health of his community. The water barrels sat under the tree with orange plastic mugs bobbing on the surface. We intended to leave them for the patients who waited in the sun, but we all sidled up to drink as the afternoon passed.

I stood outside the gate and triaged as patients arrived. Some just for water and some for water and medical treatment; left, right, right, left. I herded them into groups. The usual crowd had gathered, wanting relief from their lifelong pains — burning feet, gas in abdomen and the all-pervading general body pain. I needed a rucksack full of paracetamol to help them. But with our stocks in Muhajariya already low I could only give them water. What kind of help was that?

One old man floored me with his complaint. I thought I'd heard them all.

'I have moving ears,' he said, looking at me seriously with his old, milky eyes. 'At night they move from here to here.' He showed me where they journeyed while he slept.

I looked at him for a moment. In, out, stay, go?

'Go and see Karen,' I said with a smile and put my arms around his shoulders. 'I'm sure she's got an answer.' That would make her laugh!

By nightfall the clinic was empty and we retired to our mats around the lanterns. I still felt exhausted after the journey from Nyala that day and the shock of hearing gunfire. Peter had arranged takeaways for dinner — what a treat in the middle of southern Darfur! A local restaurant had made our dinner, bread, salad, stew and beans, and Peter and Ali had driven into the village to collect it before nightfall. We sat together and shared our feast, the best cooked meal we had eaten in Angabo. We agreed to buy takeaways every night from then on.

I prepared my night-time home while the others sipped their coffee and Ali pulled out his pack of cards. I lay a mattress in Ali's vehicle, with sheets and a thin, brown pillow from our new store-tuckul. I kicked the empty soda bottles out the door and soon it felt like my home. I remembered those first nights in El Wadi when Toby forgot the stretchers and blankets. Icy, metal floors without a sheet and my back bruised from lying on the buckles. My Angabo bed was a palace, even with a thin, stained pillow, and I wouldn't have swapped it for anything.

The wind howled during the night as a storm passed over in the dark. The vehicle rocked with every gust, but I felt safe and warm inside. Ali had woken in the night and crawled out of his sand- and rain-proof tuckul. I heard him shut my windows to keep the storm at bay.

'Goodnight, my sister,' he said as he pulled the last window shut.

'Goodnight, Ali,' I croaked and rolled over and went back to sleep.

I was woken later by the sound of voices just outside. It was still dark. I heard early-morning whispers and the sound of the equipment trunk being opened. Idriss and Ibrahim were taking care of a new patient. They would call Karen and me if they needed help, so I pulled up my sleeping bag and went back to sleep.

I woke again at 6 o'clock. When the first whisper of daylight reached into the land cruiser I couldn't sleep any more. I couldn't hide behind the cloak of darkness. So I climbed out of the vehicle and walked over to the group standing in the treatment room.

The staff stood around the patient, some holding torches, others yawning in the shadows. Ibrahim crouched on the ground beside her.

'What's wrong with her?' I asked.

'Diarrhoea, dehydration, she's stopped eating and drinking now,' said Ibrahim. He pinched her skin in the torchlight and we both watched as it gathered beneath his fingers then stayed raised when he let go. It was dry, empty skin.

Idriss knelt beside her, tied a glove tightly around her forearm and started searching for a vein. This was the team I loved. Local staff who had learned what to do, without schools or diplomas or clinical exercises. Practice through experience, patient after patient, body after body. War provided an endless line of patients, the barbed suffering on which they hung their experience.

They were managing all right, so I left them to work. Tea and custard cream biscuits were our morning staple every day. I accomplished little before my second packet of four crumbled biscuits. I sat on a mat and watched Selwa make ten cups of tea.

Karen and I returned to the treatment room again at 9 o'clock. The patient lay on a mat, against the sorghum wall. She was covered from head to knee in a vivid blue wrap, a hum and buzz of huge blowflies sat on and all around her. Fat, shiny, lazy-winged flies. While Karen talked to the others I crouched down and looked at her feet, the only living expression discernible under the blue veil.

They were long feet, dry and tired looking. Feet that had walked a lifetime in the sun. One foot rested unmoving against the other. The shadows cast by those of us in the doorway hid her feet now and then, the morning sunlight warming us from behind. Her feet were cold. They were strong feet. Sad feet. Tired feet.

A fat green blowfly came to rest on one toe. It cleaned itself in the sunlight, first one wing, then the other. Legs shrugging up one side then down the other. She didn't move. I wanted to brush it away. I stood up. Watching her feet made me feel sad. I left the others to help. I knew how frustrating it could be when too many people tried to help, interfering and confusing. I don't know what happened to her, that lady in the early-morning shadows. And I never saw her face. Only those long, strong-looking feet, lying motionless in the shadows. The day started soon afterwards, a crowded tumbling throng of patients and not enough time. And soon I forgot about her.

By the time we left at 3 o'clock the compound was nearly empty. Pieces of white paper and our empty soda bottles littered the sand. The water barrels were empty and the mats folded away. The pump was still broken and my head ached for water. But we had more than some people. Baby Idriss died. Despite Haroun's patience and his care the starving baby had simply had enough. I watched while his mother cried. She held him in her arms and rocked, her tears falling silently. An African mother doesn't grieve less because she does it often. I've heard people say, 'It's different there,' when they hear of death and dying in Africa. They say, 'Those people are used to death and for them it is just natural.' Stand listening to a crying mother as she holds her dead child in her arms and tell me if you really believe that. They cry and grieve and ache inside and the aching never goes. The difference is they have no choice, without the care we take for granted. Their children die and they can only watch. So they lift the body, tie it to their backs with a colourful sheet and carry another baby home to bury in the sand.

I wanted to cry as I listened to her. I lifted the sheet to look at him one last time. He had held my finger only the day before as I whispered to him. He had looked at me with his big, tired eyes. But his dry body was empty now. Around his ankle sat my little red bracelet. It was no use to him now. I covered him with the sheet and watched as his mother walked away.

****

Later that week we drove to Labado. It was our first clinic since the attack two weeks before. We didn't have the full story and by now I didn't care. Whether it was a government attack or Janjaweed militia or just a tribal skirmish made no difference to me. It may have been a cattle raid, on a grand and well-armed scale. Janjaweed militia had come from the north that Monday morning. Some said hundreds came, some weren't sure. They had circled the town and started firing while the cattle were being watered on the edge of town at dawn. For all the patients we received that day the militia must have had an unexpected reception. Soldiers, farmers, women and the elderly fought back. The raid failed and most of the Janjaweed were killed. We heard reports of over seventy dead. Their bodies still lay where they fell, no one would honour them with a burial.

We approached Labado from the east, along our usual route. Six bodies lay along the track. Dave had asked us to check whether they had been moved or buried. Karen and the team had seen them the week before, so they knew what to expect. I sat in the second vehicle and strained my eyes to see. I needn't have bothered. The bodies lay close to the track and Ali slowed as we passed them all.

'Roll up your window,' he said softly as we approached.

Four bodies lay to our left, on a gently sloping hill. Two lay to our right. I could smell them in the morning heat. I knew I should look away. There was no point in staring. But I just had to look again, to see if the stories were real. I gave in to that cold, sick curiosity that wraps itself around you when you really know you shouldn't. My eyes were drawn to the one nearest me. He lay on his back with his arms by his side. His eyes were closed and his mouth wide open. He wore old grey trousers held up with a long piece of string. One trouser leg was pushed above his knee, the skin looked smooth and shiny. What caught my eye, and has stayed with me since, were his thin, white socks. His boots were gone, stolen as he lay in the sun. His socks looked old and worn and they were far too big for his feet. They hung loosely where his toes should be — a man's socks for one much younger than a man.

We drove past. My vulture's gaze took only seconds. But I have never forgotten his feet and that solitary pair of socks. Karen called on the radio.

'Did you see them?' she asked.

I didn't feel like talking. 'Yep. Talk later,' I mumbled into the radio.

In some respects those bodies were no different from the corpses we saw every day — cows, donkeys and goats lay bloated in the sand. We passed them often as we drove to clinics or out looking for the displaced. The smell and the flies were normal in this land of death and hunger. But those bodies were also different. They were fathers and sons and brothers. Their shirts and belts and short white socks made them one of us. And I didn't want to think about it. Karen and

I could talk about it later, but we had a whole day in Labado to face before I could let myself think and feel and worry for those men.

We arrived in Labado on time and ran into a frantically busy day. I stood outside in triage, trying to pull the seriously ill from the crowd. We dubbed this role Mobile Bitch. Turning people away or dismissing their ills in favour of others was the worst part of any day. I couldn't make them understand why we did it this way. And I hated doing it every time. But if we were to treat those in real need someone had to do it. A local pharmacy sold a cornucopia of drugs, so those with money still had a chance to buy their health. For those with little money or serious problems, a three-hour journey to Muhajariya brought them to our hospital where the treatment was free and more professional. They were far luckier than those who lived days from any clinic or doctor. But the people of Labado wanted us there, to treat them in their community for free, taking away their every ill. Chronic pain, mysterious itches and the perennial burning feet queued for hours to be healed.

Inside, Karen saw the patients: The Mobile Princess at work. Patients loved her as she saw them, listened to their ills and tried to help them with her treatment. I was the nasty one outside, the barrier between patients and their salvation from pain and exhaustion. Sometimes women broke the rules and climbed over the back wall after I had turned them away. They sat and smiled and waited with the others on the mat, just outside Karen's door. When she saw them and their chronic complaints of pain, she knew they had sneaked in, so she sent them out again. But people rarely became angry. Instead they sat down in the shade, prepared to wait all day for their turn.

It was after 12 o'clock when Ibrahim stood on the verandah and called 'fatuur!' Lunchtime. I looked round at the standing, pushing, heaving crowd. How could I tell them that we were stopping for an hour? They would have to sit and wait and even fewer would be seen. I knew the reasons for it all. Our staff didn't eat breakfast, fatuur was the Sudanese way. They always ate mid-morning, their first meal of the day. Working until midday their stomachs would be growling with hunger, but fatuur would keep them going.

But when it was my shirt and jeans the patients pulled and touched as they asked and pleaded for help I found it hard to look into their eyes. 'No,' I would say each time, and turn away. The patients missed out on their own fatuur on Sundays as they waited for their turn. A small packed lunch and a bottle of water would be easy to bring, but some were lazy and some simply didn't have enough food to bring. So they waited with their stomachs growling. There was nothing they could do.

I climbed over the rope and walked slowly up the stairs.

'Come, come,' said Issa standing at the door. Inside the team stood squeezed around two plastic tables covered with food. We had bean stew, fresh local salad and a pot of meaty bits. Great piles of fresh flatbread were stacked in the middle of each table. When everyone was gathered we started eating, tearing chunks of bread off and dipping it in the stew. The small, hot, noisy room echoed with our talking and slurping. Outside, patients stood with their faces against the wire netting of the windows. They watched in silence.

As we were finishing we heard a shout outside. There was screaming and shouting as patients ran in every direction.

'Please don't let them hurt the patients,' I thought as I rushed outside, wiping my hands on my trousers.

Ali stood under the rakuba and he was yelling at the patients who waited around him. 'Run, run, quickly move your mats,' he shouted.

Seventy or more women had been sitting quietly waiting for us before lunch. Now the area was chaos.

'Ali, what's wrong?' I called, looking in every direction for the guns.

'Fire, fire,' he shouted and he pointed to the roof of the rakuba.

The dry thatched roof was smouldering and burning in the midday heat. Never mind the rainy nights, the sun dried and burned in the heat of the day. The whole waiting area was made of wood and thatch and the fire could spread quickly in the breeze.

I ran down the stairs and stood beside him, looking up at the smoke. It was everywhere. We dragged mats and crying babies into the open, shouted at the mothers and called the guards for help. Mona, the tea lady, hurriedly gathered her cups and coal burner and stood beneath the burning rakuba while she tried to push them into her sack. They were her livelihood.

Ali quickly climbed one of the thin wooden poles and stood on the wobbling, burning roof. He beat the flames with an old, wet towel; whap, whap, whap. Other men came running. They carried a water barrel from the front steps between them. They passed small buckets up to Ali and soon the sand at our feet was wet as the water poured through the flimsy thatch. It was all over within minutes. Ali climbed back down, his feet covered in blackened thatch and his clothes wet and smelling of smoke.

'Shukran, Ali,' I said walking over to him. 'This could have burned down if it wasn't for you. I don't want to think what would have happened if it had come down on the women.'

'No thanks for duty,' he said with a smile. 'But inshallah I can have a cup of tea now.' His hands shook with the sudden rush of adrenaline. And he sat down with his back against the wall. I ordered a cup of tea from Mona and then climbed the stairs back to the waiting crowd outside.

The rest of the day passed quickly. Order was restored and the mats rearranged in the sun. I resumed my Mobile Bitch role, turning people away by the dozen. Small aches and pains and skin lesions were beyond us. They deserved care but we didn't have the time. With our two small boxes of drugs and a long queue already waiting inside, there was only so much we could do. So I closed my ears to their pleading voices and continued my work.

When it was time to leave there were two pregnant women waiting to travel with us back to Muhajariya. Both vehicles were already full of boxes, buckets, mats and the heavy blue metal trunks. One woman was in obstructed labour. She had been struggling for three days. The other was six months pregnant and bleeding heavily. With their bags and mats and friends and family there was little space left in the small, dark room we used for our more serious cases in the clinic. The iron shutters were twisted and rusted, never open to the breeze or sunlight outside. The creaking beams above us groaned in the afternoon heat. One day the whole roof would come down on us while we worked, of that I was sure. But there was never time to look up. There were always women on the floor, labouring, bleeding or comforting those around them.

I walked through the clinic, past the empty mats and across the soot-blackened sand below the burnt rakuba. Outside the clinic, Karen stood with her hands on her hips, shaking her head vigorously.

'We can take two patients and two family members only,' she called above the chatter of voices. The two women who still lay in the clinic had a support crowd of over twenty. The crowd of women stood in the sun, arguing loudly about which two it would be. When the guards appeared, carrying the two women in a sling of mats, the crowd parted. Each mat was carefully lifted and the women slid onto the floor of the waiting vehicle. Shouting, calling, guiding advice was given through every open window.

'Put her over there, pull her this way, mind her head, cover her legs.'

The crowd surged forward once the women were settled, all still convinced that indeed *they* were the best people to come with the patients.

'No, no, no,' shouted Karen from her vantage point. She had climbed up on the rear bumper and stood frowning at the insistent crowd. 'Can't you count?' But still the crowd argued.

When we left at last the two women lay in their painful, perspiring cocoons, surrounded by blankets and mats. Two sisters accompanied them. Both had a grin on their faces as the vehicles pulled away. They had made it.

We drove past the bodies as we headed home to Muhajariya. I looked the other way this time, not wanting to see the young man with his white socks. On the hill to my right lay another young man. He wore red shorts. His body lay face up, stretched out across the sand. He looked as if he was dancing, a grotesque movement in his dying limbs. This time I could smell them, the back window was open for the two ladies lying on the floor. The two sisters sat on the back seat, looking out as we passed the bodies.

'Inshallah,' they said, taking a deep sigh at the sight. They shook their heads and closed their eyes in prayer.

We returned to Muhajariya making good time on the muddy track. We spent the rest of the evening in the hospital with the pregnant women. One baby died, six months of pregnancy simply not enough to sustain its young life. His anaemic, malnourished mother too tired to hold onto the pregnancy. Another day, another death in this land where the pain never ends. The other baby was saved by Harold's caesarian, an exhausted but healthy baby girl. A success, small but real.

Those bodies outside Labado were never buried. We drove past them every Sunday. The sun dried their skin, leaving their faces tight masks in the glare of the desert. After three weeks someone covered them with sand. The sandy mounds were hasty but incomplete, their feet still showing at the end of each mound. With wind and rain the sand moved, revealing old grey trousers and a pair of red shorts. They were probably uncovered before too long. We stopped driving along the track in the end. Karen and I couldn't face it. The team stopped looking, preferring to keep the windows shut and their eyes on the floor. The African Union wouldn't bury them — they didn't want to get involved. Their own Janjaweed tribe couldn't enter the town, so far from their own lands, to retrieve their brothers and fathers. We couldn't bury them for fear of showing favouritism to one tribe in a place where our actions were closely watched and tribal politics were increasingly volatile. There was no one else who could bury them. So they probably lie there to this day.

CHAPTER ELEVEN

There is hope in Darfur. Where there is life, there is hope. And because we believed in life we woke at dawn every morning to push and help and change all we could. Even Karen woke early as the last weeks crowded together. So much to do and such little time.

One of our first tasks was to rebuild the clinic in Labado. For too many months we had worked crouched or on our knees in small dark rooms with burnt, creaking roofs and under sooty, brittle shelters just waiting to topple in the wind. We didn't have time to plan and build or alter the clinic. It was all we could do to survive each day, treating hundreds of patients who only seemed sicker as the months passed. All this in the clinic that had made me smile on my first visit — I had called it easy in the absence of El Wadi's commander. Now we fought a different battle — with diarrhoea, dehydration and bleeding women every single day.

We sat together one evening, spinning dreams and wishes for the new team who would take over from us.

'I'd like a real latrine in Labado,' said Karen. 'I'm tired of the overflowing dung heap we've got now. I can't even get the door open any more for all the shit inside.'

The others listened with disgust, blocking their ears and wrinkling their noses.

'Stop, stop,' said Gertrude, her hands pressed firmly over her ears. 'We don't want to hear about it.'

'That's nothing,' replied Karen. 'You should see where people go now ...'

Jack and Harold made retching sounds and Ellie started coughing loudly in the corner. They didn't want to know.

'I'll build you a new one,' said Jesse. 'What colour do you want?' It was as simple as that. Jesse was our new logistician. He was bursting with energy and ideas in the first weeks of his new mission. Where would we have been without new faces and boundless enthusiasm. Our own enthusiasm for solutions had certainly paled.

In a single day Jesse mobilised a dozen workers in Labado. They dug and sweated and carted away buckets full of hard, rocky soil. Towering posts were driven into the ground and soon the makeshift walls were up. A bright orange tarpaulin billowed from the posts by early afternoon as the breeze tugged at our new, secure latrine. The old, full latrines sat nearby, heavy padlocks on their rusting doors. No one would venture in there now. They were tombs for spiders, lizards and scorpions.

'Not bad, Jesse,' I said as we gathered to examine his work. I followed him inside, along two short corridors before we emerged in the pristine open-air latrine.

'Ta da,' he shouted, his arms in the air. 'You ask and I deliver.'

We stood over a cavernous pit latrine, the ground covered in packed earth with a neat hole in the middle.

'I can guarantee you two years of happy toilet use,' he said with a smile. 'Now, what else can I do for you?'

I felt tears well up in my eyes. Small solutions to small problems were all we needed. Latrines, repairs and simple structures would make our lives so much easier. But after the grinding frustration of overcrowded clinic days and my own feelings of inadequacy in the face of never-ending needs even those small solutions seemed impossible to achieve. Darfur had nearly beaten me, no effort was ever good enough, the suffering just dragged on. But Jesse had reminded me — change is possible if you just focus on what is in front of you.

'Thank you, Jesse,' I sniffed. 'I think I need to be alone now.' I sat on the freshly packed earth, my back to the tarpaulin and looked up at the sky. Only three weeks to go and I'd been reminded of another lesson in Darfur — never give up.

****

The following morning I woke early and lay watching the first light as dawn unfolded through the trees. My bed was outside. The night had been cool and I reached down to pull up my sleeping bag. The Milky Way lay on its side, almost ready to fall as it gave way to the new day. Behind the fence I heard the clatter of a teapot and the steady whoosh-whoosh as our neighbour fanned her charcoal fire back to life. Under the bed my friendly hedgehog sneezed then waddled out after his next easy meal. The lazy black beetles didn't survive long enough to learn the lesson that would save their lives — hedgehogs made short work of beetles that sat and rested on the ground.

I climbed out of bed and stretched. Time to get to work, I thought. Less than three weeks left and we had so much to do.

A short while later I was sitting in the office, a solar light flickering on the table beside me. The monthly report was almost due and its spreadsheets took hours to fill. I looked up when the screen door opened, creaking on its rusty hinges.

'Cup of hot chocolate for you?' asked Jesse. He carefully lowered a white china mug, almost full to the brim with frothy hot chocolate.

'I gave you extra sugar for energy,' he said. 'I will be next door if you need anything.' And he disappeared out into the darkness again, the door swinging behind him.

Moments like that slipped unasked into a day and lit them with such kindness. I sat warming my hands on the mug, breathing in the sweet, chocolate-flavoured steam. And I listened as Jesse hummed to himself next door. When life is good in Darfur you just smile with gratitude. What more could you want?

****

On Tuesday morning we started the day early. We planned to go to Angabo, but to add an extra day. Villages to the east were still a mystery to us. Where were they, how many people lived there and why were most of our patients from the east so sick with water-related illnesses? Diarrhoea, vomiting, dehydration and malnourished children arrived in Angabo each week. They waited patiently in the sun after walking for hours to see us. And each time they gathered their paracetamol and rehydration sachets together at the end of the day, rounded their tired children into a group and set off for home. We wanted to know more.

Muddy, trench-filled tracks took us almost to Angabo, then suddenly stopped as sandy paths followed a dry river bed into the bush. Few vehicles ever passed this way. The whole team was bruised and braced themselves for the next dip or crash as we made our way closer to El Noor, the biggest village in the east.

After five aching hours of driving we finally arrived in El Noor. We climbed out of the vehicles and stood quietly in the small deserted marketplace. My teeth ached from the long, shuddering drive.

The team wandered off in search of fatuur, the meal that cost us an hour or more of each working day. With time so short I sighed as I watched them disappear into the market.

'Don't worry, Lisa,' said Peter. 'The work will happen faster when their stomachs are full.' Peter could read my mind. We would never change their routine, with the team starting the day with breakfast. It wasn't the Sudanese way. So there was no point to my frustration; just accept what you can't change and move on. With a smile and a shrug I followed Peter to the shade and we sat down to wait. We never had to go searching for local leaders, invariably they found us more quickly than we could move.

Within minutes we heard shouting. An SLA soldier ran towards us, his shoes untied and an AK47 rattling against his hip. An orange toothbrush bounced against his chest, pushed through his leather protection pouch that hung from his neck. Clean teeth and bulletproof protection in one tidy package, I had to smile at the sight. We quickly realised that he posed no threat.

'Who are you?' he asked, still panting from his run. 'Why are you here, where is your permission?' He must have been on duty, his job to keep watch over this faraway village. Judging from his ill-prepared state he didn't get many visitors.

Jack explained who we were and why we had come to visit. He stepped forward as our leader, our negotiator and the responsible male. He talked about the water point and the sick patients who came to see us in Angabo. The soldier looked over Jack's shoulder and in through the vehicle windows. He obviously saw nothing of interest and realised we were pretty harmless.

'So are you a doctor?' he asked Jack. 'I have a pain in my side, down here. Can you give me some tablets?' We sat talking a while longer, reassuring our weary soldier that he was not seriously ill as a crowd began to gather.

The village leaders eventually arrived, bringing the Oomda with them. They sat around us, their jelabiya gowns drawn tightly across their knees. A group of children stood behind them, excited by our arrival in a village where little action happened. They pointed and giggled and nudged closer to us. An old man lashed out at them with his stick, muttering in a tribal language words that surely meant the same in ours. 'Bloody kids, no respect, must have something better to do...' The boy squawked and ran, hiding behind trees a little distance away. But slowly they edged closer again, too curious to keep away.

'Water is our problem,' said the Oomda. The men around him nodded in agreement. 'Our pump is very bad. A man came from the city to tell us what to do. He told us not to use it, said the pump is very old. But we have 11,000 people in this area. I cannot turn off the water. What am I supposed to do?' He looked at us with rheumy eyes and shook his head slowly.

We talked for a while to learn more. The city official had in fact told them to reduce their use to eight hours a day. The pump ran for sixteen hours now and that was just enough. They couldn't use it less or the cattle would die of thirst. In a land where wealth and hope for the future lay in the number of cattle a man owned they were reluctant to make a decision that would cause their cattle to suffer.

The pump was old and maintenance was probably unheard of. So we agreed to take a look to see what could be done. Fortunately Jack was with us, his logistician's eye would see more than ours. Karen and I knew little of mechanics and pumps and borehole management.

We climbed back in the vehicles, with the Oomda and two of his local leaders, and drove slowly back through the village. We passed big compounds with newly mended fences. Cattle pens were neatly swept and dogs sat at every entrance, sleeping in the sun. Lush, broad-leafed creepers grew over rakuba shelters, covering them in a cloak of green. Tiny, white flowers tumbled over rooftops, tangled in the creepers' arms. From a distance the village looked like Eden, ordered, fertile and abundant. But remember, in Darfur nothing is as simple as it seems.

We arrived outside the water point and parked beside the gate. Most of our team was still in the market, preparing their fatuur meal and talking to the locals while they waited. We could learn a lot about a community in the calm of a local restaurant, about safety, food supplies and general community worries. So we left them to it. There were also pretty girls there to talk with and laugh and smile at, to help them pass the time.

The water point was fenced, an old chain-link structure to keep cattle out at night and the crowds out when the pump broke down. Families would wait for days when the borehole was closed. They were given enough water to drink while they waited, but they couldn't take any home. They waited for up to a week recently, just sitting in the sun. The men and boys drove the cattle further east to another borehole when El Noor was down.

The ground was sandy and coughing clouds of dust rose as we jumped out. Standing at the gate my ears were overwhelmed by a cacophony of sound. The pump roared and shuddered, its diesel-powered frame thundering in the shade. Cows, camels, goats and sheep filled the compound, slowly herded closer to the troughs of water by the young boys with sticks and whistles. A crowd of women stood in one corner, their jerry cans stretched across the sand. Talking, shouting and whistling, mooing, grunting and camel-sighing groans mingled with the engine's incessant noise. I stood with my fingers in my ears, my head starting to ache with the heat and sound.

An old man walked towards us, beckoned by the Oomda. His jelabiya gown was wet, and muddy sand stuck to his feet and legs.

'You have to shout. He's a little deaf,' said the Oomda, pointing to the old man. 'His ears are getting old.' Surrounded by that noise all day it was no wonder his ears had aged ahead of the rest of him.

'I've been here for maybe forty years,' said the old man as we sheltered behind the vehicles. 'It's my job to keep everything working. I try my best but I have no tools and sometimes I don't know what is wrong. We go to the city when everything has stopped but sometimes they can't help us.'

They couldn't afford a brand-new pump, that much was obvious. The village managed to get by, but there wasn't any spare money. And this diesel machine had worked almost non-stop for over sixty years. Its solid parts and meticulous care had nursed it along this far, an extraordinary feat in remote Darfur. When the boundaries were drawn between north and south Darfur over a century ago, the line cut this town in half. To get help to replace the pump, the Oomda needed government help, both financial and technical. The northern administration insisted the town was more in the south, therefore not their responsibility according to their map. The southern administration said just the opposite, not our problem. That left the Oomda with few choices.

We wandered over to the water trough, passing animals and stepping over jerry cans. As we walked closer the ground became boggy with water that leaked from the cracked concrete troughs. Steaming piles of animal excrement covered the ground, soft fresh droppings on top of years of old. Soon my boots were heavy with sand and mud and excrement.

Standing beside one trough I watched the green churning water as it swirled and frothed. A woman stood beside me, her jerry can pushed deep into the water as it filled. The animal dung on the outside of her jerry can washed away in the swirling water. She reached out to smack two cows on the nose as they drank, their noses nudging her container.

Green algae, excrement, animals and people all mixed together. The crystal-clear water thundered from the borehole's pipe into the trough, drawn from 70 m below. But by the time it reached the trough it was a toxic blend of bacteria-, parasite- and dung-filled pollution. We had the answer to our question now — we knew why so many people from this place presented in Angabo, exhausted by the walk and made sick by their only source of water; why their children were malnourished and so many died from dehydration. Their water was poisoning them.

We stayed a while longer, examined some sick patients who were carried from their homes and dispensed tablets from the back of one vehicle. We ate fatuur in the market, surrounded by curious children in a dim and quiet restaurant. Bean stew and bread and salad had taken the team a long time to find from various stall-holders. There wasn't a lot of surplus food in the village, each man had enough for his own and little else. But we paid handsomely for our food, leaving them with dinars to spend in the city for more.

All too soon we had to leave. Their water pump wasn't strictly our business and district politics not our game to meddle in. We were focused on health and medical intervention. But we promised to talk to others and to return with what we found. Their water had become our problem.

It was nearly 5 p.m. when we arrived in Angabo, tired, thirsty and with our bones aching from the journey. We were all asleep early, after local takeaways and brief goodnights. Jack disappeared into one tuckul, Karen into her usual Angabo shelter. Her tuckul was chaotic, bags and shoes and books lay on the ground. Her giardia still caused her pain and cramps, leaving her exhausted and drawn at the end of a hard day. Her weight continued to drop, safety pins now held her trousers up.

I kicked the usual rubbish from the floor of Ali's landcruiser, lay the thick foam mattress down and fell heavily onto my sleeping bag.

The night passed far too quickly. When I woke the next morning my boots were still on, covered with dried mud and excrement, too much bother to remove in the aching darkness the night before.

****

Our two days in Angabo were the usual clinic days — long queues and endless chatter with the occasional donkey cart reversing in with someone injured or unconscious. Karen, Ali and Issa waited inside to treat them. As the Mobile Bitch, I trawled the crowds, searching for the sickest, but each time I was waylaid by calls and smiles and shouts. Haroun walked beside me, rubbing his hands with enthusiasm.

'Today is good,' he smiled. 'Very good today.'

He said that every day and very little else. So I smiled back and nodded. 'Yes, Haroun. Very good today. But we have a lot of work.'

He patted my hand and nodded sagely, his smile gone for the first time. 'No problem, Lisa,' he said. 'If you want no work, no problem. I will tell them all to go home now.'

'No, no, no. That's not what I meant,' I said hurriedly. 'Work is good, work makes me happy.' And it was true. If ever there was a sense of purpose in my life, it was Darfur and the work that I could do. Small steps and small successes. That was all I could claim and I wanted to keep going. I wanted to try.

A young woman tugged at my shirt behind me. I turned. On her hip she carried a little girl, perhaps four years old. Her hair was tightly braided and she hid her face when I turned. What caught my attention was the smell that surrounded them both and the buzzing hum of flies. The little girl had her right hand wrapped loosely in a cloth. I suspected that was the source of the smell.

While Haroun talked to the young woman I lifted back the cloth. Beneath it the little girl's hand lay still, her fingers drawn into a blackened claw. All over her wrist and hand and fingers grew a thick coat of white fur. Fur. On a four year old. Now that was something new!

I led them through the gates, with Haroun in tow as he told me what was wrong.

'She says her brother's child was burned by a fire many days ago. It's no problem now, no pain or fever. But she is asking please can you give her some tablets for the smell,' he translated.

I raised my eyebrows. 'And the fur? Was she always half cat?'

Haroun shook his head. 'Not cat. Rabbit'.

The little girl had fallen into a fire two weeks before and her hand was badly burned. A traditional healer had caught a white rabbit, blessed and killed it for her treatment. He tied the freshly skinned rabbit pelt onto the weeping burn and waited for it to heal. The family was convinced the hand would heal if only the smell would stop. As the rabbit meat rotted, the flies were attracted in droves. Beneath the flurry of buzzing activity, her little fingers were hard and black, too damaged to ever heal.

We left her in a corner, playing with empty bottles and eating biscuits while the young woman went in search of the little girl's parents. They had already chosen to treat their daughter with traditional medicine and we knew it wasn't always easy to convince patients that our treatment was often better.

Rabbit-skin dressings, burning welts, scarification and dehydration were traditional treatments that increased our workload no end. But this was one problem too much for us in Angabo, burns and rabbit skin, however blessed. If the little girl was to have a chance to use her hand again, she needed surgery and care in Muhajariya. We had to try.

We returned to Muhajariya the following day, new patients filling both vehicles. Burns, malnourished babies and infected snake bites were beyond our little metal trunks, even with an outstanding mobile team. Working on our knees, overwhelmed with patient numbers, we knew how much we could do and when it was simply too much. Karen and I stood at the gates to the hospital and watched as the patients and their families slowly clambered out.

'Bloody hell,' said Bridgette, walking out to meet us. 'Is this the mobile clinic bus service? Are you going to bring the whole of south Darfur next time?'

'No, just a few at a time,' said Karen with a tired smile. 'These are just the easy ones.'

We spent the rest of the evening admitting our patients, walking from ward to ward as we searched for translators, weighing scales and after-hours meals. We let the rest of the team go home. It wasn't safe for anyone to be out on the streets after dark since a local staff member had been abducted. She had been taken from the hospital by a group of men after shunning their advances earlier that week. Jack had retrieved her with the local commander's help. She was unharmed but frightened; Jack had arrived just in time. So now all staff were told to be vigilant, and that meant no one was out at night.

Around us the hospital slowly settled for the night. Kerosene burners were lit and Hawa, the tea lady, made her last rounds calling 'Chai, leben, kerkedei' through every open window. Tea, milk and sweet drinks were a treat that settled patients for the night. Karen and I called for tea and went back to work in our respective wards.

The nurses and assistants dragged their chairs outside and sat waiting for Bridgette's evening ward round.

'Hey, Karen and Lisa,' called Salah, one of the health assistants. 'Come and sit with us.' He leaned back in his chair and waved at us lazily. 'It is dark now, stop the work.'

We were both exhausted. Two days of work in Angabo after the bruising drive to El Noor left us feeling like robots, eyes heavy and shoulders aching. It was nearly 9 p.m. as we finished writing up our notes.

Karen walked over slowly and fell into the plastic chair.

'Shukran, Salah,' she sighed. Thank you.

He smiled, his face lit from below by the lantern on the ground. 'How are you, my sister?' he asked. 'You are working too much, I think.'

I dropped my bag and empty water bottle in the nurses' office and walked out to join them.

'Everybody works too much in Darfur, Salah,' I said, sitting down beside him.

'This is true,' he nodded. 'This is how the life goes. But now we sit with friends and stopping thinking about the work.' He reached down to dim the kerosene lantern and the five of us sat together in the shadows and forgot about the day.

All around us patients and their families lay in the open, their mats stretched across the sand. Quiet murmurings were interrupted now and then by a crying child or a sudden burst of laughter somewhere in the dark. About twenty patients remained from the attack on Labado, only seven from the one on Arto. They lay on their metal frame beds, their damaged limbs carefully pulled with sandbags as the traction helped to heal their broken bones. With their families sitting beside them they looked like any other patient, healing from an infected abscess or an amputated toe. They talked and smiled and said thank you when their beds were dragged outside at the end of every day. But everyone knew their wounds went much deeper than their smiling faces showed.

****

We travelled more in the days and weeks that followed. With the rainy season progressing and who knew what changes in security as rumours of attacks and rising tensions grew, we wanted to get out while we could. We talked to small village leaders, asking them what life was like. Sitting cross-legged in a small, dim tuckul we spoke to an Oomda to see what help they needed. Karen and I wouldn't be able to help, but surely the new team would take our lead and try.

The Oomda was obviously a man of great wisdom and his people respected him highly. He was by far the oldest Oomda we had met. When he spoke he paused often, searching for the right words. He looked at me with such piercing eyes I had to look away. He only wanted to take care of his people, he told us. To watch the children grow and keep his people safe. But it was hard, almost too hard for this old man.

'Who do you trust now we have war?' he asked. We all sat in silence, contemplating the question with no answer.

'Who are you?' he asked, looking at me directly. 'And what do you want of your life?' My answer would seem empty compared with any other wants around me. I wanted a good life, yes. A house. Even a husband who loved me. But I couldn't share my own heart's desires, not in the face of their hunger and fear and loss.

'I only want to help Darfur,' I said at last. 'I think I am too small to help but I would like to try.'

He leaned back, hands resting on his knees and looked at me. 'If you need help then you can be my daughter,' he said at last. 'And I will help you.'

I didn't know how to answer. This wise, strong, war-weary man would help me live my dream if I asked. He would help me find purpose and meaning at a time when my life was confused, exhausted and almost defeated. I whispered my thanks and looked away, knowing I was not strong enough to help Darfur beyond the next few weeks.

His people wanted tools and seeds to help them with their

farms. The rainy season had begun but most farmers did not have the equipment to start working their land. It had all been stolen in the past, in raids by other tribes. With rising tensions some were nervous about planting again, for fear of losing their crops again and being left with nothing.

'We will ask about seeds and tools,' said Karen as we left.

'Inshallah you can help us,' said the Oomda. God willing.

The rains came every day that week, leaving the hospital and tracks great squelching bogs of sand, bricks and long white feathers. I lay in bed at night and listened to the symphony of sound that rose from the marketplace. Frogs of every description croaked and squeaked and roared from the pond that used to be the meeting place in the market. Bull frogs, tree frogs and tiny, green I-want-to-pick-you-up frogs. I loved the sound.

Bashir, our resourceful local logistician, engineered a Darfur-experience for me to take home to New Zealand. One night after a particularly heavy rain, he walked down to the pond and he crouched at the water's edge with a tape recorder. There in the dark he waited patiently, the little red recording light flashing as he recorded the night sounds of Muhajariya. I have it with me now. Somewhere in the background I can hear him yawn, this man who sat listening to frogs for a crazy, homesick expat. On and on the frogs croak, singing and splashing in their new home. Recorded for posterity so that I can smile in the months and years to come.

'I made this for you, Lisa,' he said the next day, holding out the tape. 'You said you love the frogs. I don't know why. They make me annoyed. But now you will have our frogs in your country and maybe you will remember this place when you listen to them.' He stood with me outside his office, this broad-shouldered man with his wide smile. And he touched his heart.

'For my sister,' he said.

I blinked back the tears and touched my heart with thanks. More kindness and love when I knew I could never repay him. My body was exhausted, my heart broken in a thousand ways and I ached already with grief for the friends I would leave behind.

'Shukran, Bashir. Thank you for your kindness.' Thank you.

'No thanks for duty,' he smiled even wider. 'Don't forget us, my sister. Don't forget Darfur. And inshallah we will see you when you return.' God willing. With that he turned and left, a heavy bag swung over one shoulder. I walked to the gate and watched him leave. I kept watching until my eyes began to water and he disappeared into the distance, a tiny speck on the sandy track to town.

****

Some stories have happy endings and some you wish could change. The little girl with her rabbit-skin wound spent nearly three weeks in our hospital as Harold slowly repaired her hand. Lying in her father's arms on the operating table several times each week, she lost her fingers as he cleaned the burned skin away. With a skin graft and a lot of loving care she healed and started to play and run and laugh again. The day she was discharged her parents stood at the hospital gate, ready for the ten-hour walk back to their village.

'Shukran for my daughter,' said her father, bowing and touching his heart. 'We have no other children and my daughter is my life.' Thank you.

'Alawajip,' I replied. You are welcome. And we watched them walk away. The little girl watched us shyly from behind her father's hat, her right hand reaching out to wave as they walked along the track. Karen and I smiled at each other. Another small success.

The old diesel pump in El Noor was replaced for free and a technician came to train the old man in its care. A government grant of seven pumps to various villages in South Darfur was timely. We walked into a government office in Al Dein and pleaded their case as villages were being selected. An international organisation planned to return and redesign the water point in El Noor. No troughs, no mixing of animal and humans. They would have clean taps that gave pure borehole water and a series of drums for the animals in a compound next door. They have clean water now and the knowledge to keep it that way.

Most farmers didn't get their tools or seeds to plant that year. Some equipment was distributed by organisations, but few and it was never enough. World Food Programme rations were cut further to try to make their small stocks last. But with ever-growing numbers queuing patiently, the rations only got smaller, with some receiving nothing at all.

A new attack on Saleem sent another wave of families running for the hills. They had withstood attacks, intimidation and growing aggression over the previous months. But when the attacks became more vicious they had to run. Many tribes, not just one, escaped by cloak of darkness. Some sent the children ahead at night, then joined them with donkeys and food they had managed to gather. Others tried waiting outside the African Union in Saleem, hoping for protection and help. A Janjaweed militia attack outside the compound sent them running. One of our old clinic workers in Saleem was shot, a quiet lady called Miriam who swept the clinic and made tea for Sam and me. She was running from the attack outside the African Union's compound that day, but she couldn't scale their fence to get away from the men on horses. Miriam made it to Muhajariya, she was a survivor. But how many others limped and crawled away, into the hills to live or die far from help or protection. How many children ran after their parents or waited in the bush for family who never arrived. We will never know.

My own ending in Darfur was quiet, a gentle absence rather than anything grand. Darfur is so used to saying goodbye that striking celebrations are for life and for those who stay. I stood crying in the kitchen with Hawa, our desert-beauty cook.

'My friend, my friend,' she said, over and over as she cried and we hugged. 'Please come back to Darfur,' she said and she held my face in her hands. 'Please do not forget us.'

'I will try to come back,' I said, not willing to say never.

Amna stood behind us, she who swept and stole our toiletries.

'Goodbye, my sister,' she said and we hugged each other. 'I will miss you.' Then she linked her arm through mine and we walked towards the gate. 'Can I ask you a small favour?' she said when we were far enough from Hawa. 'Can I have your lotions and creams and all your things? You will not be wanting them now.'

'Mamumkin, they are all finished,' I laughed. Not possible because you stole them long ago.

My night-time farewell with the hospital and clinic staff had left me feeling exhausted with sadness that we would never meet again. The stars above us had shone for Africa, another rain-free night. Donkeys called mournfully from their tethers outside the hospital gate. And in the trees above us great white cattle egrets murmured and shuffled in the dark. Tens of thousands of these birds were migrating to and from somewhere, pausing to rest in our part of the newly lush desert. The town's trees were full of them. At dawn each day they flew to the east, to the wetlands that slowly filled with each passing storm. Dozens of them flew out together, in low-flying clouds of white. At dusk they all returned to town, taking roost in trees and huts and mosques. There in the dark, surrounded by my friends, laughter and the balmy evening calm, I fell in love a little further with the beauty that is Darfur.

I walked slowly out of the compound on that last morning and up to Ali's waiting vehicle. I had said goodbye to the team, to Dave and Jack, Jesse and Harold, to Gertrude, Ellie and Bridgette. The new team had arrived to take over and I had no idea how they would work. To be honest I didn't care by then.

****

My time in Darfur was over. Karen had left the week before. Her tuckul lay empty, tidy for the first time in months. The curtain door was tied up with string, revealing the bare room inside. We did our best, but was it ever good enough?

We ran clinics, looked for families who were hiding and those on the run from the war. We tried to give them what they needed, plastic sheeting, blankets and food. We lobbied for more food, for seeds and tools and for new diesel engines. We rescued some who would have died without us and we missed others who died out of sight, far away. We sat in the presence of wisdom, cross-legged before Oomdas, sheiks, old midwives and healers who tried to keep their people alive. We tried to treat women and watched while they died, victims of brutal female circumcision. But we were unable to stop them cutting young girls and causing the needless deaths. We worked in the heat and the rain and blinding sand storms to try to bring relief to some people in some place that most people have never heard of. Did we make a difference? Was it worth the effort? And should we even have tried?

With my heart broken and my soul still bruised by all we saw and did and failed to do, I can only whisper yes. There were small steps and small successes, granted. And sometimes our successes were swept away in a breath. Our clinic in Angabo was burned to the ground, looted and destroyed not long after we left. The gentle, grey-haired guards and smiling Haroun are gone, and we don't know where they are. Our work with local healers, to encourage and teach and share knowledge has stopped. The mobile clinics don't run in Angabo, or El Noor or any villages to the east or south. Insecurity, troop movements and attacks are common and no organisations venture out unless they have to. The people still wait and hope we will return, the MSF vehicles with their boxes of life-saving treatment for people who have none.

Muhajariya was attacked twice as tribes moved on the town from the south and east. Heavy weapons, automatic gunfire and rocket-propelled grenades sent the local staff running and the remaining team hid in our bomb shelter on and off for days. Nearly 4000 people fled from the barren, sand-storm-torn camp to the south of town. Those beautiful people with their white linen-wrapped faces, their eyes peering through the sand. Gone. Over 7000 fled from the camp to the north, afraid to stay through another terrifying attack. Many were survivors of the attacks on Saleem, people already exhausted and drained by the war. Our staff were beaten, some abducted and threatened, their lives at risk for simply doing their job. Those who could return to town came to bury their belongings deep in the sand before leaving again, not planning to return for some time. The hospital was empty on the eve of the first attack, everyone running for fear of being killed where they lay. Our damaged and broken patients from Arto and Labado, the pregnant and bleeding women we brought from Angabo on our last day — they are all gone, but I can't imagine how they ran.

The bodies of militia lay in the market after the first major battle. In the place where Bashir sat and recorded my frogs, the dead were lying, a frightening spectacle in a place where we had felt safe. Then the remaining militia regrouped and sent warning, they were returning for the bodies and they wouldn't be stopped. The killing continues, the running and hiding and waiting and fear.

Did we make a difference? To Hawa and Asha, to Mona and Issa and the thousands of nameless, faceless others we touched and met and treated, we did make a difference. I held Hanan's baby in El Wadi and knew that I had made a difference. His malnourished, dying body was too much for his abscess-stricken mother in the marketplace that day. He lived because we were there, albeit for a short while.

Was it worth the effort? How do you measure worth in a place where tears fall every day and life hangs by a thread? Bashir's tape of frog song, the Oomda's intense eyes while he offered to help me with my life. Are they worth it? The endless queue of thirsty children as they shared my cup outside the African Union's shame. Were they worth it? It's an empty question, one that has no answer.

And should we even try? Should we spend endless billions to help ease their pain? It is not our war, they don't accept our offers of peace and compromise from afar. Every attempt falls short of perfect and every cry is another mother grieving for a circumcised daughter or a dying child, no matter how hard we work.

I have been to Darfur only briefly. Nine months is the blink of an eye. Yes, it was worth the effort, for all the chaotic, overwhelming mess. It's easy to make a difference, easy to save a life in Darfur. Clean water, warm blankets and good food are simple solutions that can change a life in an instant. With my broken heart and feeling almost defeated I nearly gave up on Darfur. But who am I to give up? Me with my warm home, dry clothes and full stomach. What of my friends still in Darfur, Hawa and Bashir who begged me to not forget them? They are not asking for money, or for gifts or wanting to waste our time. They are living, breathing, faith-filled people who are desperate for a chance to live. They would hold your hand, listen to your stories and give you their last glass of water if you asked. They are grieving and loving and forgiving brothers and sisters who ask for our friendship.

The politics of war are complicated, too complicated for a nurse like me. I just know what my friends look like, how they laugh and how much I loved being with them. Politics mean nothing and everything to me. I just want my friends to be safe and for others to remember them too. So that when my time is over I know that I made a difference in this world that tries to shake compassion and hope from our bones.

****

When I returned home I received an email from Bridgette. She wrote to say don't worry, that she and the others were safe, no matter what the reports said. Despite the bombs, the fighting and the intimidation that filled Muhajariya, they were fine. The hospital was still working, albeit with a skeleton staff. She told me of a town meeting, in the slowly collapsing feeding centre we used to run on the edge of the marketplace. After the meeting, where various people talked and shouted and worried about the situation, a young boy stood up. His name was Al Haj. As a child he had no voice in a meeting of adults in this time of war. But he had a message and he wanted to share it while others could listen. He sang in front of the crowd of almost a thousand people, a little boy of eleven years old. And he cried as he sang.

Bridgette wrote: 'When he had finished singing he ignored all the applause and sat down again with his head in his hands. I was speechless. I had no idea what he was singing about but his performance was so powerful I felt tears in my eyes. Everyone had tears. We recorded him singing and then we made a translation. There is still hope in Darfur. With forgiveness and love like this little boy has, there is hope. When you write your book, tell people that. Please don't forget us here.

This was his song:

'For the sake of our mother — we learn
For the sake of our father — we learn
For the sake of our brother — we learn
For the sake of our sister — we learn
Even if our house is burnt down — because of this we should learn
Even if our house is burnt down — because of this we should learn
Our villages are empty and for this we should also learn
For the sake of our mother — we learn
For the sake of our father — we learn

We should make our voices heard so that we can learn
We should make our voices heard so that we can learn
For the sake of Darfur, for the sake of Darfur — we learn

For the sake of our mother — we learn
For the sake of our father — we learn

Even if the school is damaged — we learn
We hope the bullets to become chalk — we learn
We hope the bullets to become chalk — we learn

For the sake of our mother — we learn
For the sake of our father — we learn
For the sake of our brothers and sisters — we learn

For the sake of Sudan — we learn
For the sake of Darfur, for the sake of Darfur we learn'.

Please don't forget Darfur, or the people you have met through
my words. When I return and stand with my friends, I will look

them in the eye and say no, I didn't forget you. And others care for you, more than you know. Tangled politics, indifference and a complicated, unjust war can destroy our compassion. Why bother to try when it's impossible to really make a difference? Because when our lives are weighed and measured we are worth more than the sum of ourselves. We are filled and measured and brought to life by the love and the loss and the hope of our friends, whoever they are. Hold the story of Darfur in your heart and you will grow in love and grief and hope. I know it for sure. Apathy steals hope. But to make a difference you have to care and you have to try. To try will bring you tears for certain in this world of overwhelming unhappiness. I have cried an ocean of tears for Darfur. And it was worth every teardrop.

Acknowledgments

Dreams come true when we believe in ourselves. Too often we just survive, stumbling and hesitating through our lives. Self doubt, apathy and chaos drag our dreams down, leaving us with an aching emptiness. My dream was to make a difference in the world, to somehow make it better. It was a way to fight off the emptiness I felt. After the crashing self-doubt, the crying injustice and the world's numb indifference during my time in Darfur, I doubted that I would ever find a new dream. I achieved so little amongst the chaos. But dreams don't die easily.

Writing this book has given me an opportunity to share my dream, however imperfect or impractical. There is so much love and wonder and forgiveness in the people of Darfur — I could never give up on them. Their dreams and hopes and quiet patience deserve to be heard.

I would like to say thank you to the people who have walked with me, sharing my dream both in Darfur and at home.

Thank you to Rowena Webb and Helen Coyle of Hachette Livre, who saw in my words a story that needed to be told. My friends, colleagues and patients in Darfur have a voice because of you.

Thank you also to my agent, Glenys Bean, who first heard my voice as I talked and cried about Darfur.

Thank you to Kevin Chapman, Margaret Samuels and the team at

Hachette Livre in Auckland. Your calm confidence, smiling faces and patience has kept me writing and believing I could actually do it.

Thank you to Fran and Andrew Brown for holding me gently on my return from Darfur. You gave me the space and encouragement to start sharing my disjointed stories and bruised dreams.

Thank you to Melanya, Jette and Richard. Your endless patience with my wandering life and your open-armed love when I return each time means the world to me.

Thank you to Ian and Gloria Hurst for sharing Willowpark, your cottage and your wide open spaces with me. I spent hours, days and weeks writing and dreaming in a little stone cottage that still feels like paradise. You were an answer to a prayer.

Thanks also to Jonno and Emily Alford, Paul and Sheryl Baker, Trudy Froger, Sue Mann, Bruce and Alison Albiston. Each of you has helped me, with small steps or big ones, as I have walked and stumbled towards my dream.

Thank you to my family, to Mum, Dad, Jeannie, Andrew and Claire, to Grandma, Di, Adrian and Marion for home cooked meals, candlelit dinners and love whenever I have roamed back home. You have lived and worried and waited each time I leave, but you've always been there when I've returned. How could I ever repay you for that?

And my biggest soul-filled gratitude and love to the people I lived and worked with in Darfur. Your lives and dreams and memories are part of me now, and my heart aches with love and loss for you. We may never meet again, but through you I have learned to love, to be patient and to believe in myself. I can't change the world. I have barely managed to cause a ripple. But I still believe in dreams and I refuse to give in to the chaos. It's what I wish for everyone. I have learned to live because of you, one small step at a time, with my eyes on the stars. Shukran. Inshallah we will meet again. Inshallah.